Reflections

by Felix E. Oppenheim

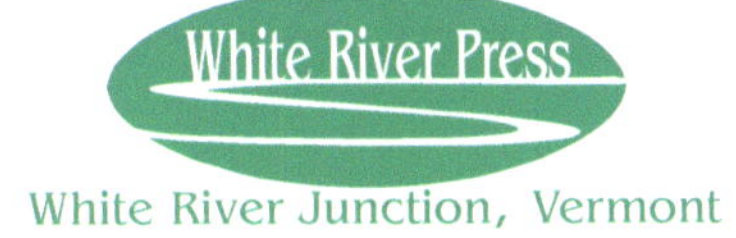

Reflections

Felix E. Oppenheim

published January 2008 by White River Press

cover and interior design by Peter Hutchins, Litmus Designs

White River Press
PO Box 4624
White River Junction, Vermont 05001
www.whiteriverpress.com

ISBN: 978-0-9792451-6-9

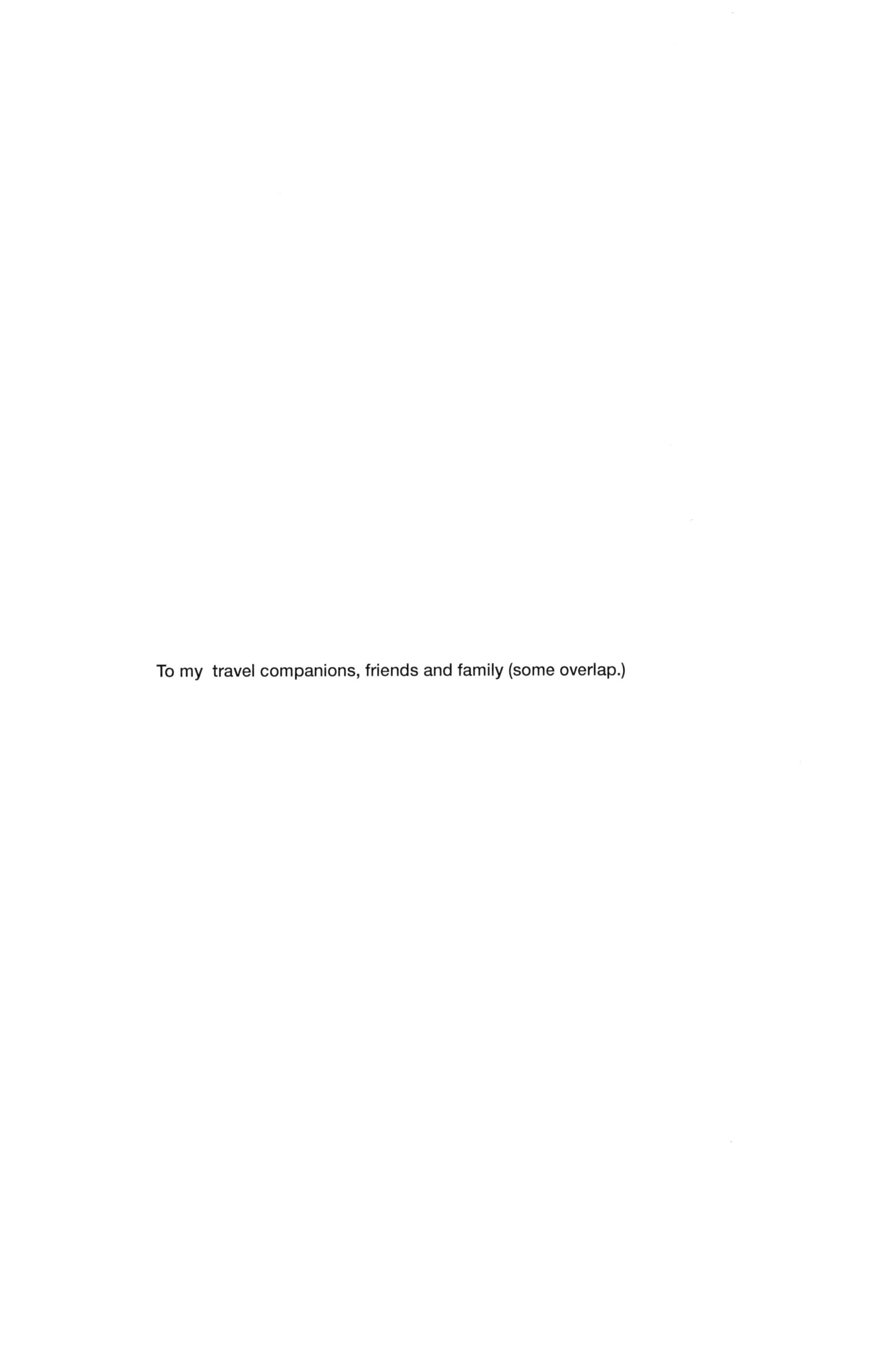

To my travel companions, friends and family (some overlap.)

Introduction

Why do reflections of buildings in water surprise and delight us? These palaces, guild houses, cathedrals, mosques, and bridges, together with their reflections, do not constitute simple sums of two distinct parts but form new and unexpected wholes, aesthetically, on a more enhanced level than their constituent elements.

These reflections tell us that the building with its scenery "makes sense" even in reverse, as does the reverse theme of a Bach mirror fugue. Yet, the reflection is not a mirror image. Unlike glass, the water's texture "plays" with the original, while remaining essentially faithful to it. When the water is moving slightly, the reflection creates images of yet greater variety, like variations on an already familiar theme.

In either case, we remain startled and pleased, as were perhaps the builders themselves, whether the reflecting water was natural–sea, rivers, lakes–or artificial–canals for commerce, basins for ritual ablution, moats for defense, and, later on, for the explicit purpose of enhancing a château's beauty.

The photographs span eleven countries and various periods. They are not meant to form a systematic whole, either geographically or historically, but to provide characteristic samples of reflective delights a traveler might discover on his journey.

There is no connection between my professional activities and my photography–an avocation which has been with me from youth on. I still remember my first camera, a clumsy Kodak my grandmother gave me when I was thirteen, and I still have the album with my first three pictures–of Bruges: one of them with the main church tower reflected in the lake–just by chance?

I was born in Frankfurt, Germany, on 14th June, 1913. My mother was Belgian: hence, I grew up bilingual (German and French). I learned Italian on my first trip to Florence (the city of my maternal grandmother) when I was fifteen.

I had little affinity with Weimar and pre-Nazi Germany (except for its music–and Heine!) and felt integrated with the more Western part of Europe. I visited my grandparents in Brussels every year after the First World War, moved there with my family as soon as Hitler came into power in 1933, and acquired Belgian citizenship.

I studied law at Brussels University, obtaining my law degree in 1938. Immediately afterward, I started (compulsory) military service, prolonged after general mobilization in 1939 (Field Artillery). On the first day of the German invasion of Belgium (May 10, 1940), I was taken prisoner-of-war and was shipped with thousands of others by freight car to a camp near Hanover–my only "trip" back to Germany! For obvious reasons, I changed my name, assuming Flemish identity because of Germany's pro-Flemish occupation policy in World War I. Indeed, I was released with all Flemish prisoners after four months and shipped back to Belgium.

After four further months, I was able to leave occupied Brussels and, surmounting many obstacles, I reached the United States on 1 January 1941, and joined my parents in Princeton, New Jersey, where they had come in 1939. Even though my English was still rudimentary, I was admitted as a graduate student to Princeton University, due largely to my law degree. After one-and-a-half years, I received a Ph.D. in Political Science in 1942, followed immediately–again!–by military service, now in the American army, becoming an American citizen. After a number of temporary assignments, I was transferred to the Research and Analysis Branch of the OSS (Office of Strategic Services), first in Washington, then in London, and finally in liberated Brussels.

I was responsible for analyzing political developments in occupied and liberated Belgium (my reports went also to the U.S. Embassy in Brussels). Who could have foreseen that some day I would stand as an American officer at the very spot where I had been taken prisoner five years before? I was commissioned a second lieutenant at the end of 1945. Four months later I was demobilized, and returned to the United States. (For more details on my life so far, see http://fmo.qeh.ox.ac.uk/FMO/Reader/Viewdoc.asp?Path=Oxford/1609/10/20)

In 1949 I married Shulamith Levey, who became a well-known author of children's books and short stories. We have a daughter, two sons, and five grandchildren.

After a number of positions and visiting professorships, I came to the University of Massachusetts at Amherst in 1961 as a Professor in Political Science. I had visiting appointments at Amherst College, Princeton, Columbia, Yale, Stanford, Oxford, LSE, Turin, and Florence Universities (twice a Fulbright Lectureship). I was a Guggenheim Fellow, a resident fellow at the Netherlands Institute of Advanced Studies, and at the Bellagio Center (Rockefeller Foundation).

After my retirement in 1983, I taught for eighteen years every spring at various Italian universities (in Italian) and gave lectures in France, England, and Spain.

My main teaching and writing interests are in Analytic Political Philosophy, especially the logical analysis of political concepts and the logical status of moral judgments in foreign policy. (For Bibliography, see I. Carter and M. Ricciardi, eds. Freedom, Power and Political Morality, Essays for Felix Oppenheim, pp. 234-236.)

From 1948 on, I took my Leica on my yearly trips, some in connection with my teaching abroad, others purely "touristic." Never guided! I traveled with family, friends, or alone. I stopped to take photos, now in color slides, whenever a building, landscape, or both "spoke" to me. I often returned to the same place I had "discovered" to catch it in just the right light (especially sunset!). It is only a few years ago, when I sorted my slides for transfer onto DVDs that I discovered how many were "reflections." Hence, this book.

My warmest thanks to Peter Hutchins, Graphic Designer, for his expertise and patience in putting this book together, Sonja Hakala, Book Project Manager, for her skillfull guidance, and to my wife Shulamith whose steady encouragement dispelled my innate skepticism.

Plates

Italy

57. Venice A canal
58. Venice Cà d'Oro
59. Venice Cà d'Oro
60. Venice Near Rialto
61. Venice Toward Chioggia
62. Montagnana
63. Verona Bridge over Adige
64. Portofino
65. Portofino
66. Settignano Garden of Villa Gamberaia
67. Rome Foro Romano
68. Villa Adriana (Hadrian's Villa)
69. Villa Adriana
70. Tivoli Villa d'Este
71. Tivoli Villa d'Este
72. Molfetta
73. Ascoli Piceno Duomo

Croatia

74. Dubrovnik
75. Dubrovnik

Spain

76. Granada Alhambra
77. Granada Alhambra
78. Granada Alhambra
79. Granada Alhambra
80. Granada Generalife
81. Granada Generalife

Morocco

82. Fes Medersa Bou Inania
83. Marrakech Medersa Ben Youssef
84. Tinghir
85. Ait-Benhaddou Near Quarzazate
86. Taroudant Village near town

Iran

87. Isfahan Mosque Mother of Shah
88. Isfahan Friday Mosque
89. Isfahan Friday Mosque
90 Isfahan Mosque of Shah Abbas
91. Isfahan Mosque of Shah Abbas
92. Isfahan Mosque of Shah Abbas
93. Isfahan Mosque of Sheikh Luttallah

Greece

94. Methana View fom Peloponnese
95. Nafplion
96. Sunion View on Temple
97. Near Delphi View on Peloponnese
98. Kalymnos Sponge-fishing boats
99. Kalymnos
100. Poros View on Peloponnese

Egypt

101. Dendera View from Nile
102. Assuan Nile and Elephantine Island
103. Near Assuan Nile
104. Nile
105. Near Assuan Nile

U.S.A.

106. Pelham, MA Pond near Amherst
107. Pelham, MA Pond near Amherst

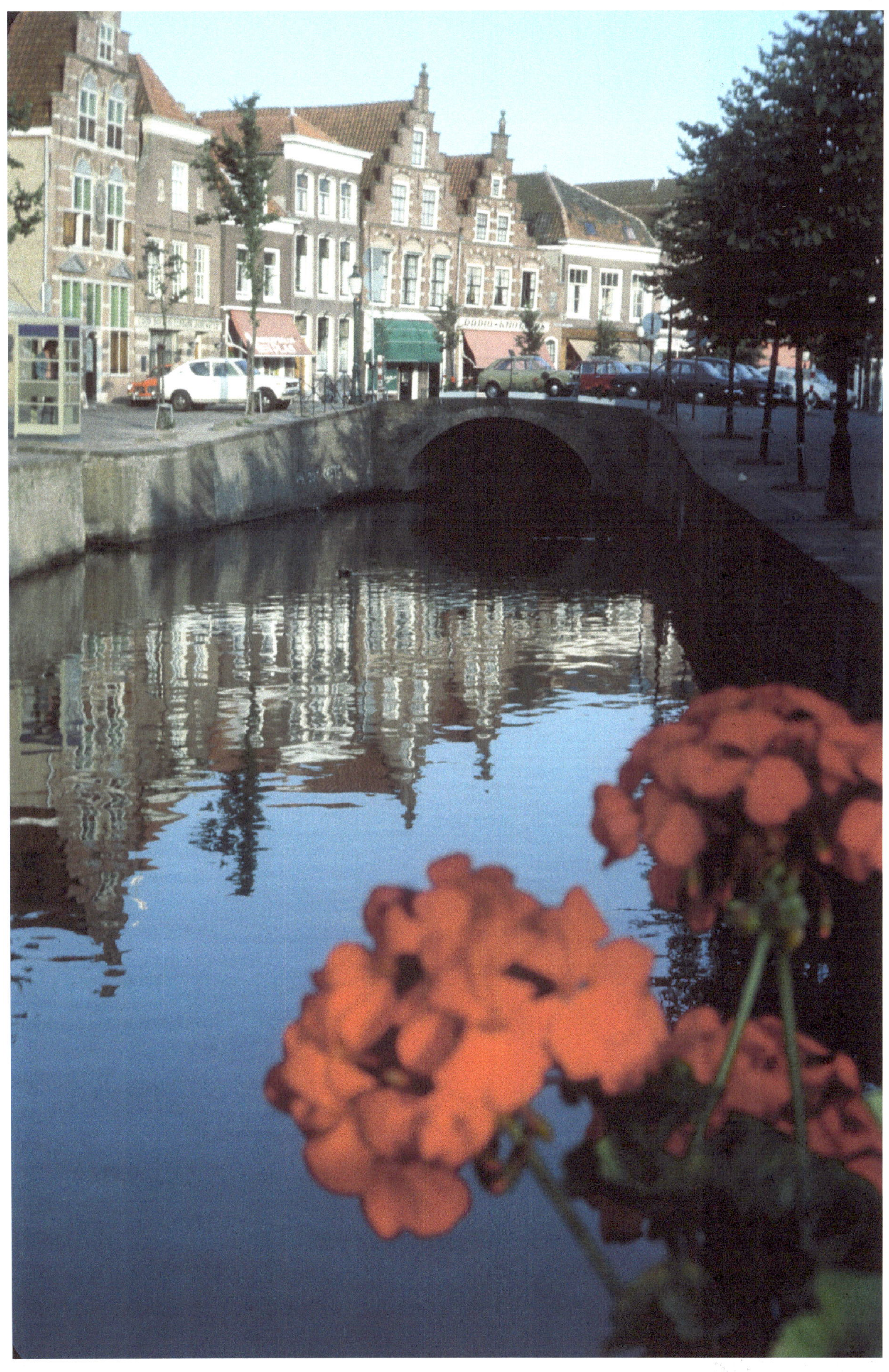

1. Oudewater near Utrecht

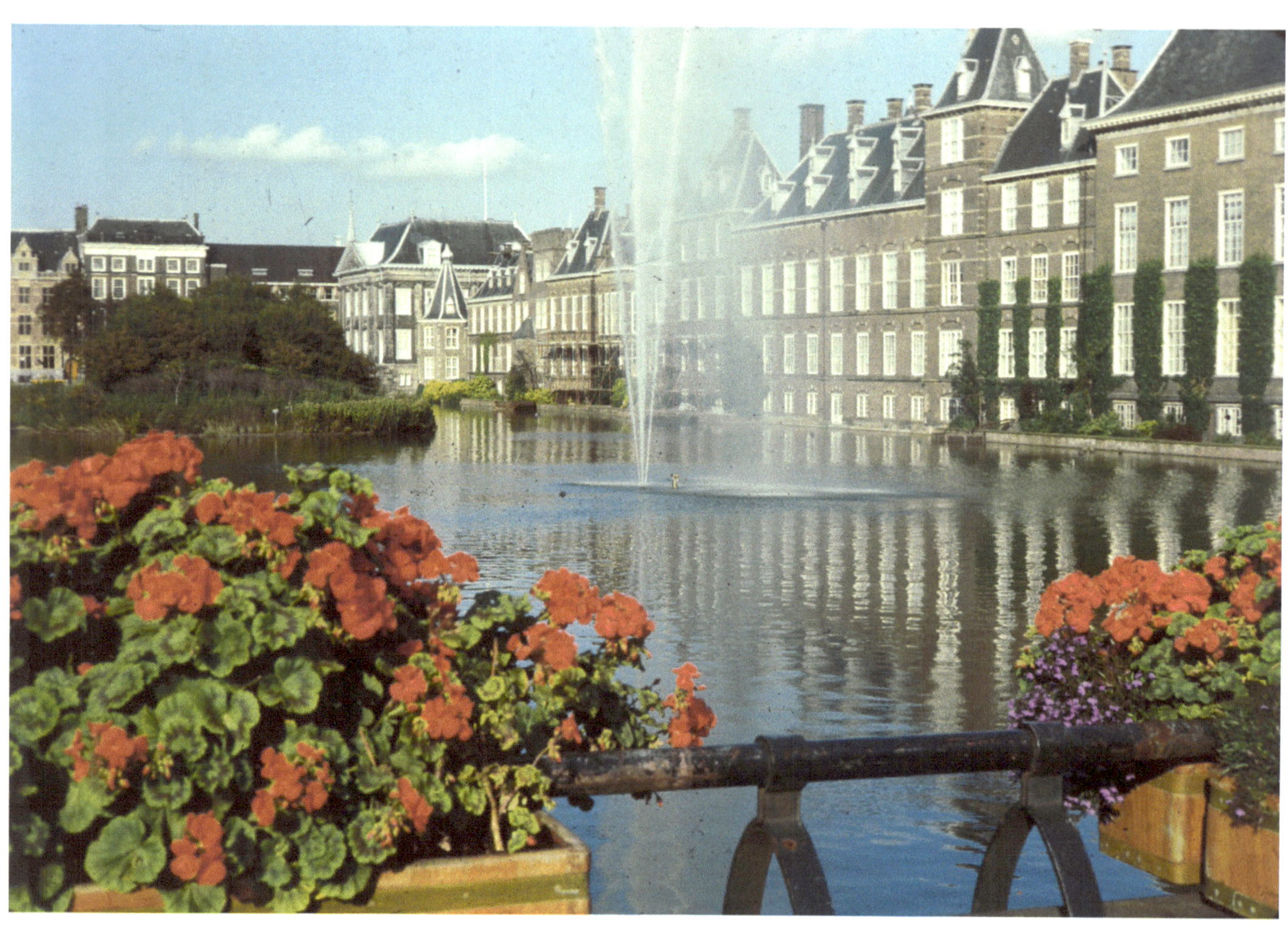

2. Den Haag Binnenhof (Parliament)

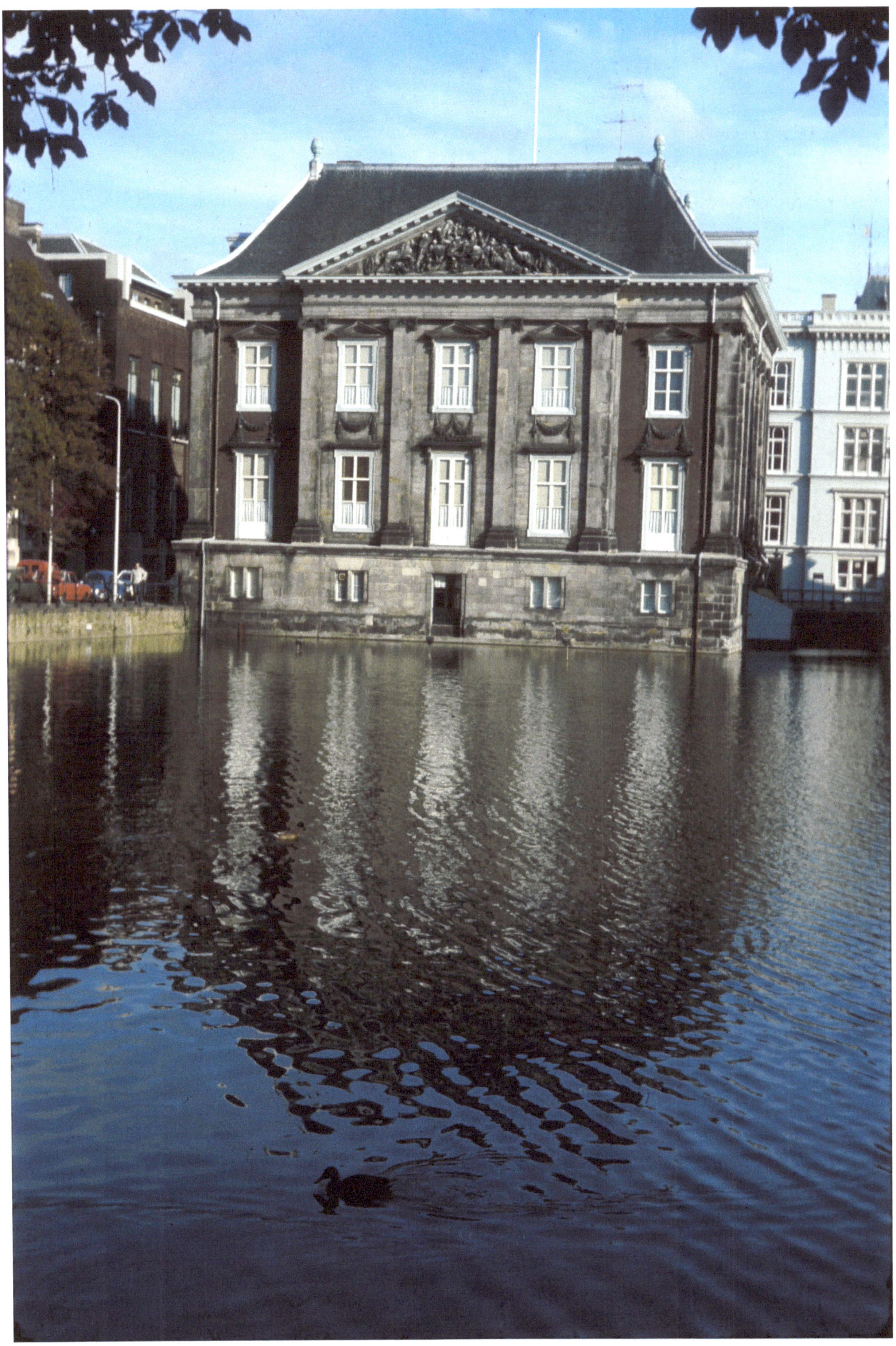

3. Den Haag Mauritshuis (Museum)

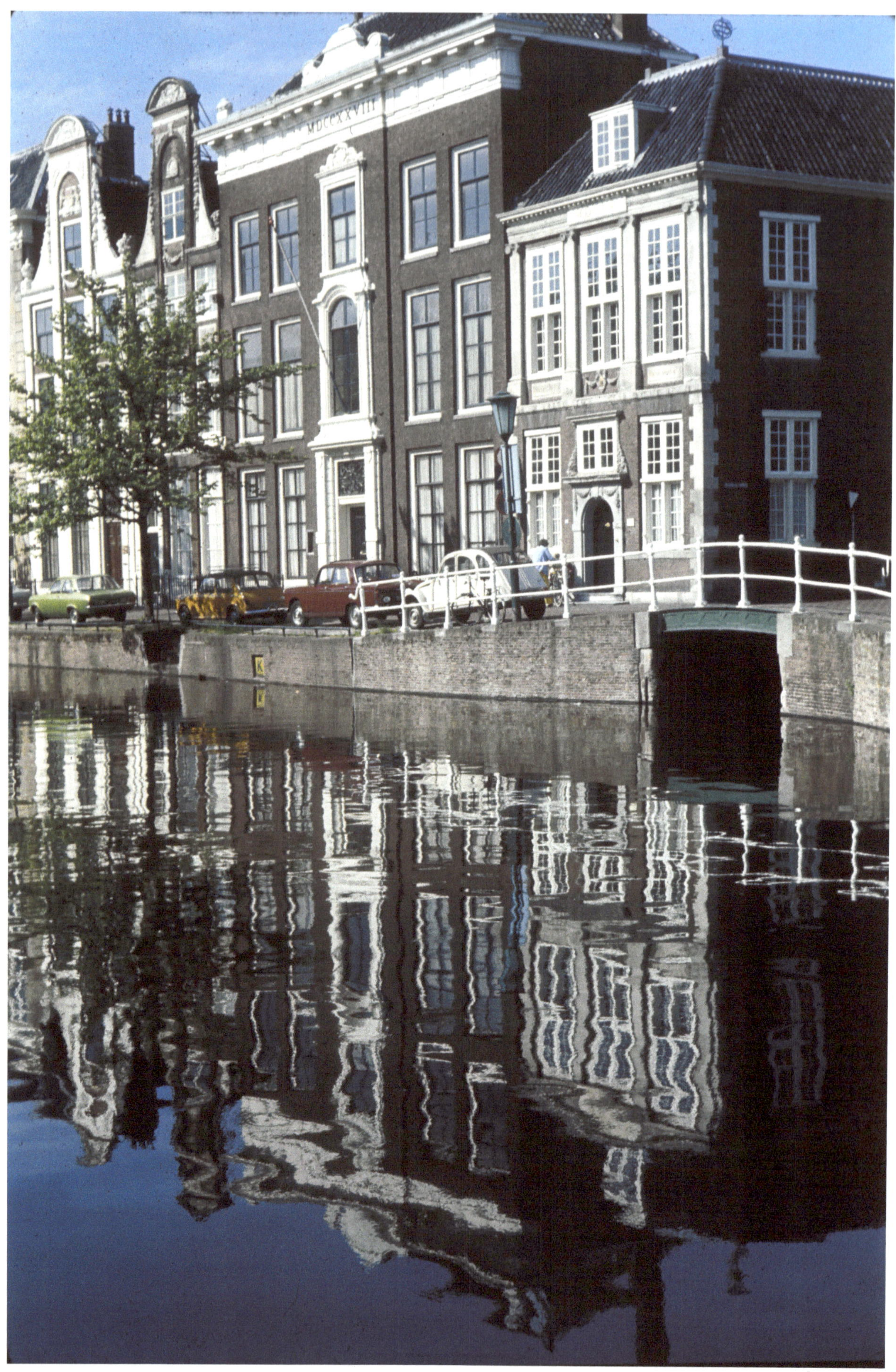

4. Leiden Rapenburg

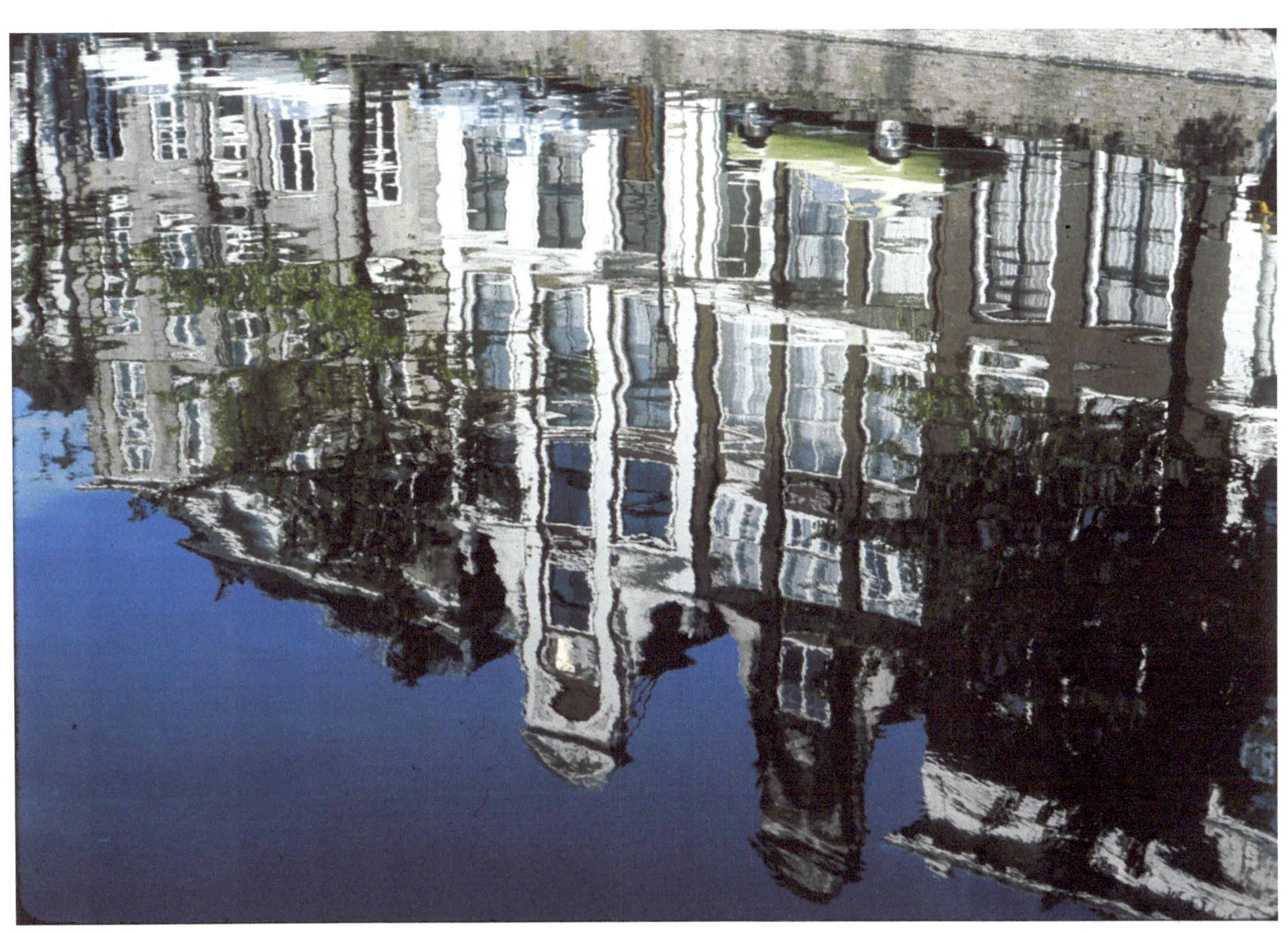

5. Leiden Rapenburg

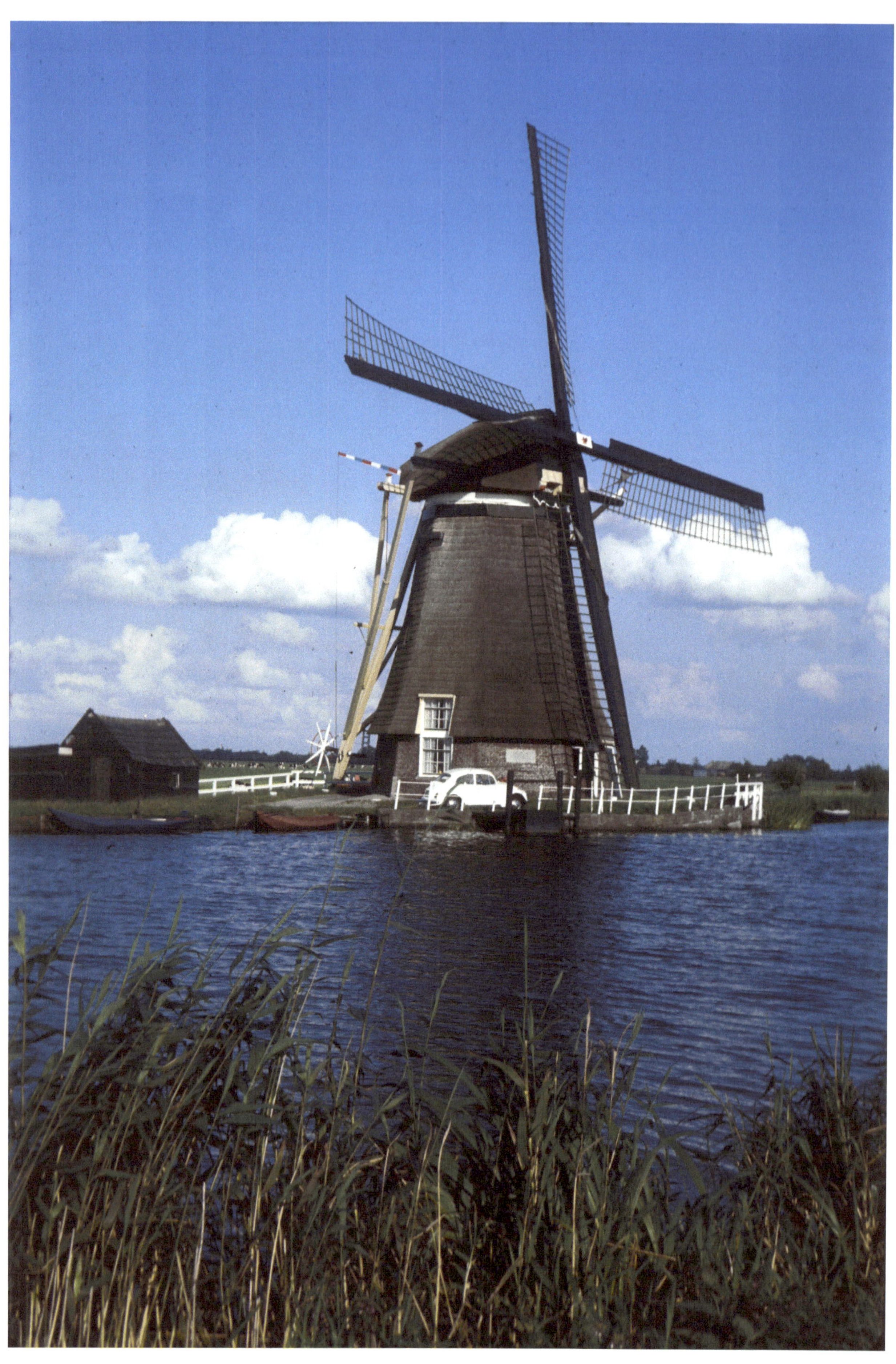

6. Near Den Haag Windmill

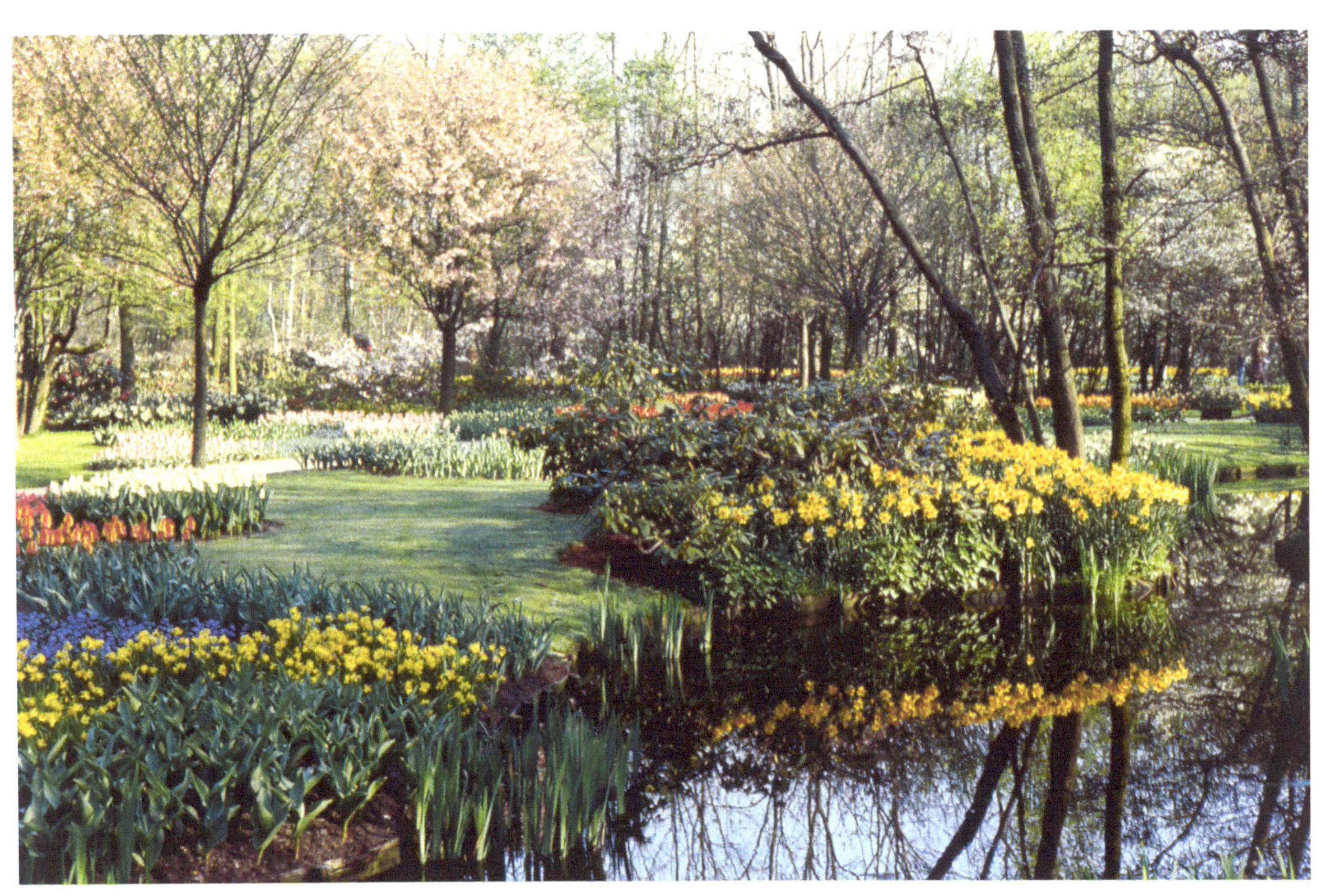

7. Keukenhof

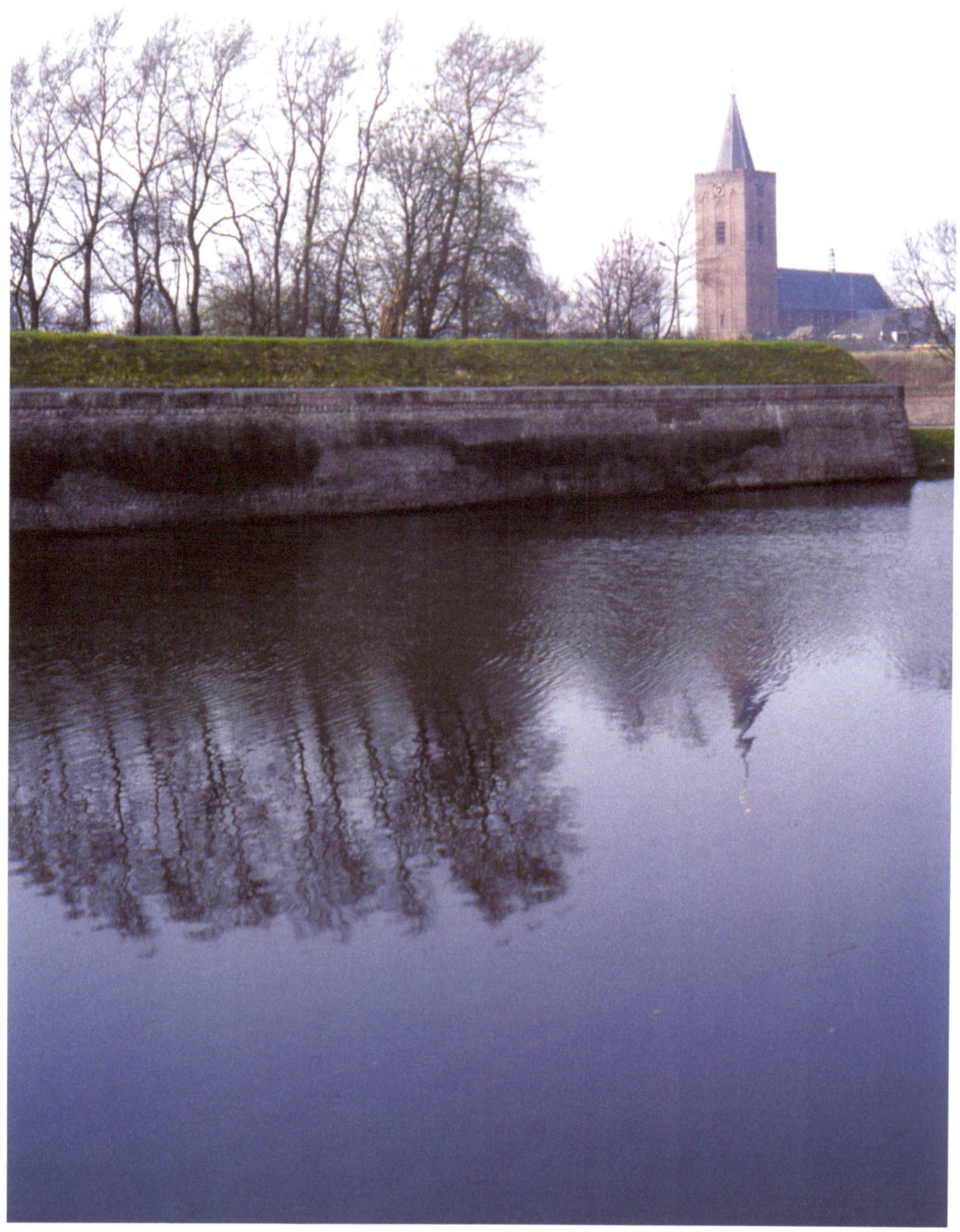

8. Naarden

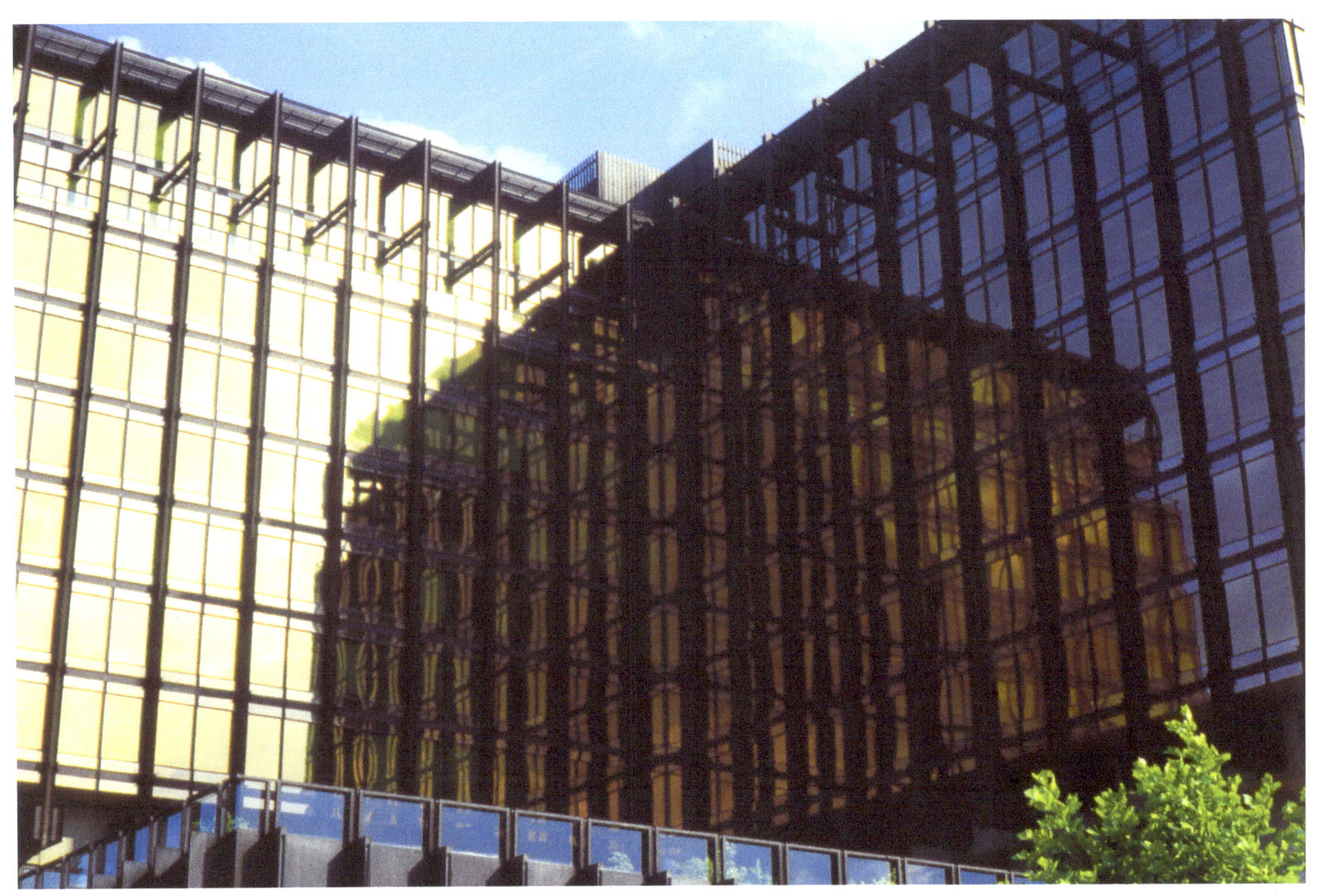

9. Brussels Royale Belge Insurance Co.

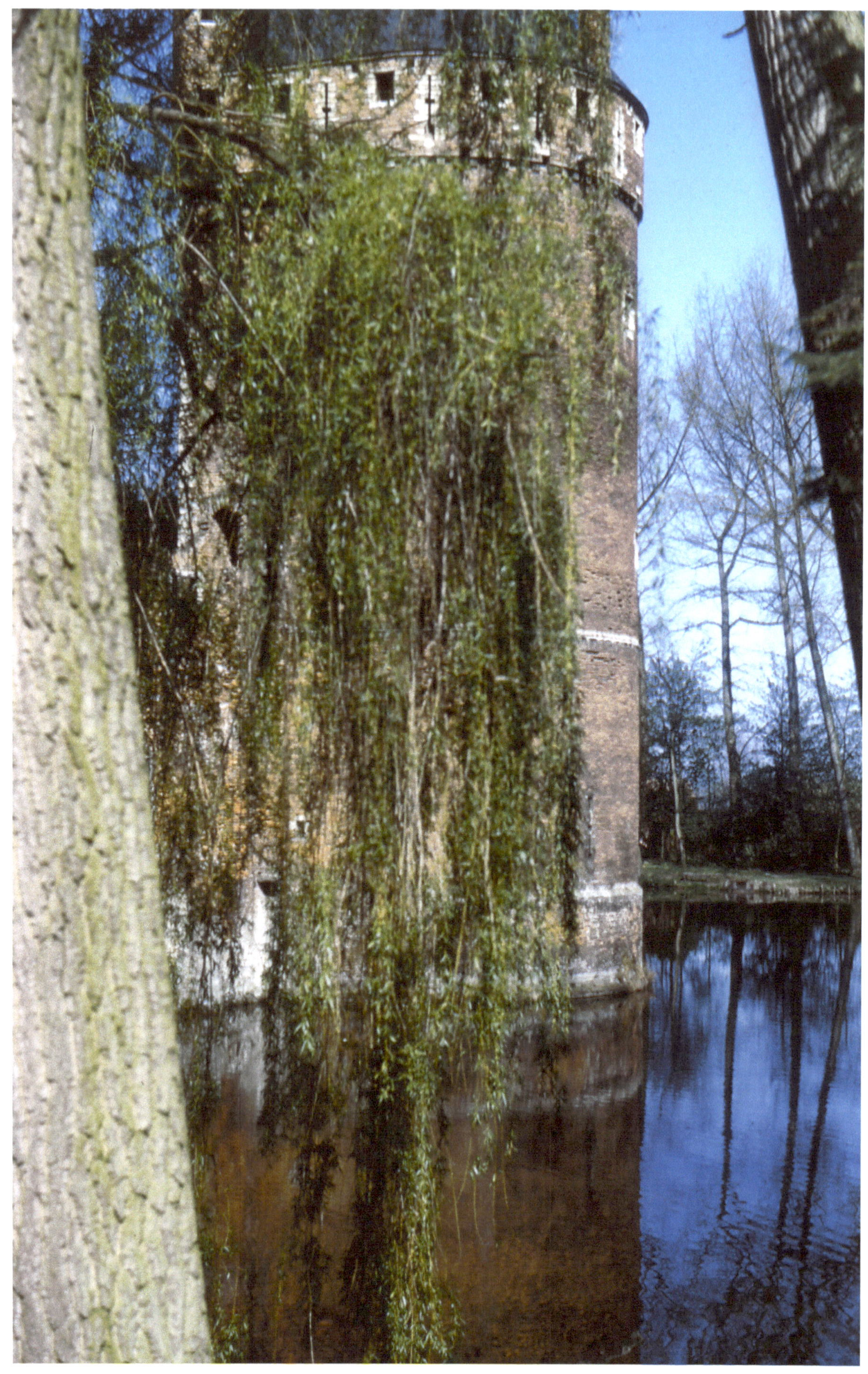

10. Near Brussels Beersel

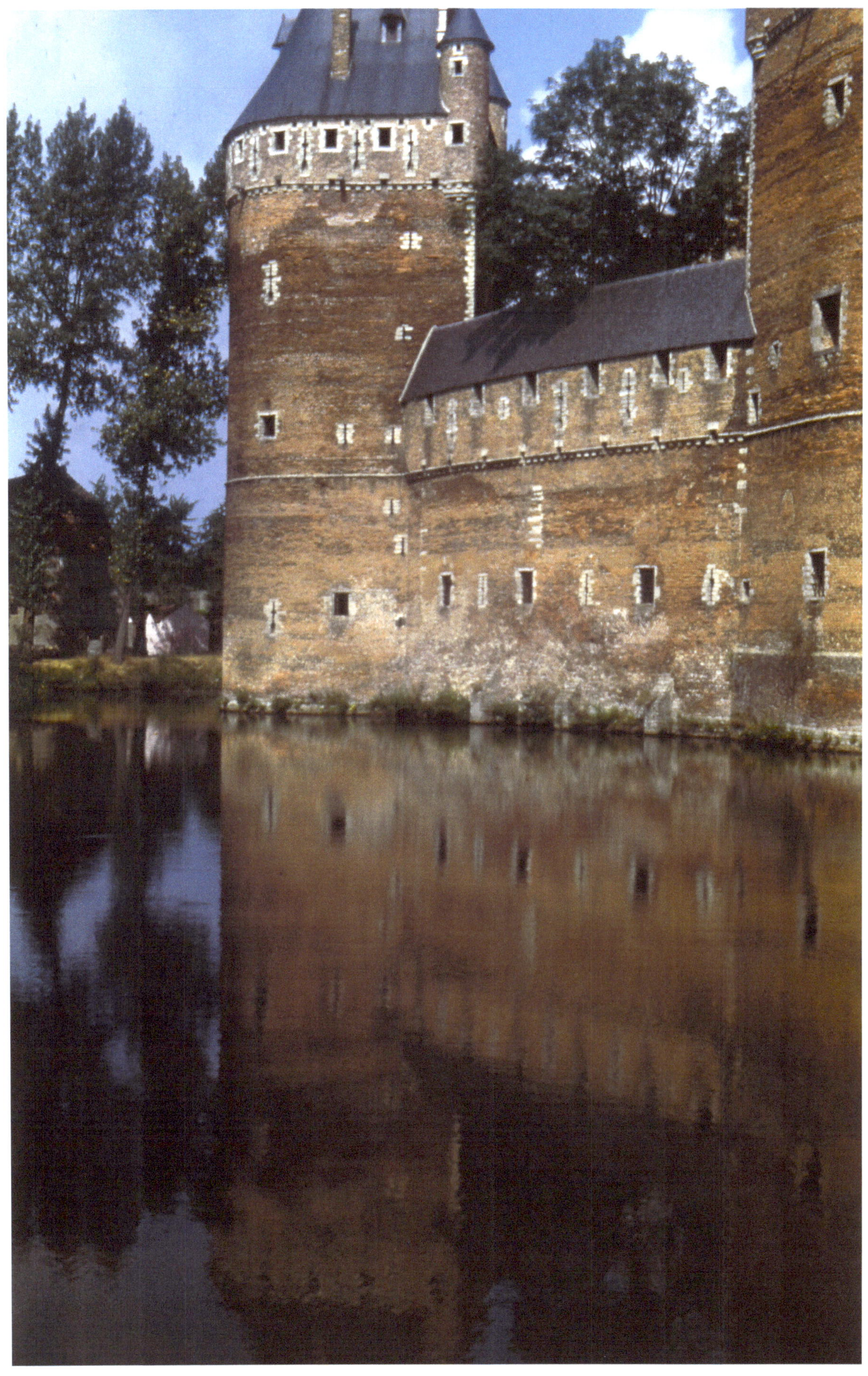

11. Near Brussels Beersel

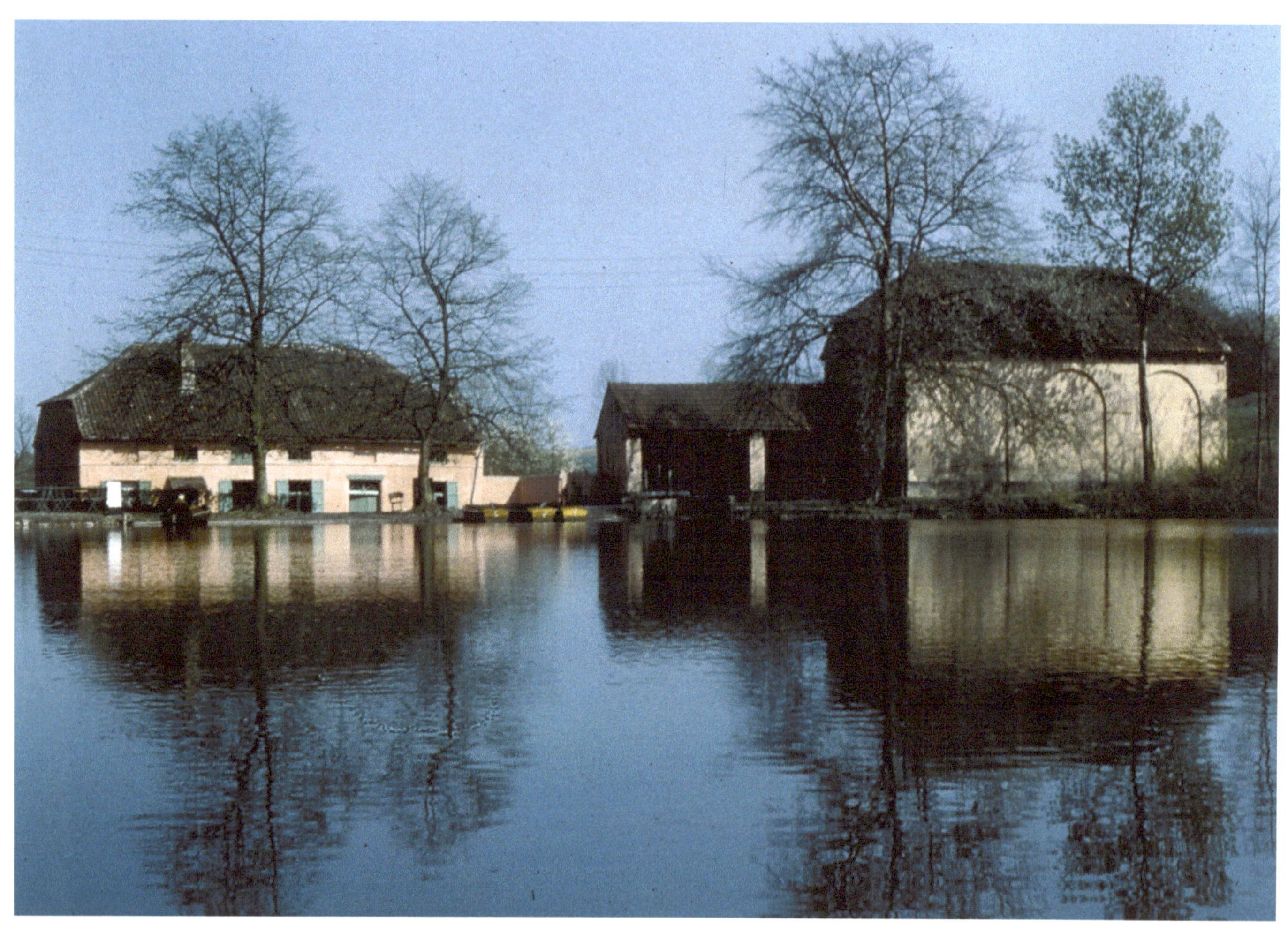

12. Near Brussels Sept Fontaines

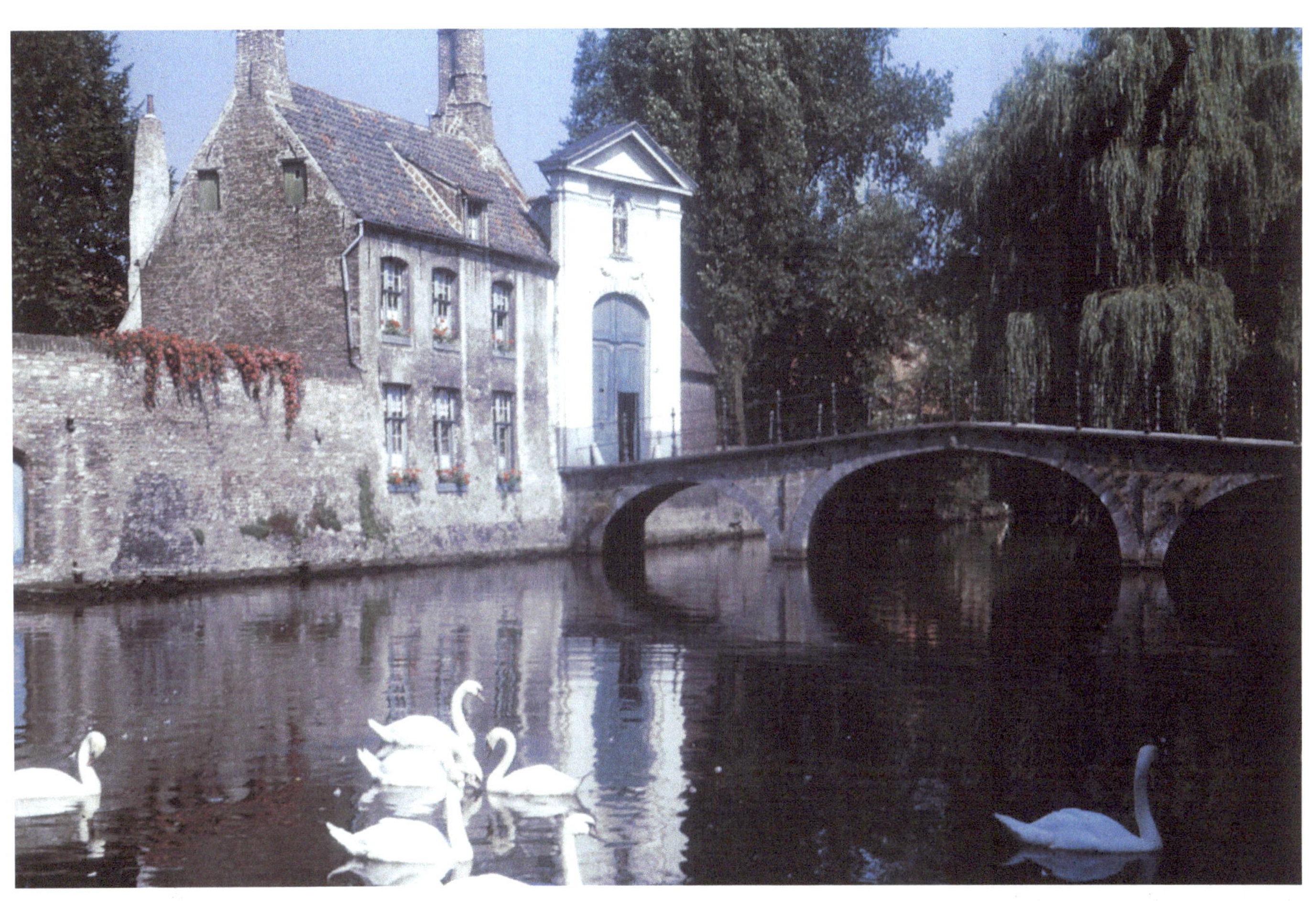

13. Bruges-Brugge Begijnhof (Entrance)

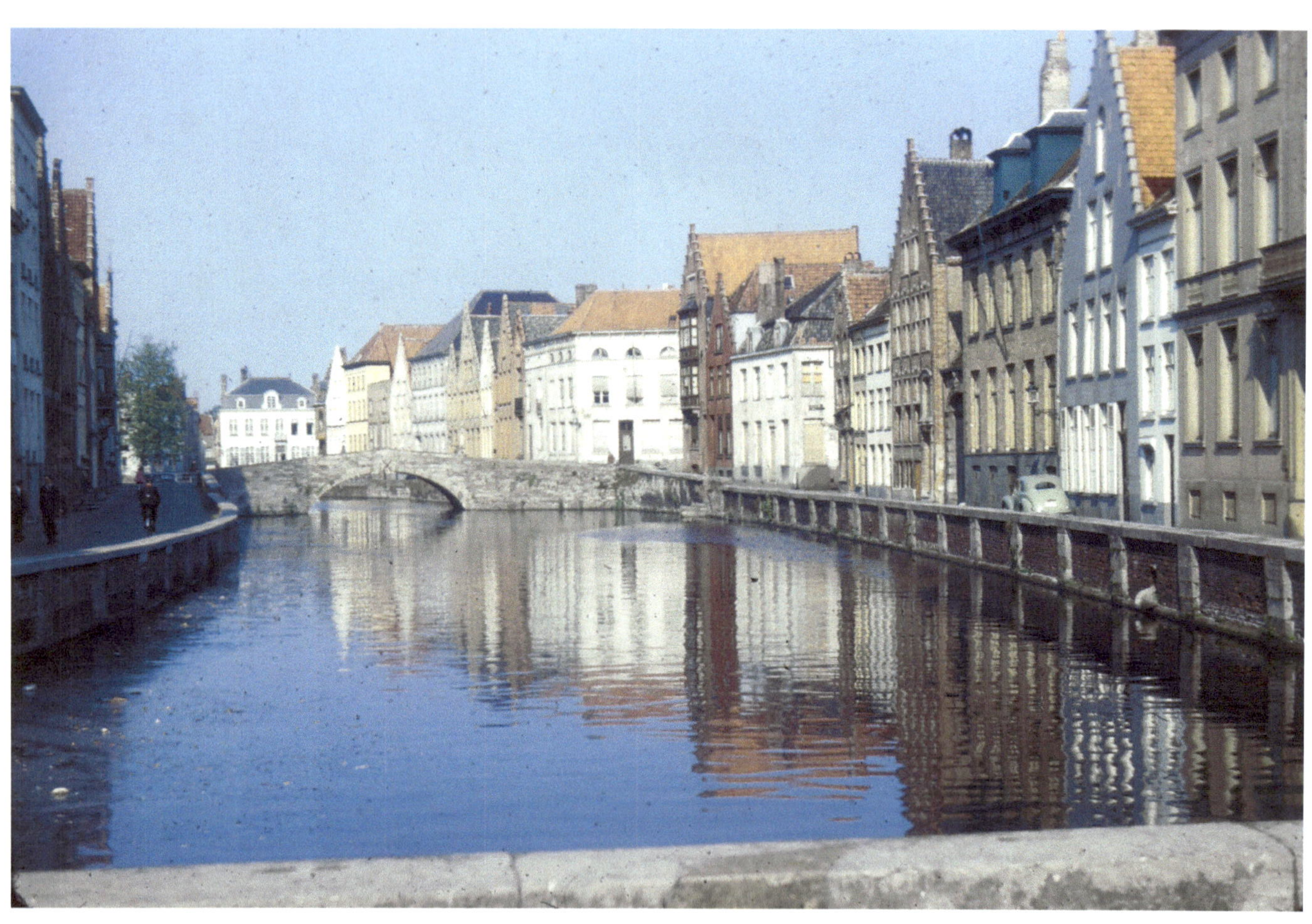

14. Bruges-Brugge Spiegelrei

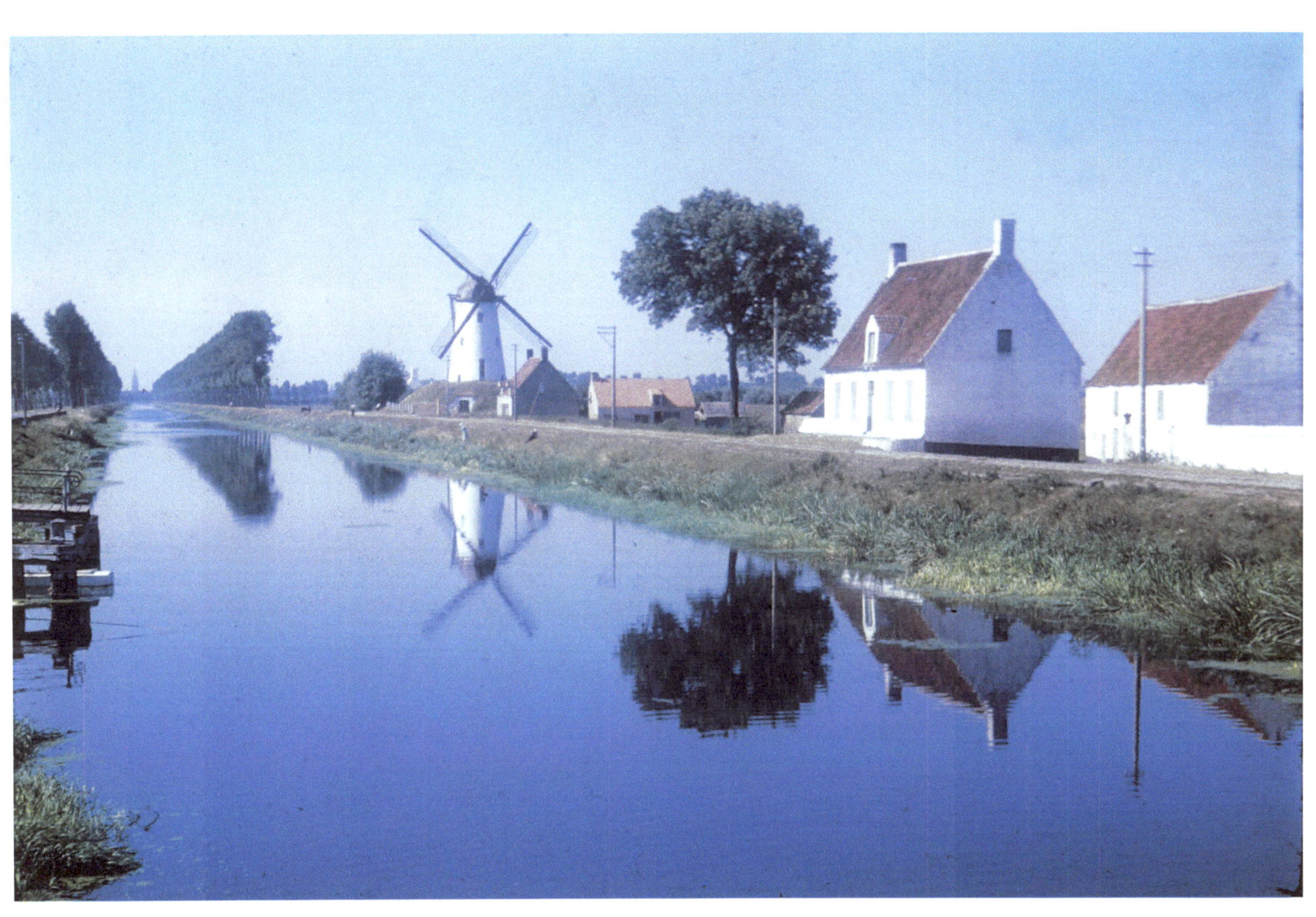

15. Damme Canal toward Bruges

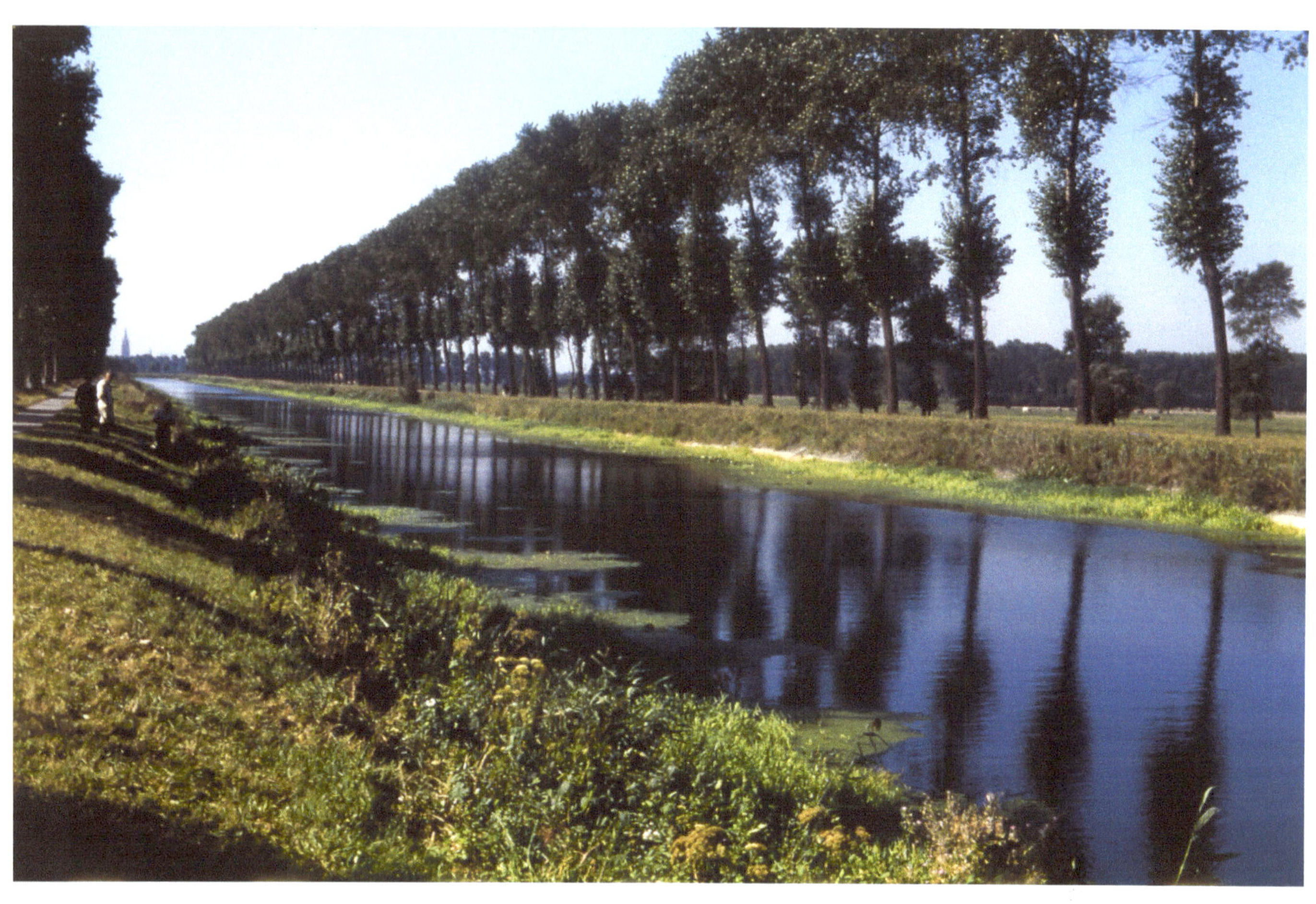

16. Damme Canal toward Bruges

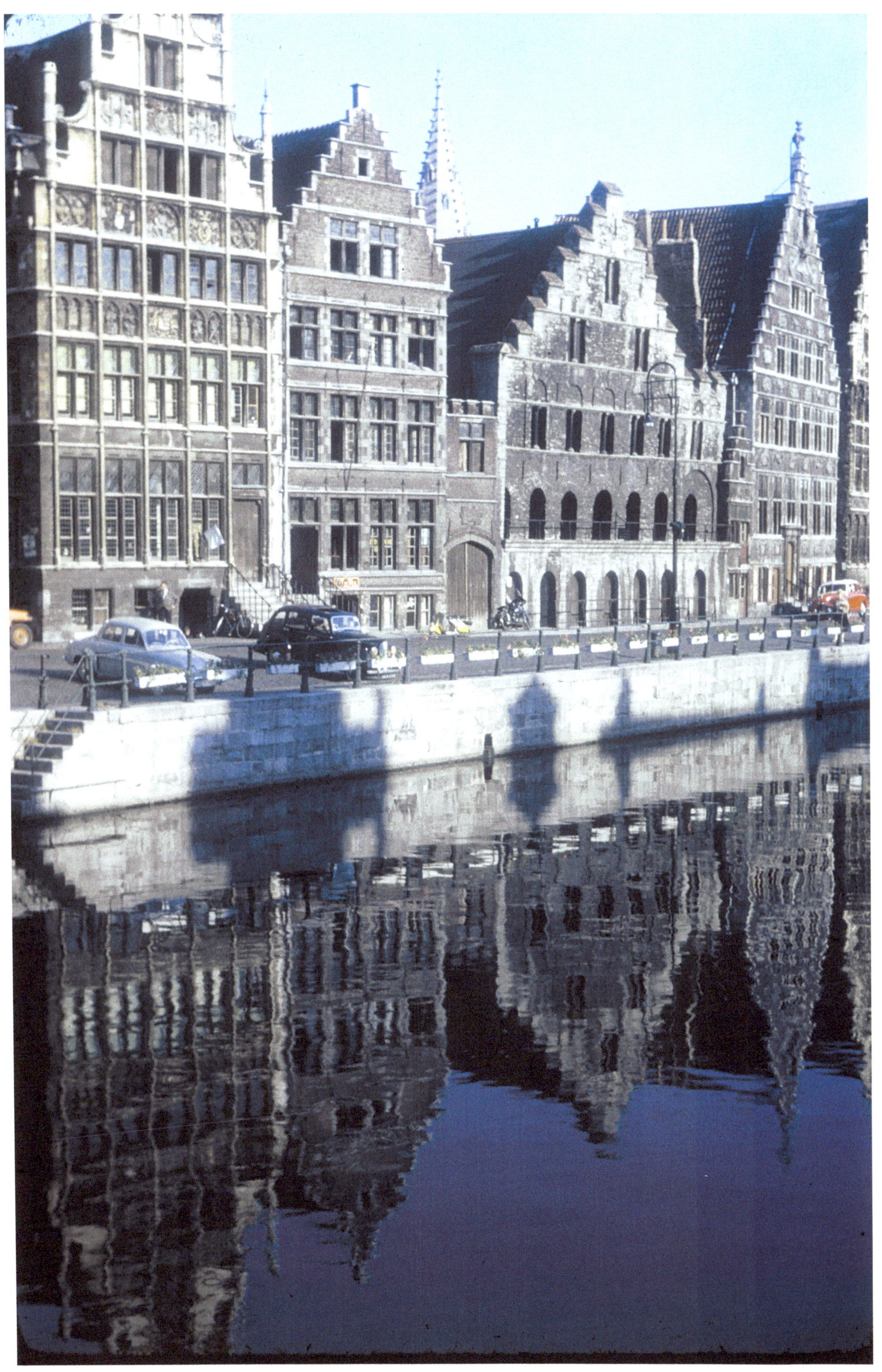

17. Gent Graslei (Guildhouses)

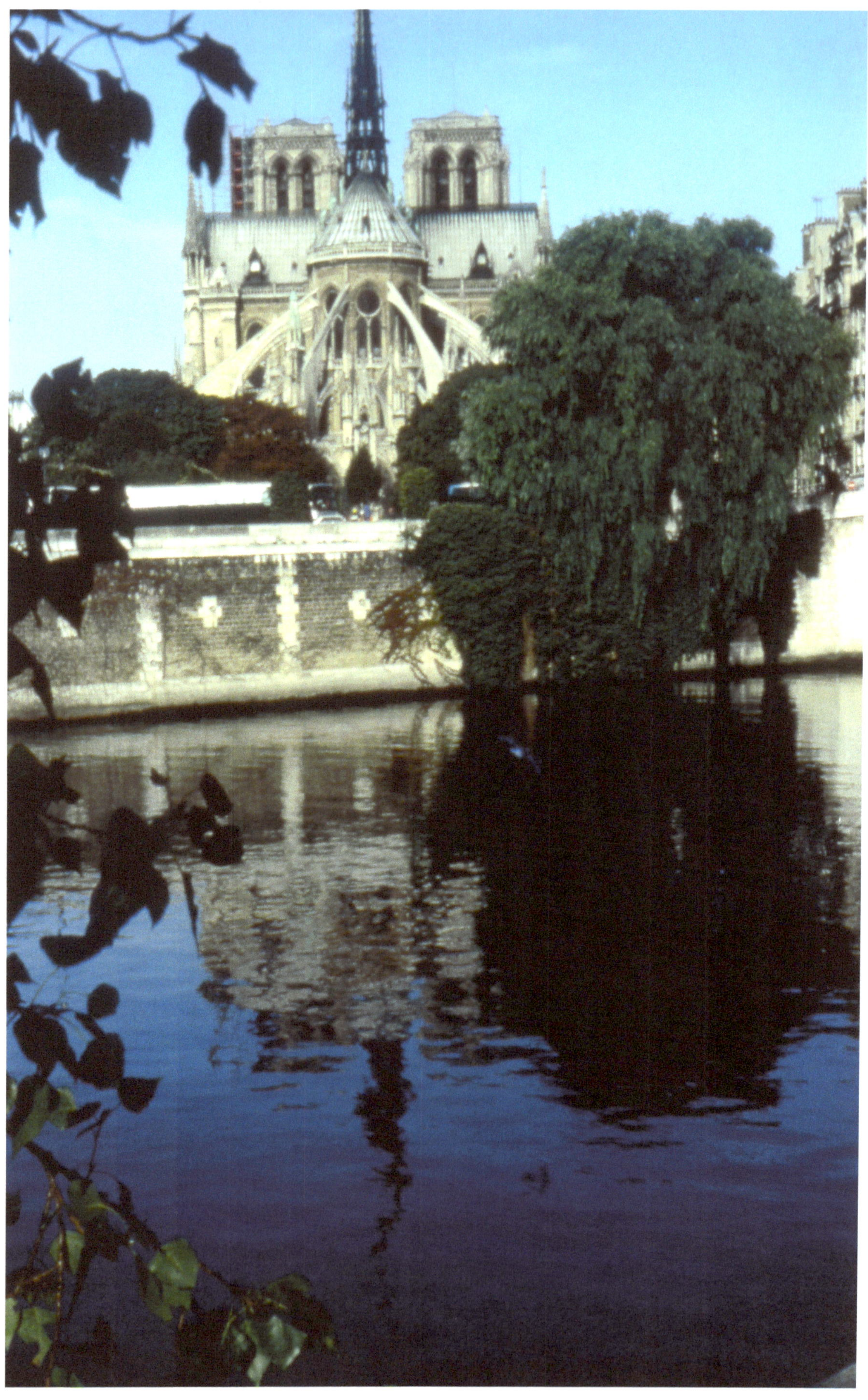

18. Paris Notre Dame (View from Ile St. Louis)

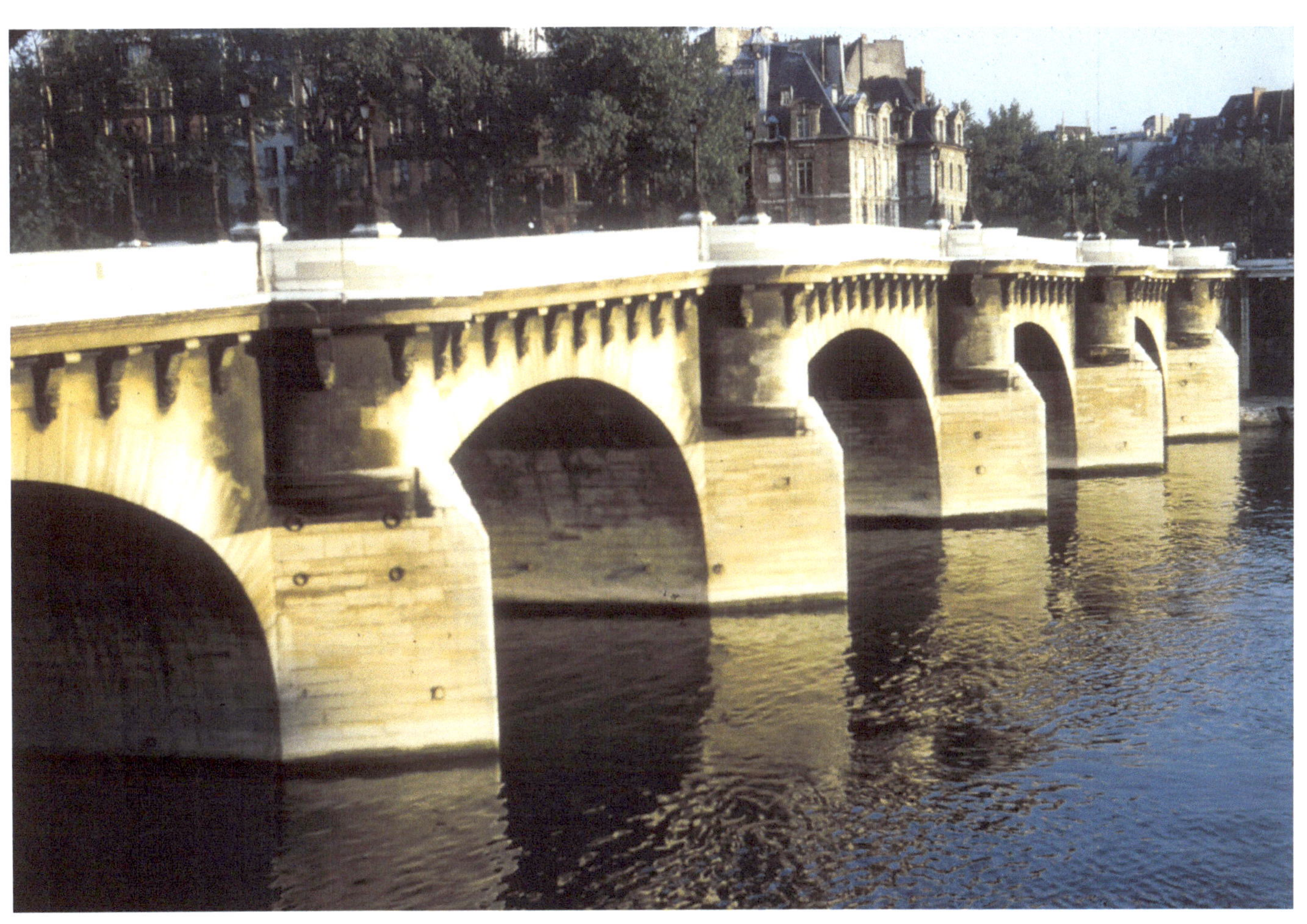

19. Paris Pont Neuf

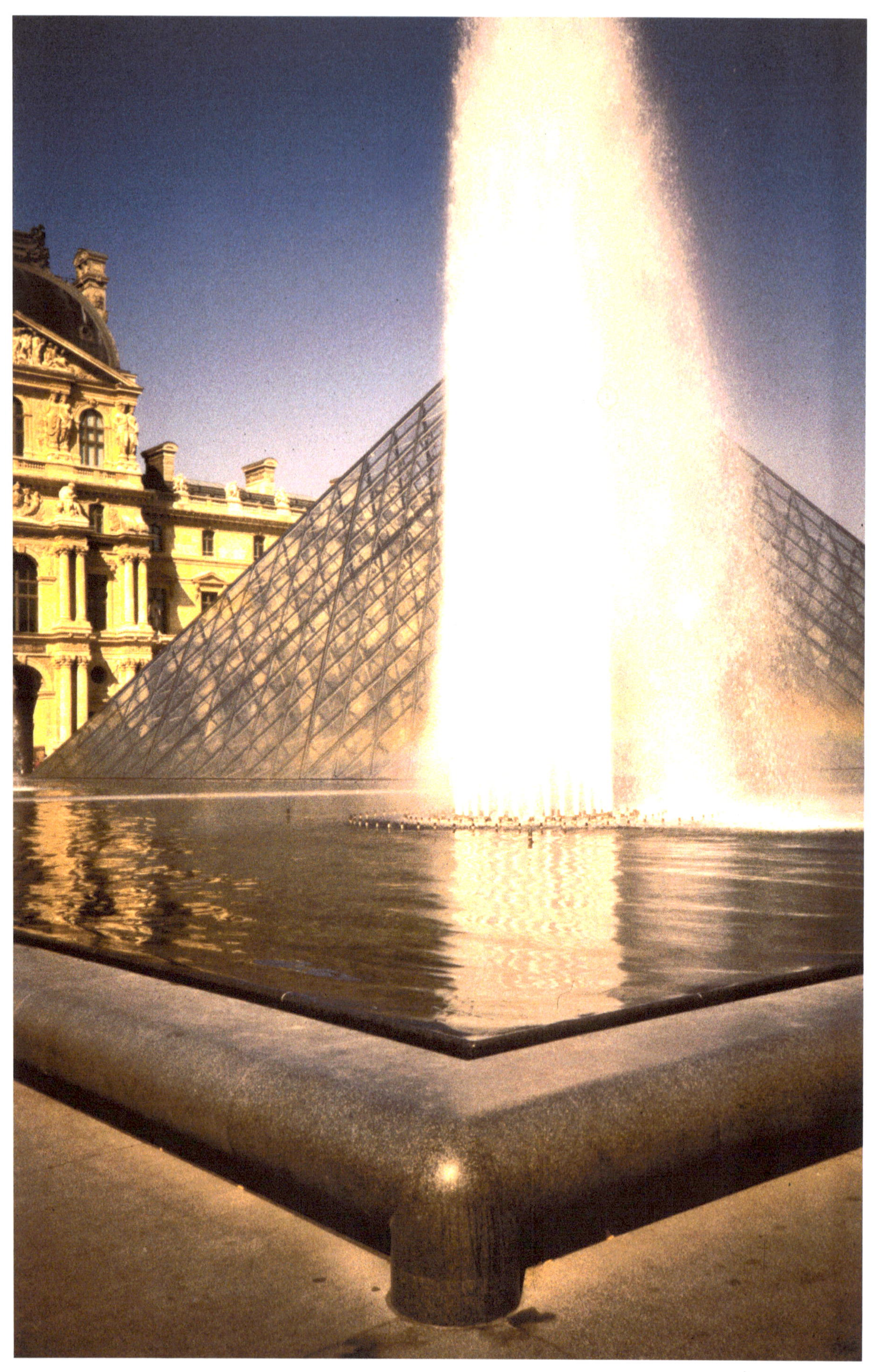

20. Paris Louvre (court yard)

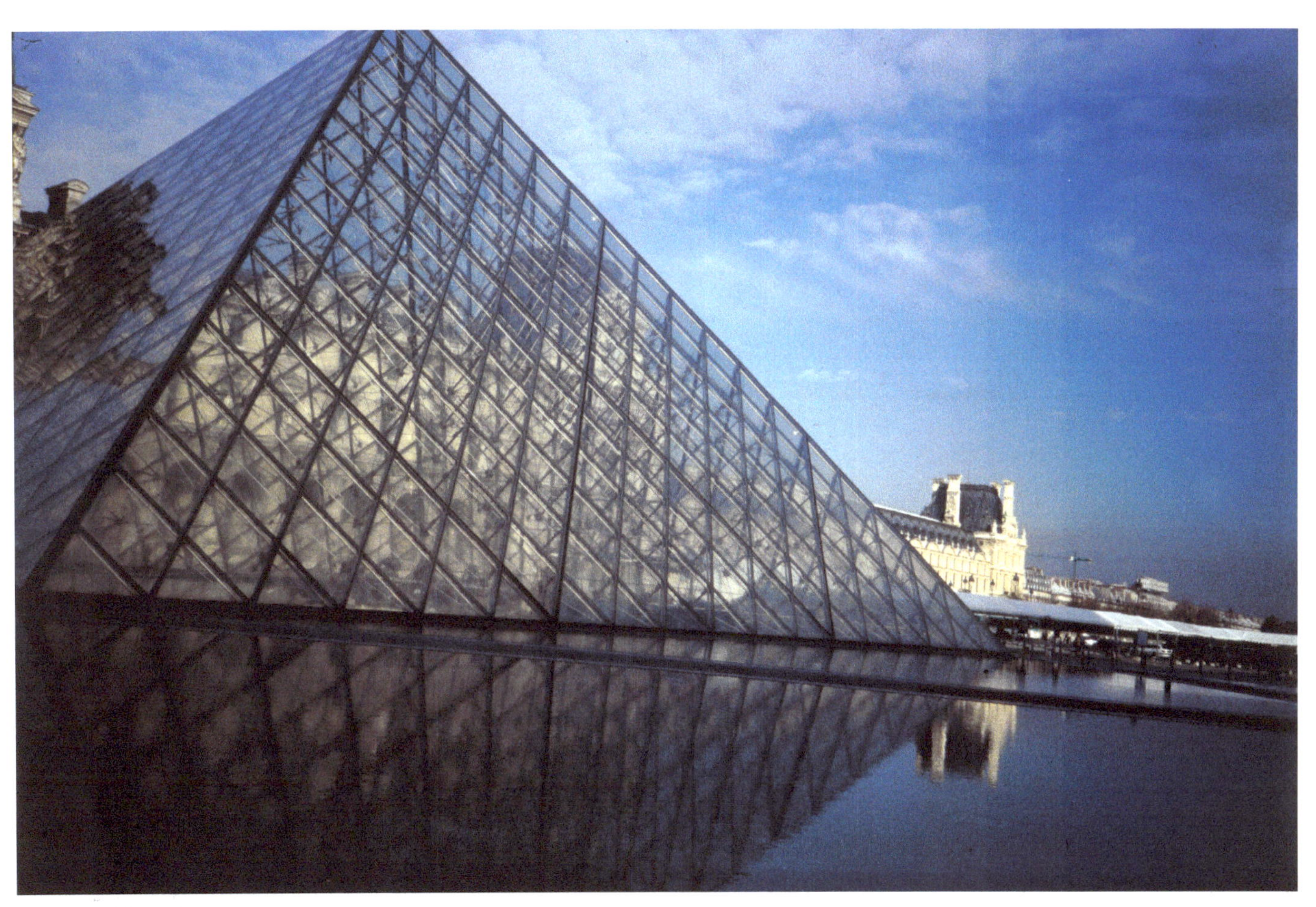

21. Paris Louvre (court yard)

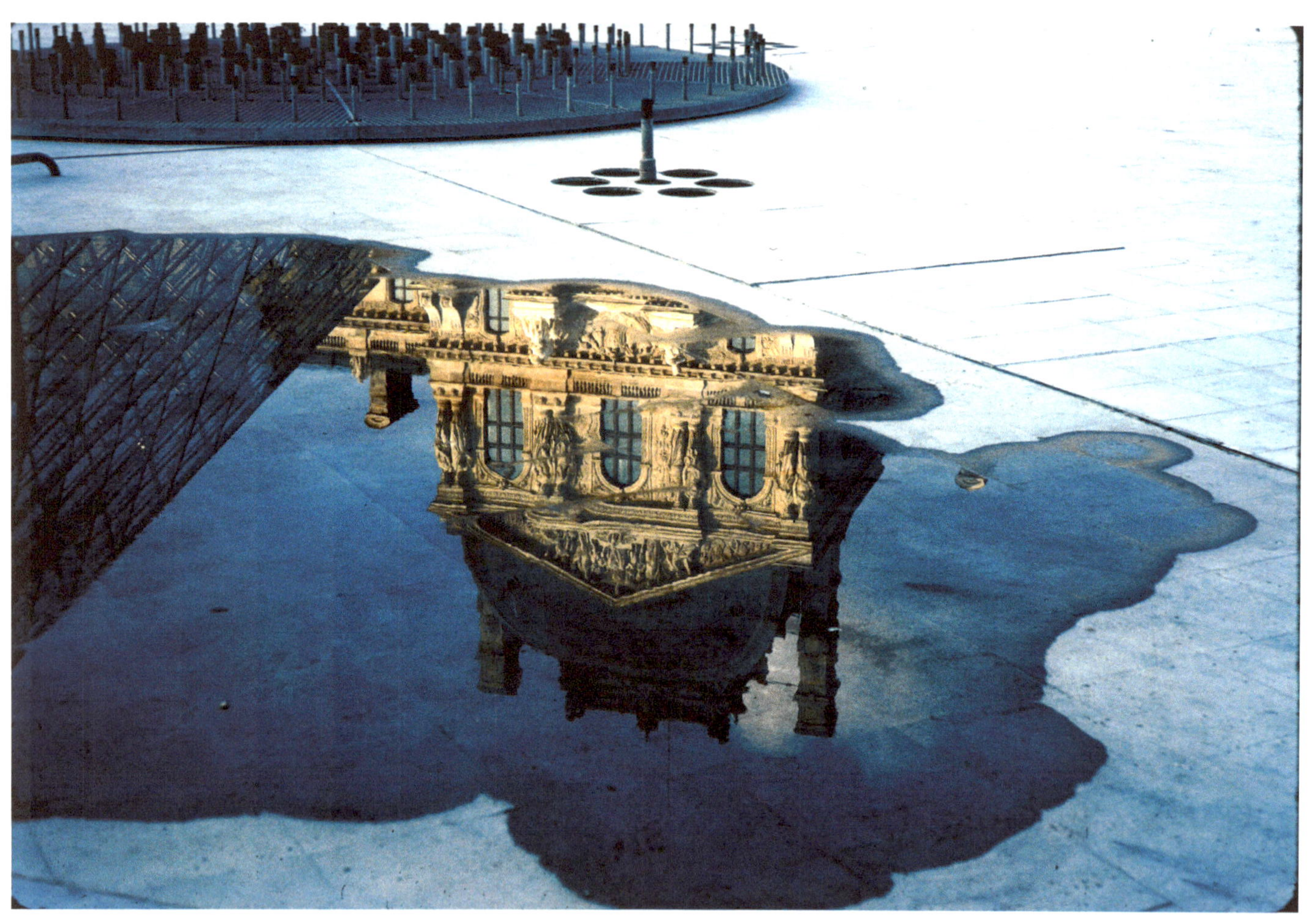

22. Paris Louvre (court yard)

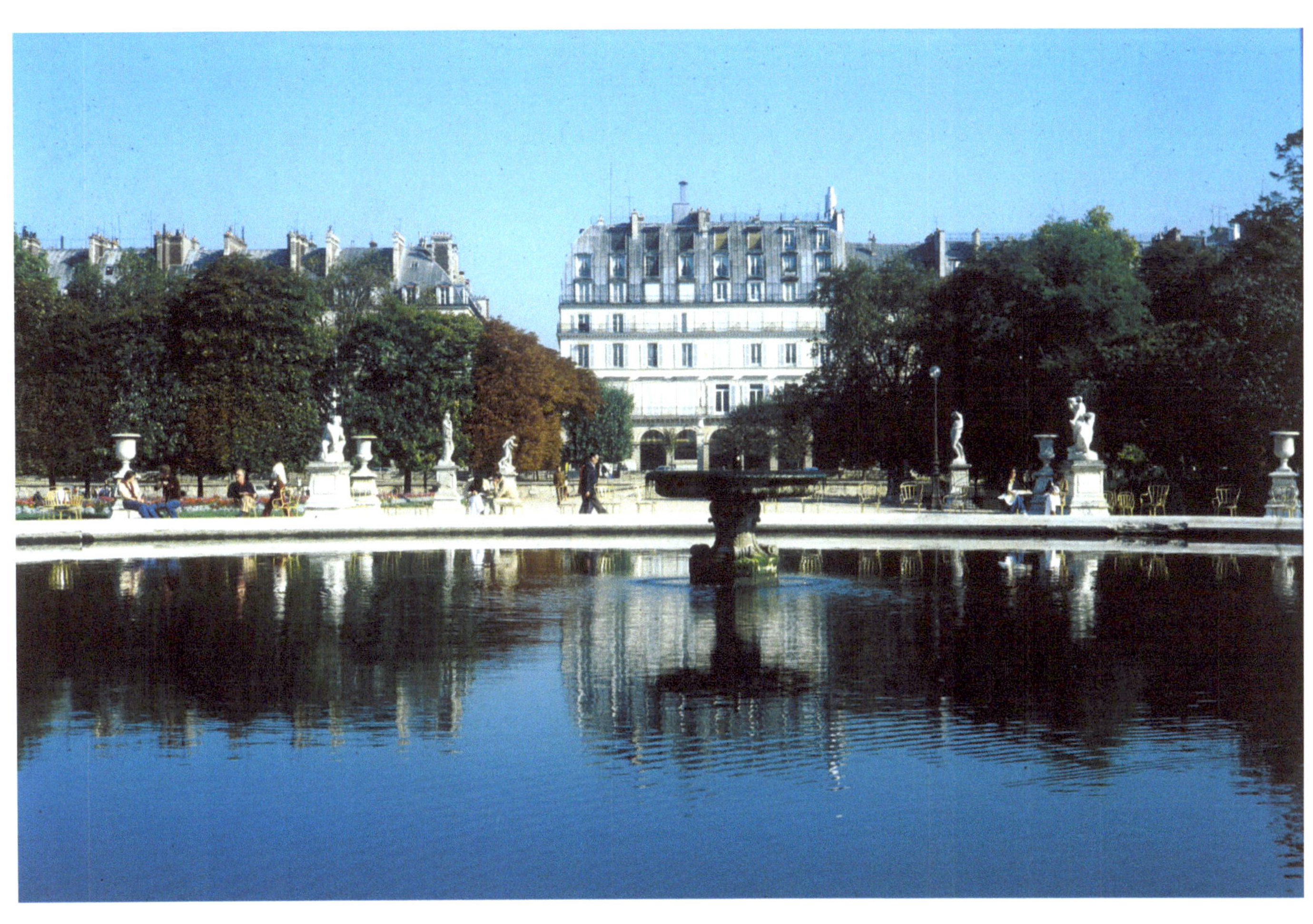

23. Paris Jardin des Tuileries

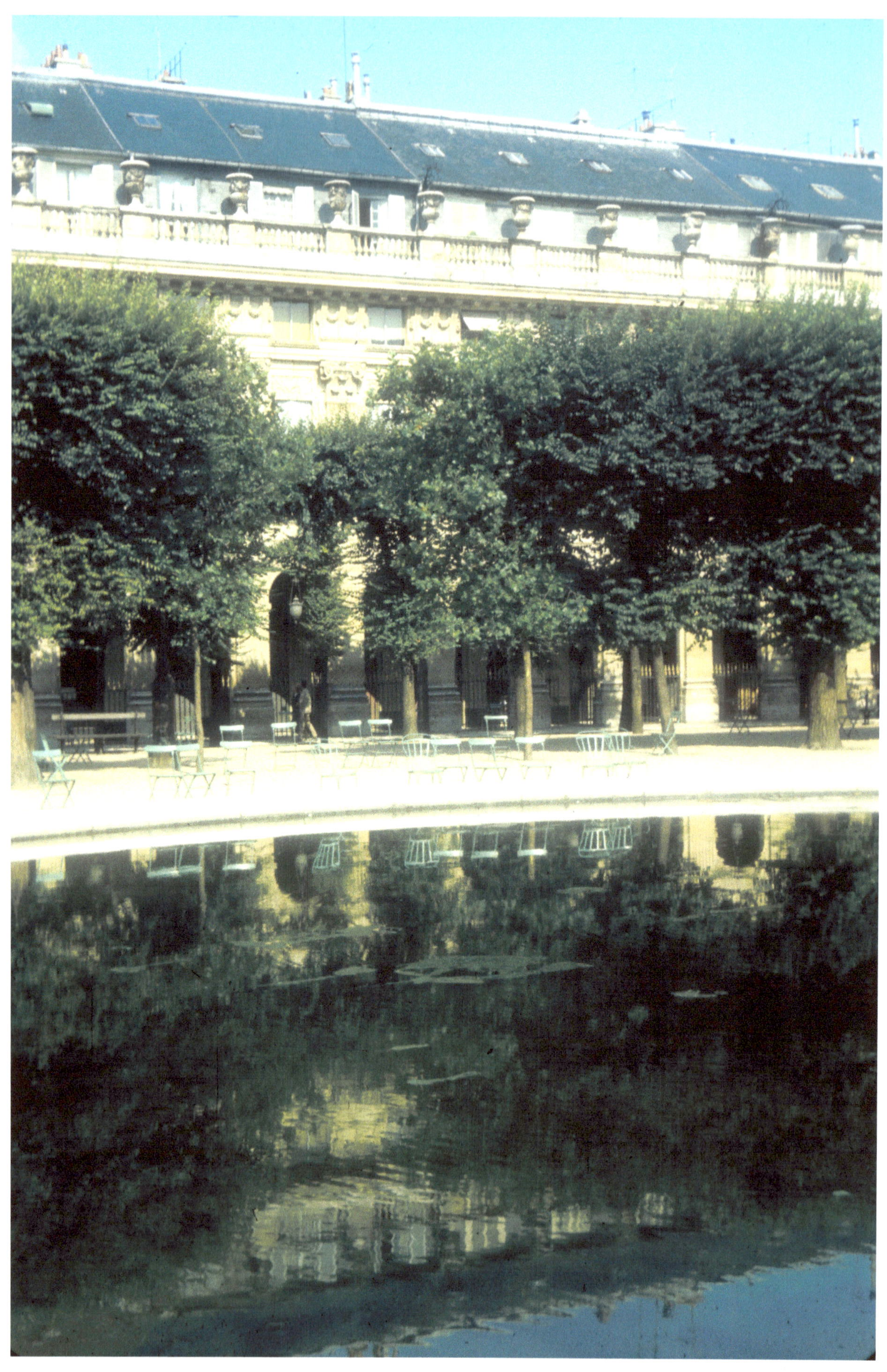

24. Paris Jardin du Palais Royal

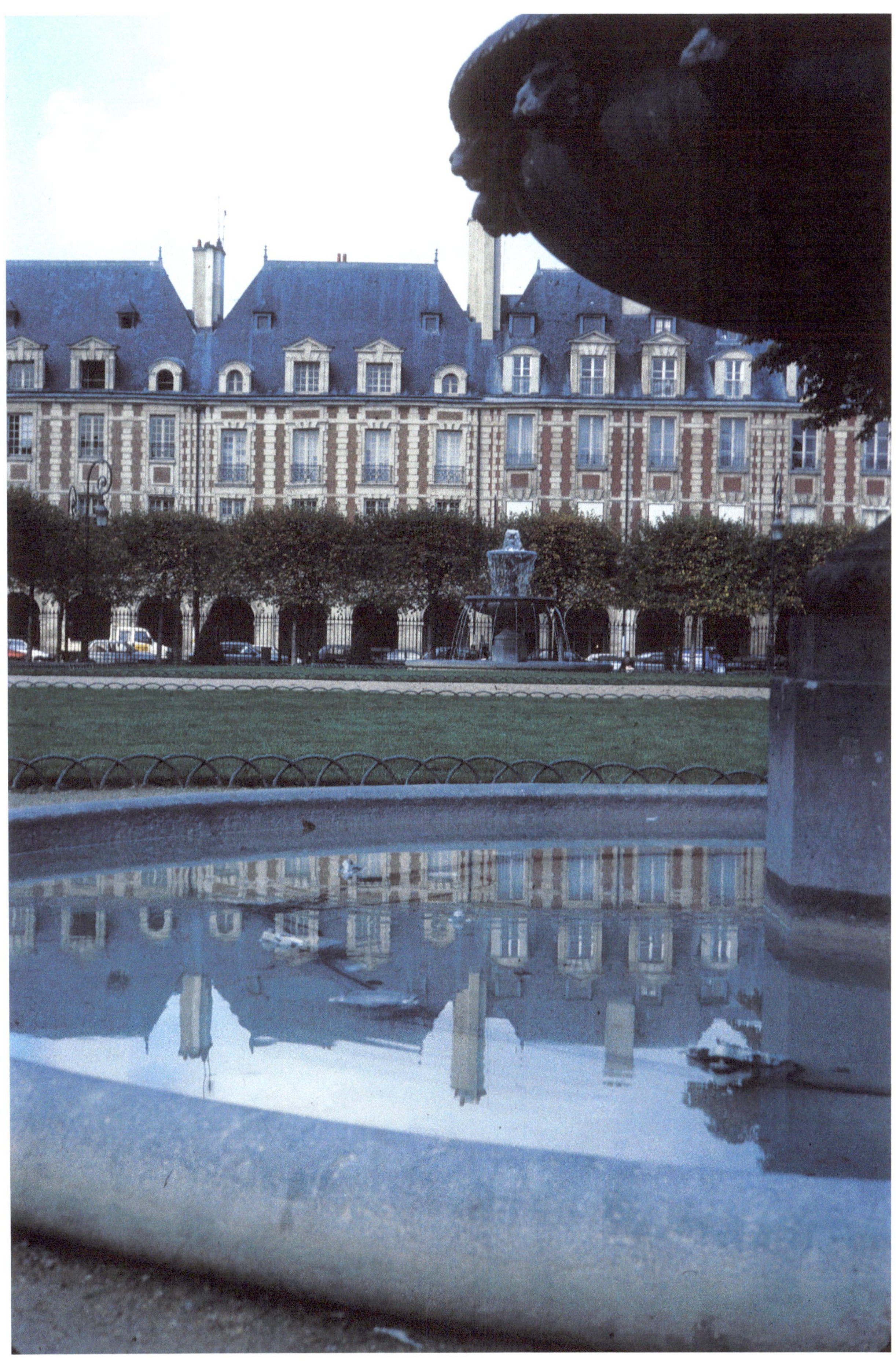

25. Paris Place de Vosges

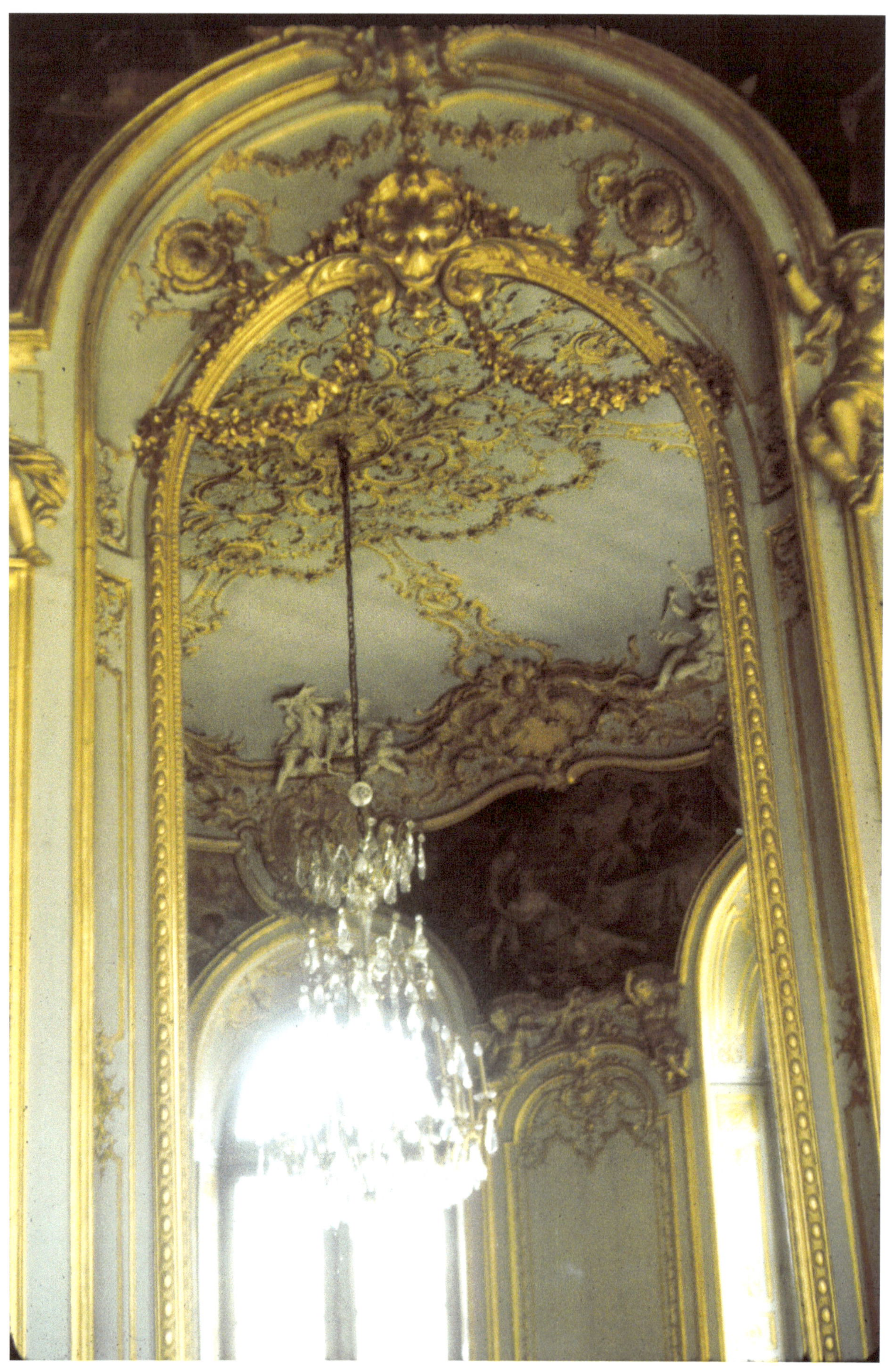

26. Paris Hôtel de Subise

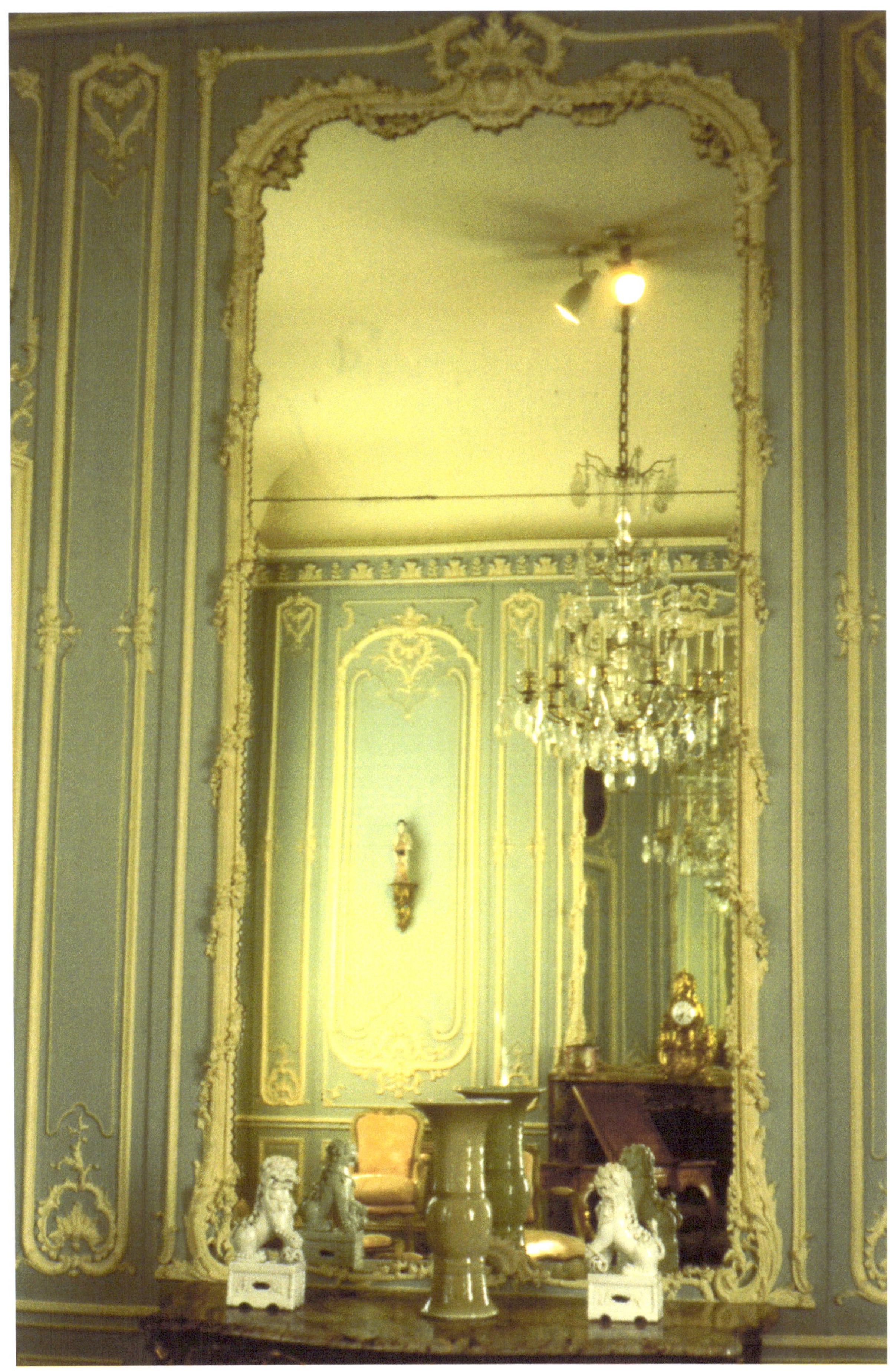

27. Paris Musée Carnevalet

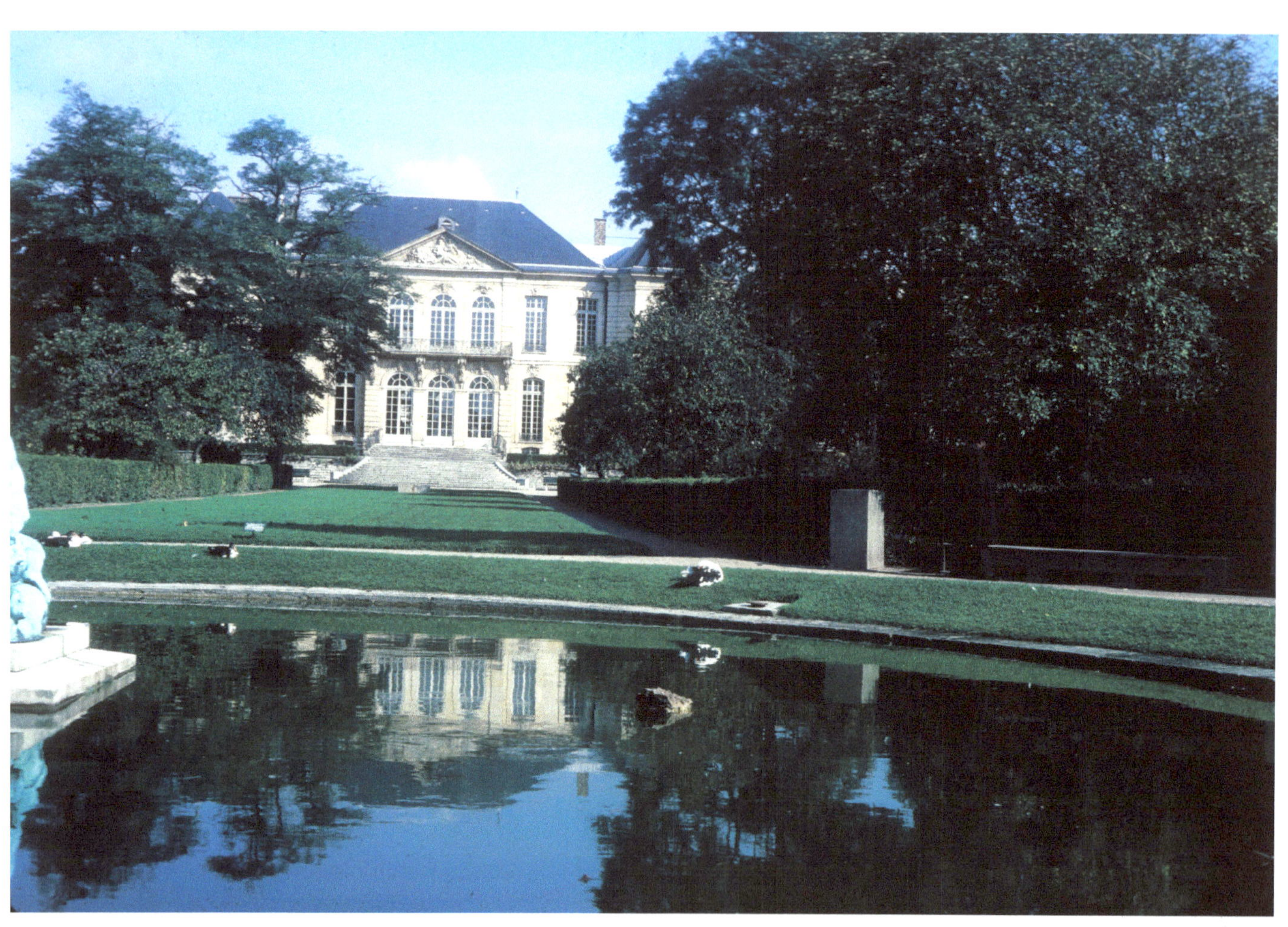

28. Paris Hotel de Biron (Rodin Mueum)

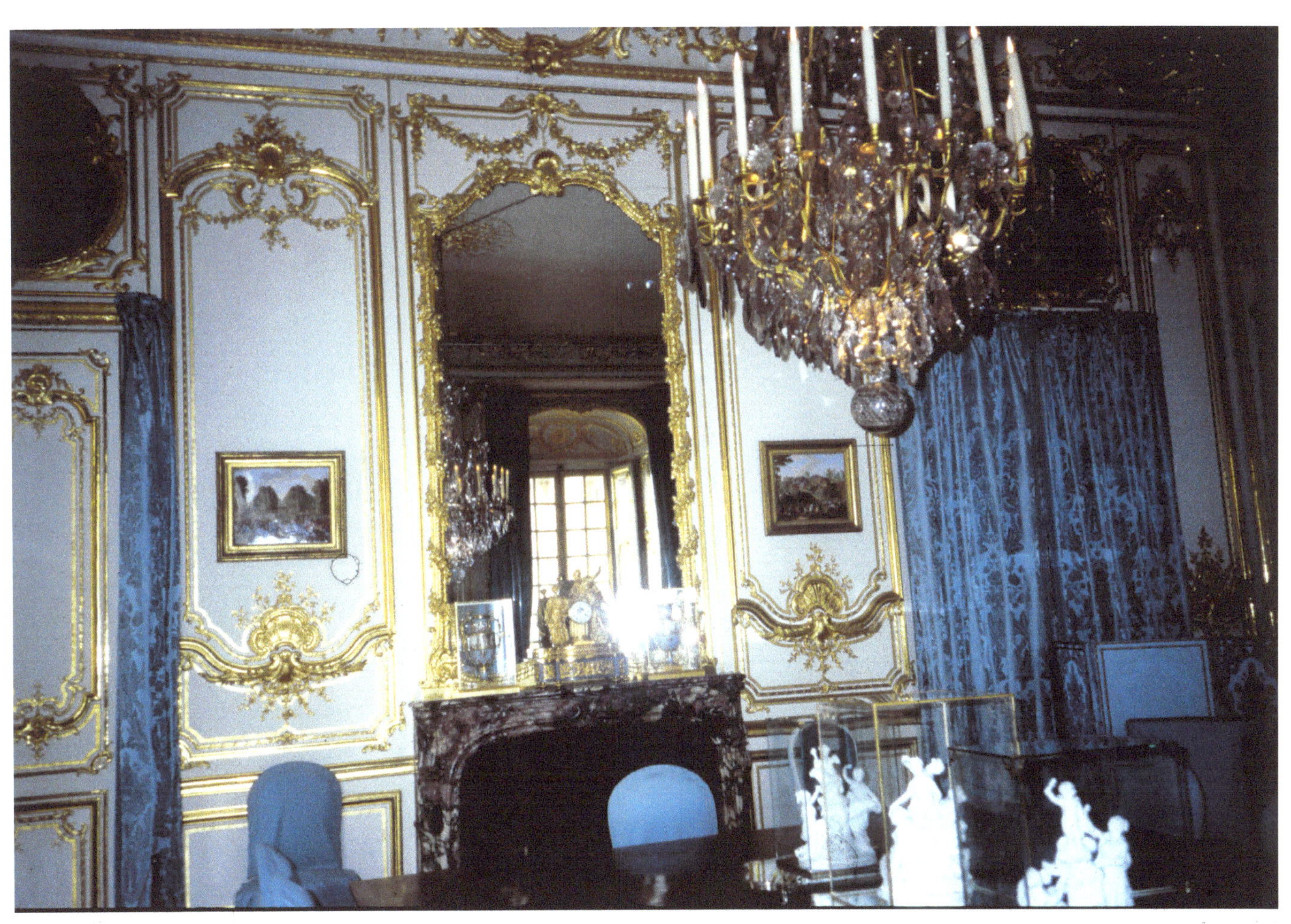

29. Versailles Château (Apts. Du Roi)

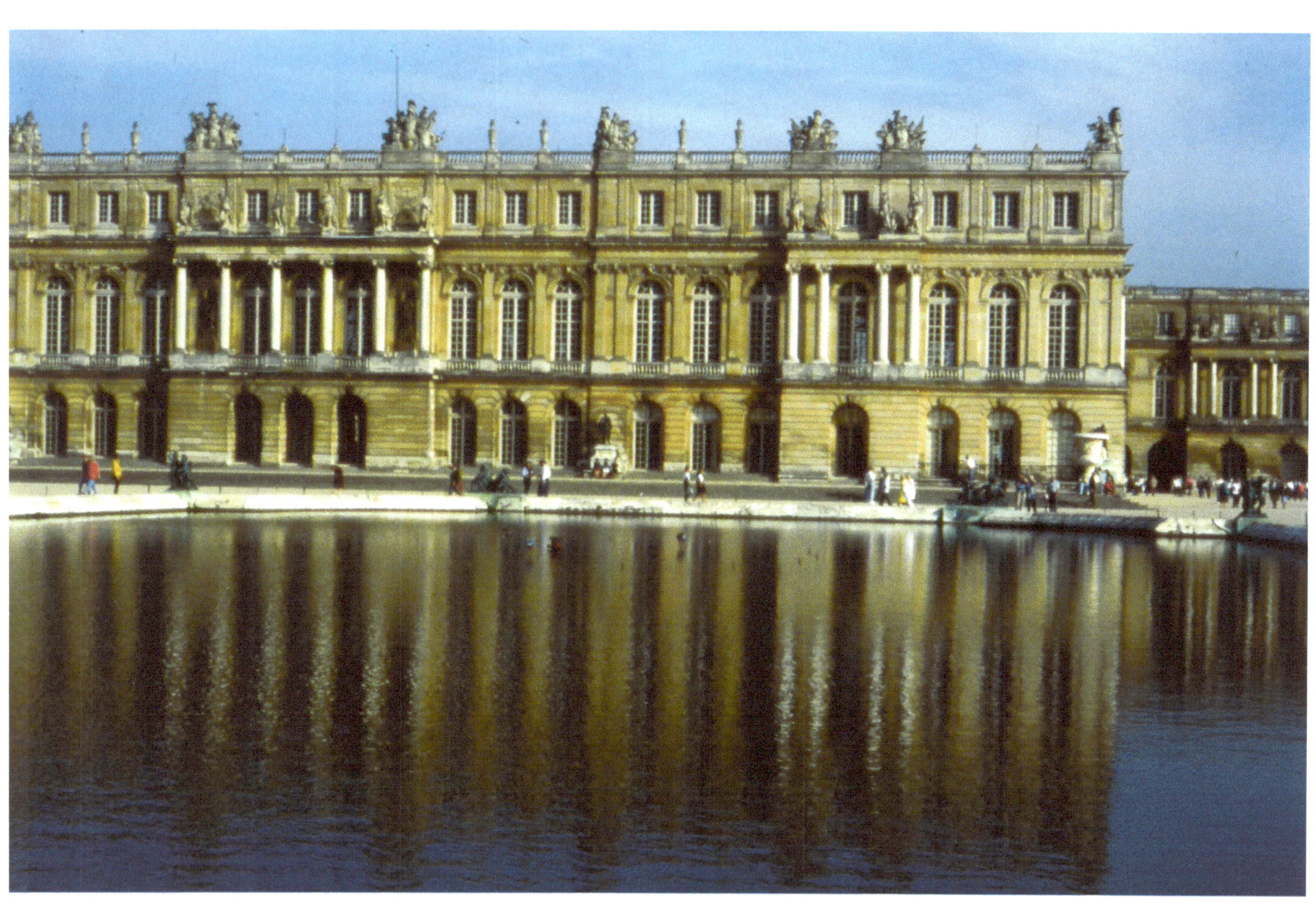

30. Versailles Château

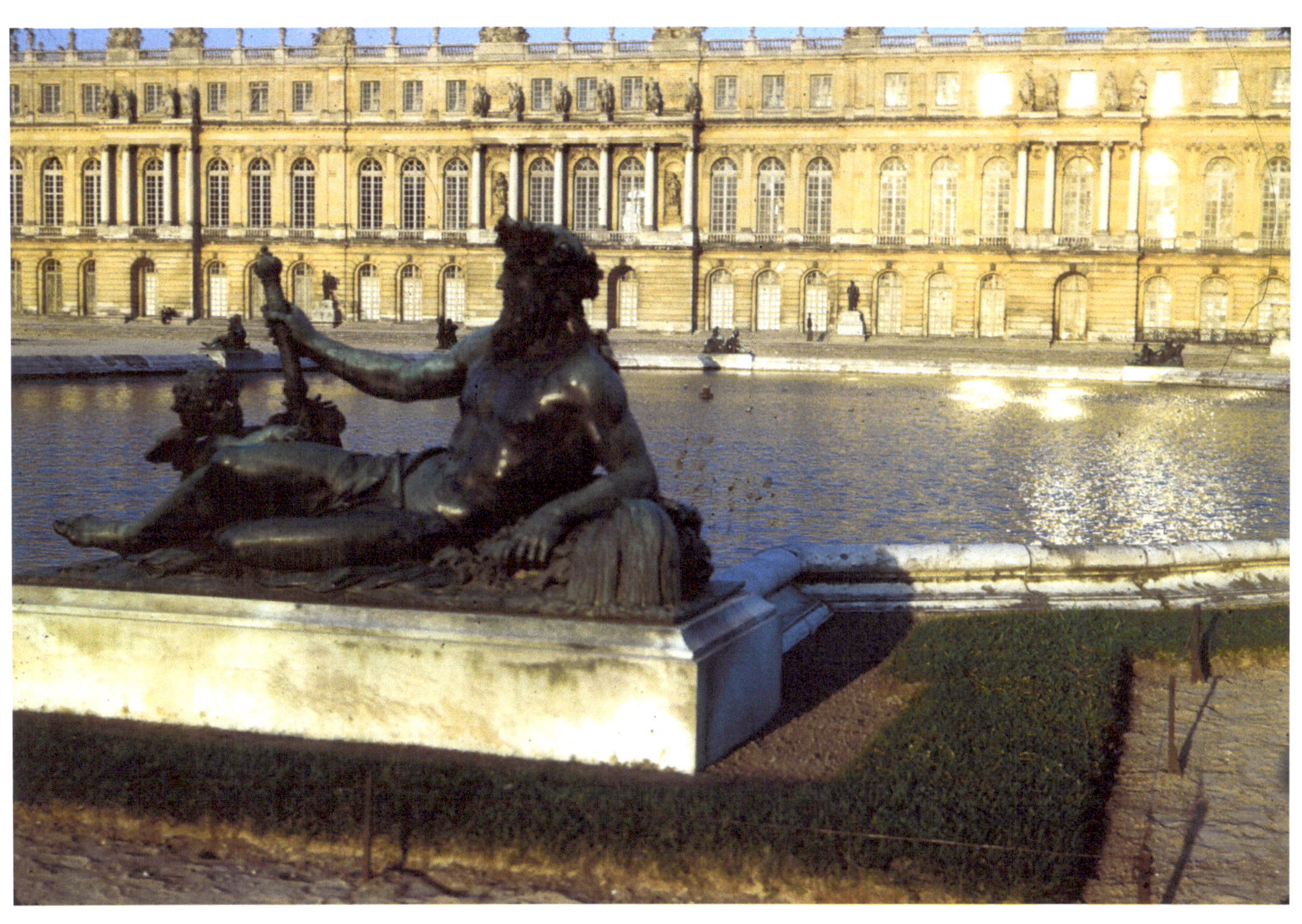

31. Versailles Château

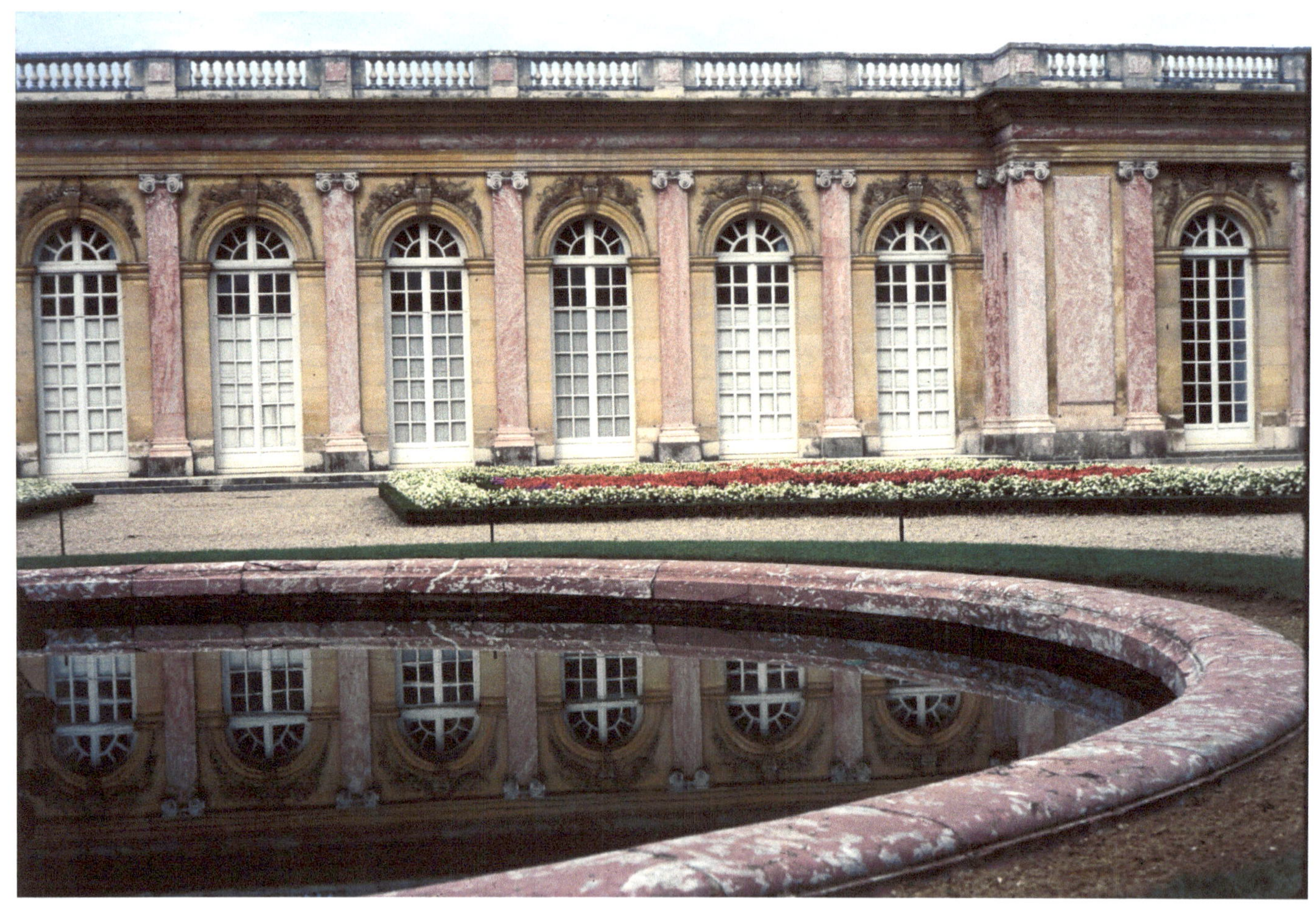

32. Versailles Grand Trianon

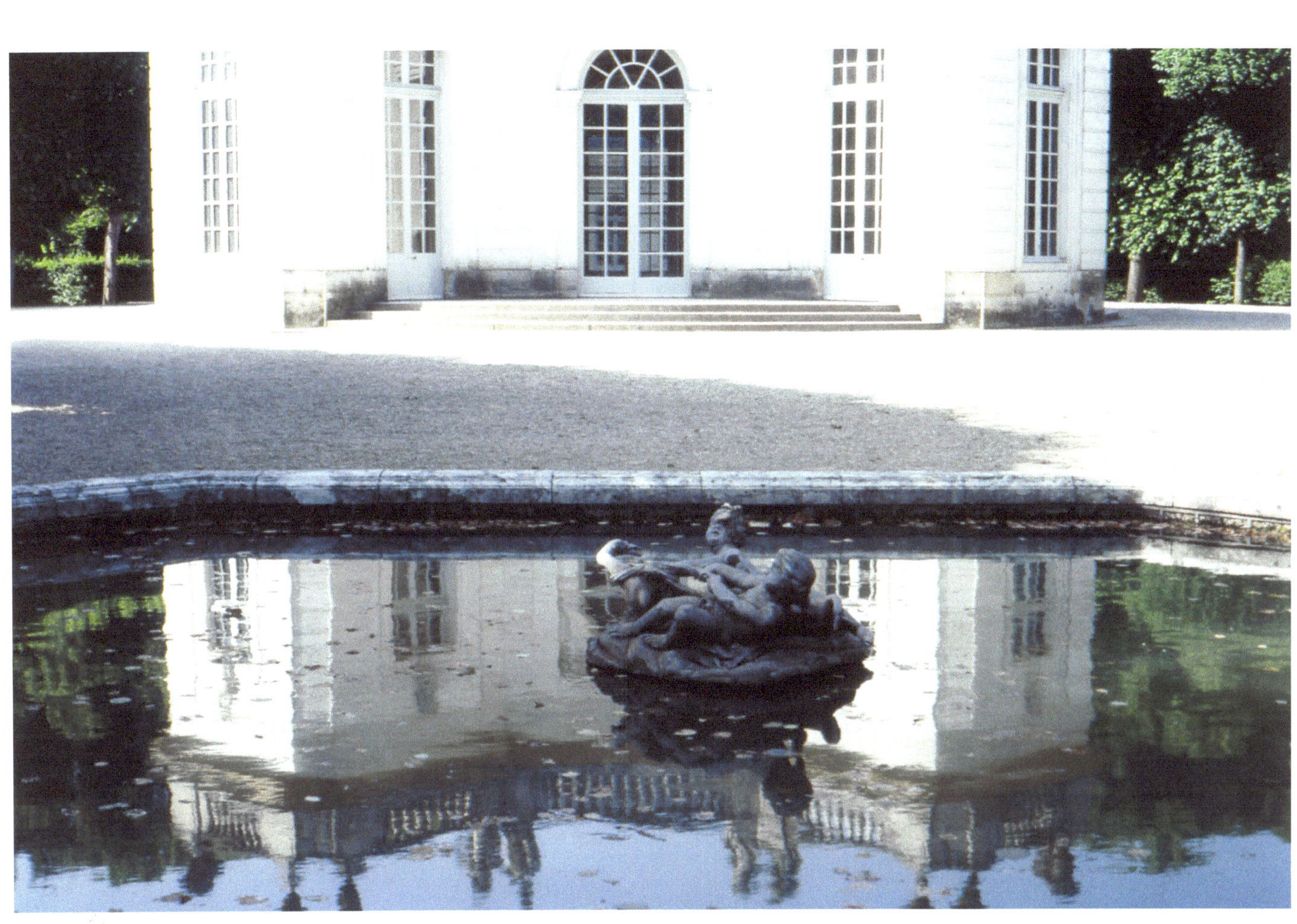

33. Versailles Pavillion Français

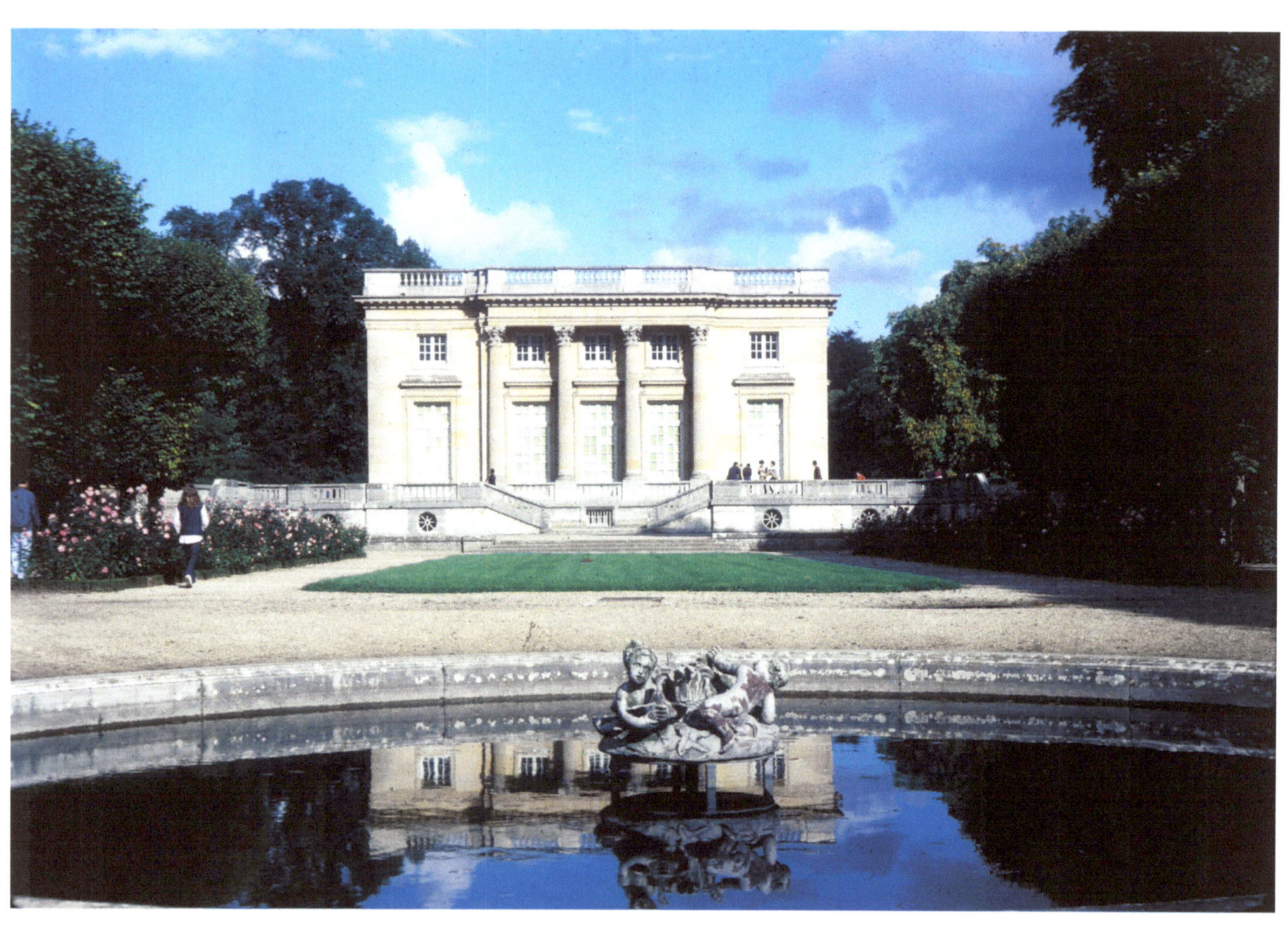

34. Versailles Petit Trianon

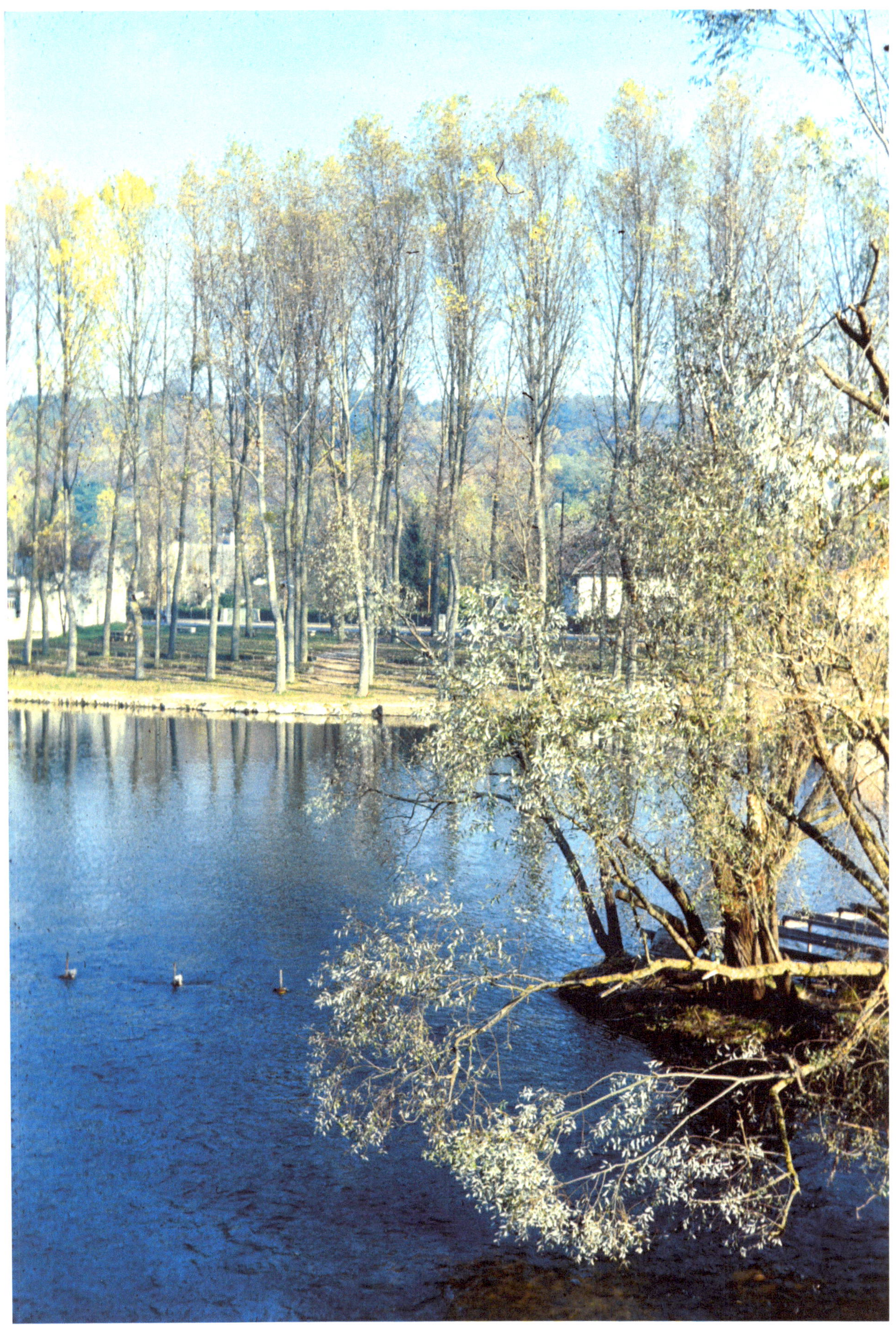

35. Moret-sur-Loing

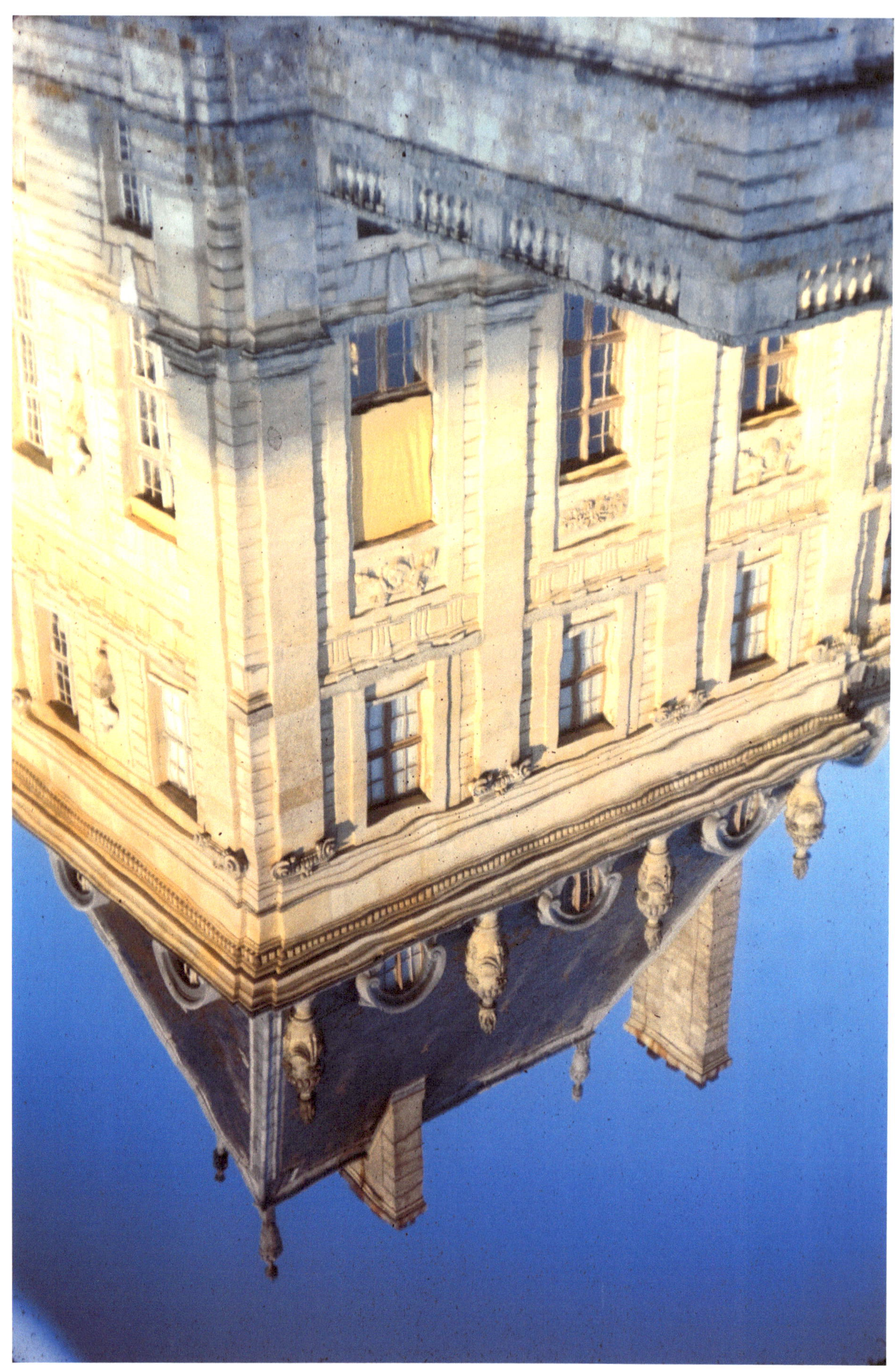

36. Vaux-Le-Vicomte

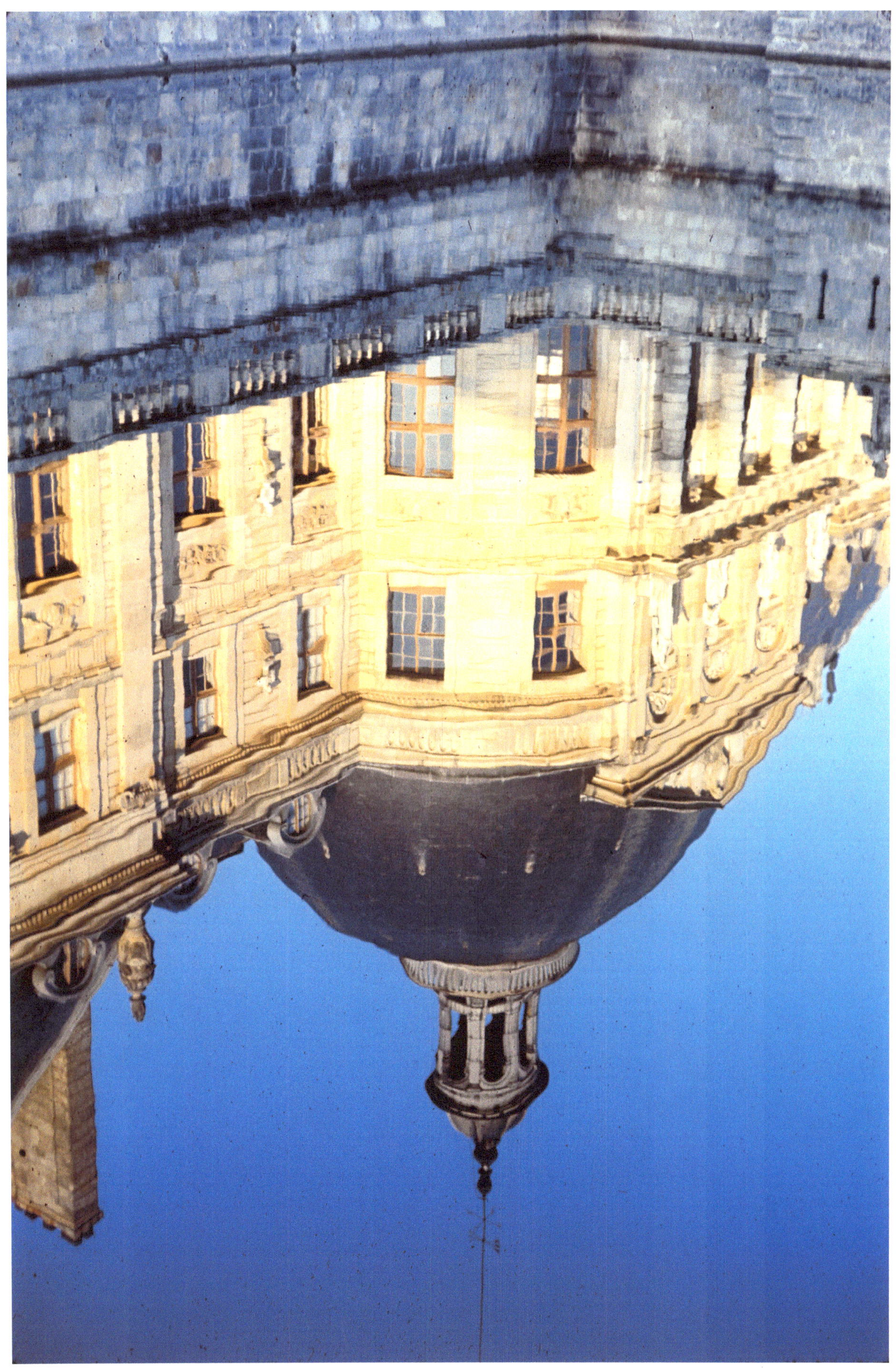

37. Vaux-Le-Vicomte

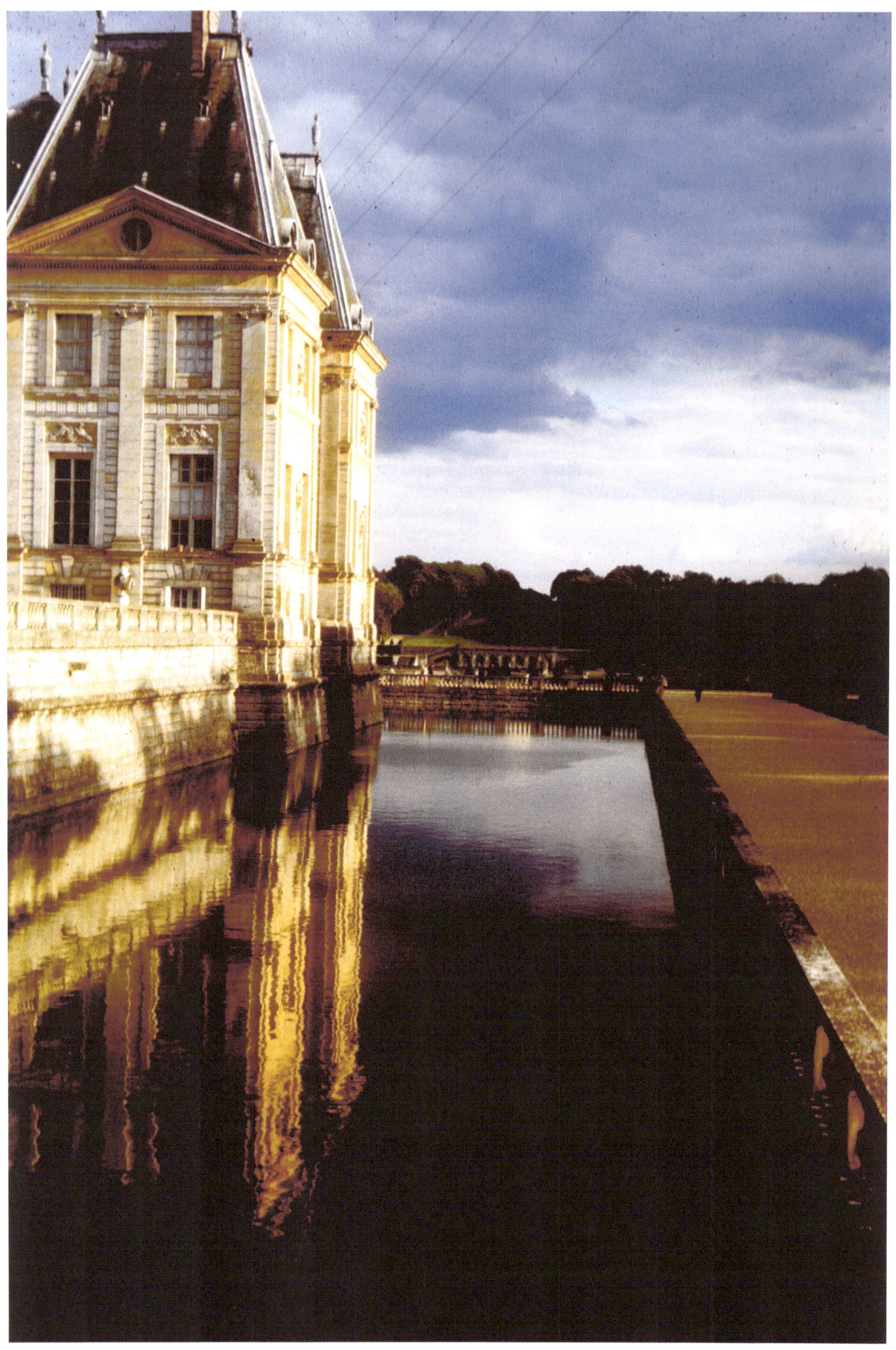

38. Vaux-Le-Vicomte

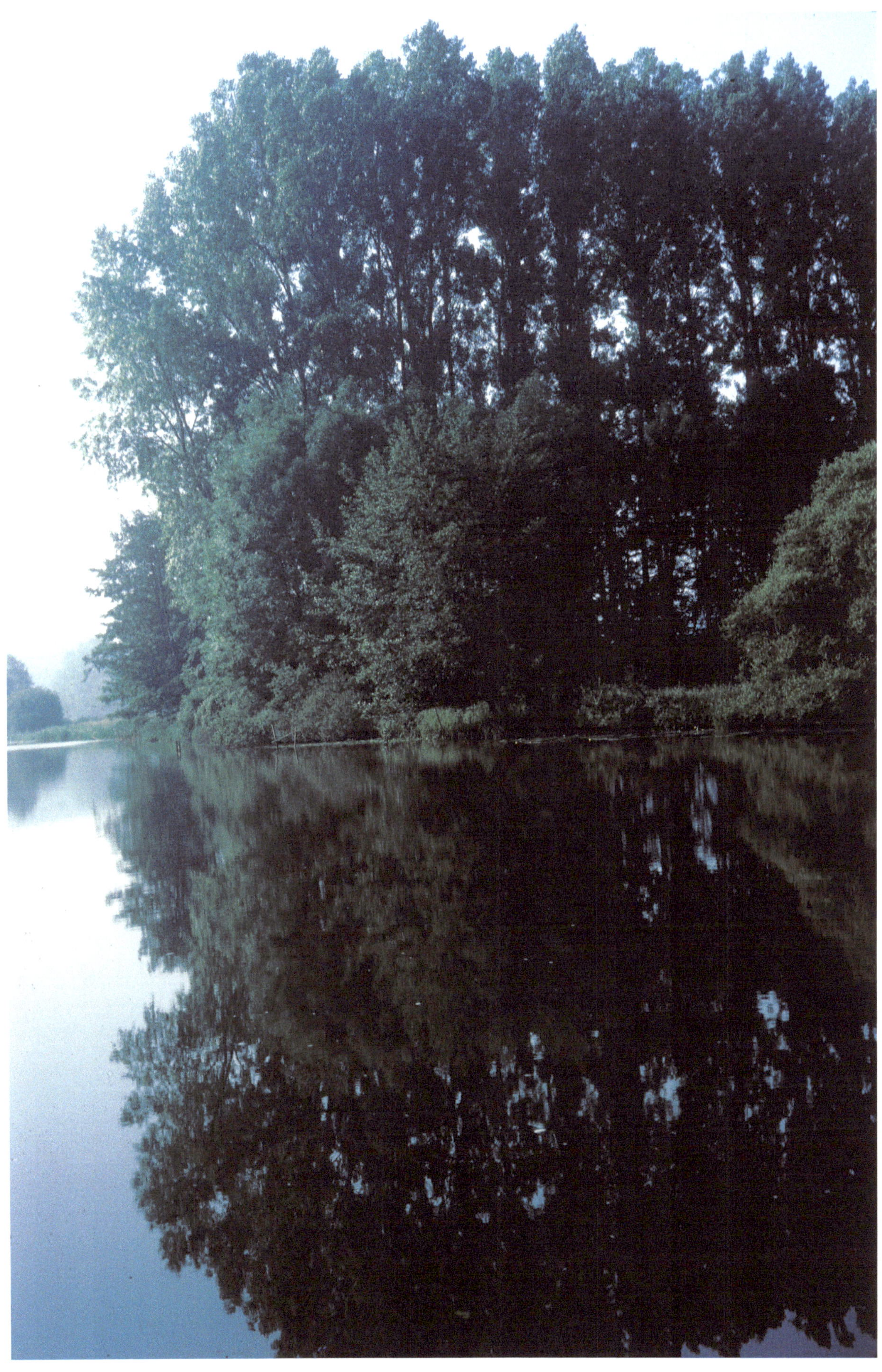

39. Canal Du Nivernais

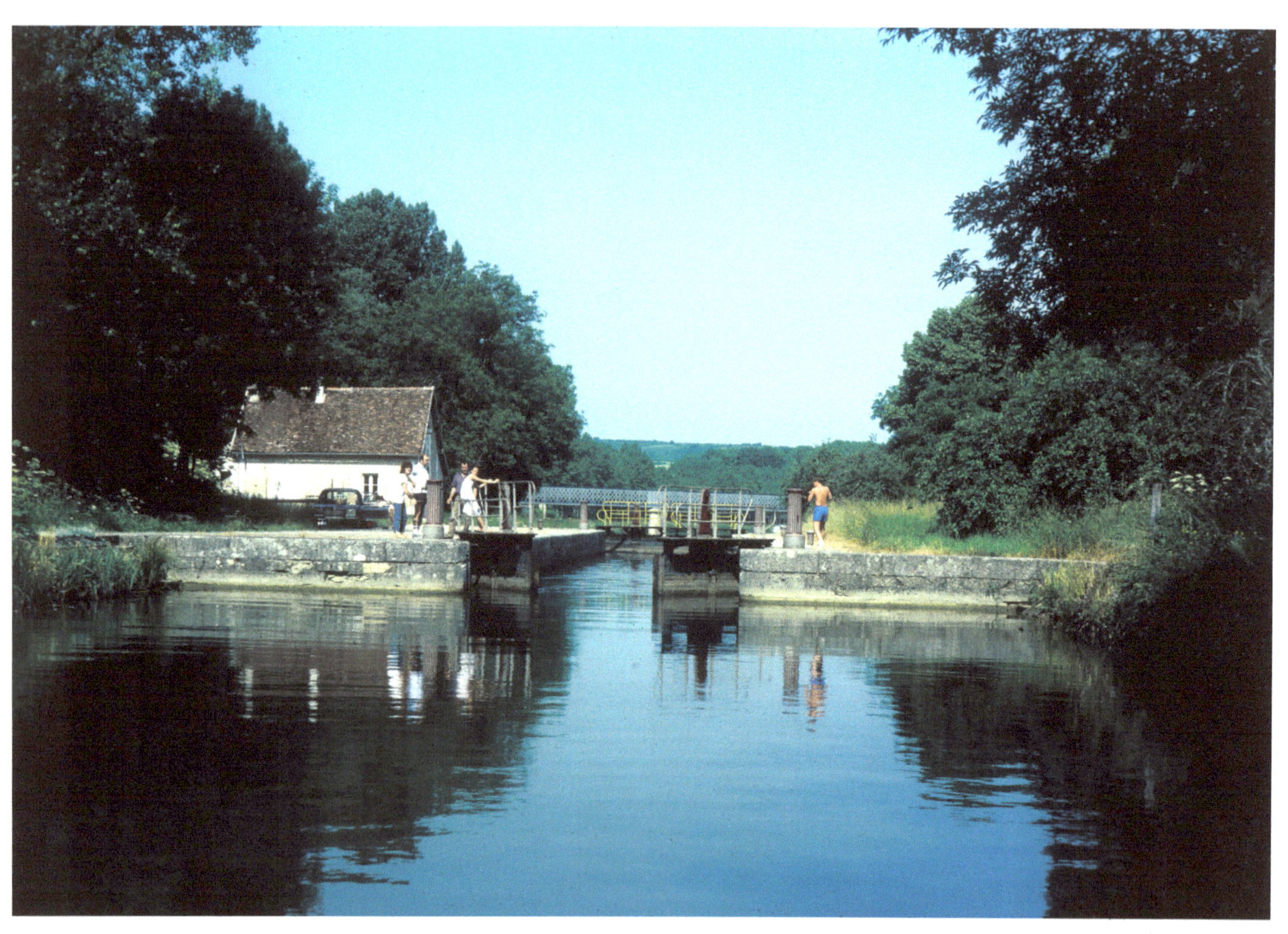

40. Canal du Nivernais

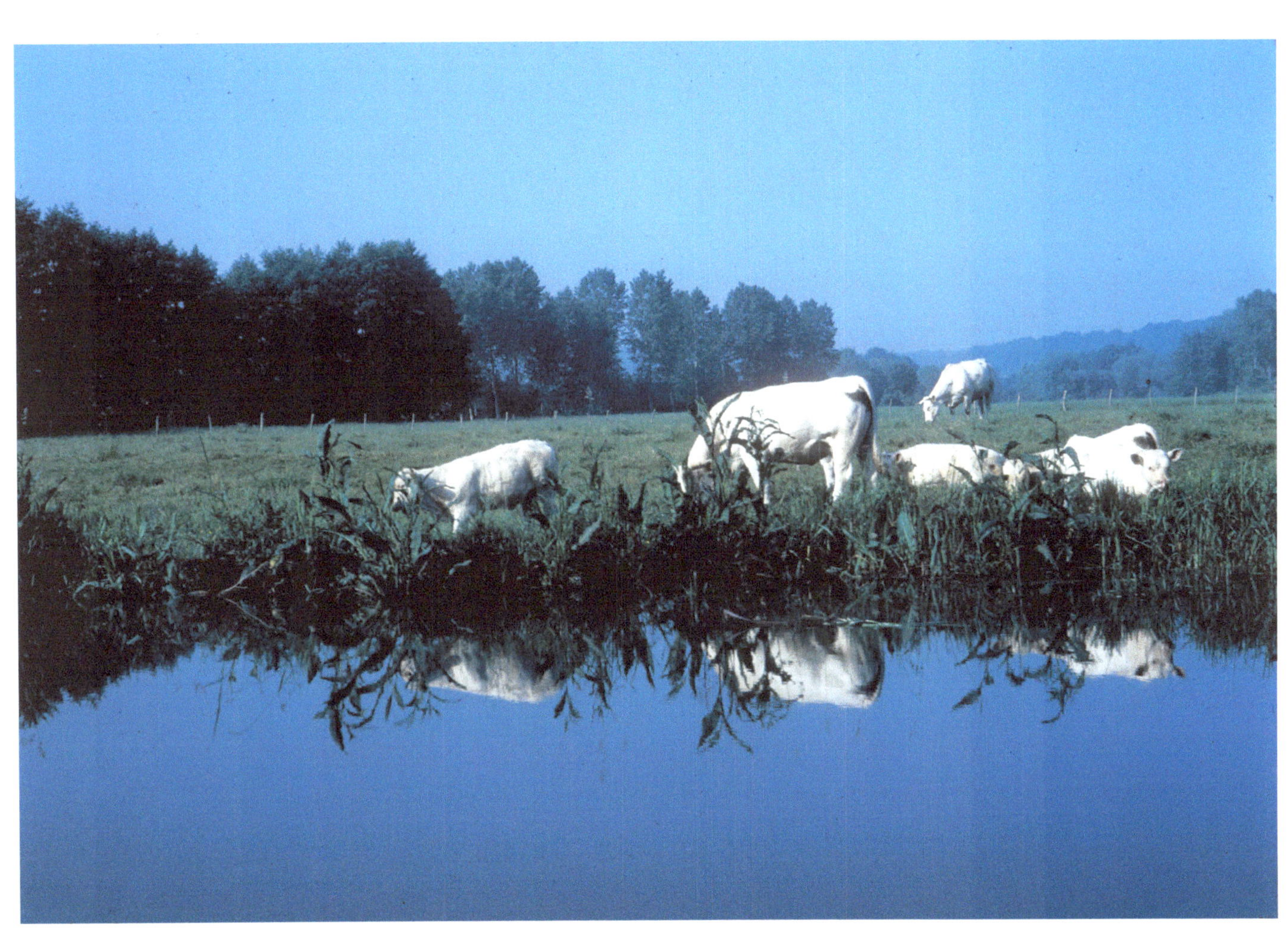

41. Canal du Nivernais

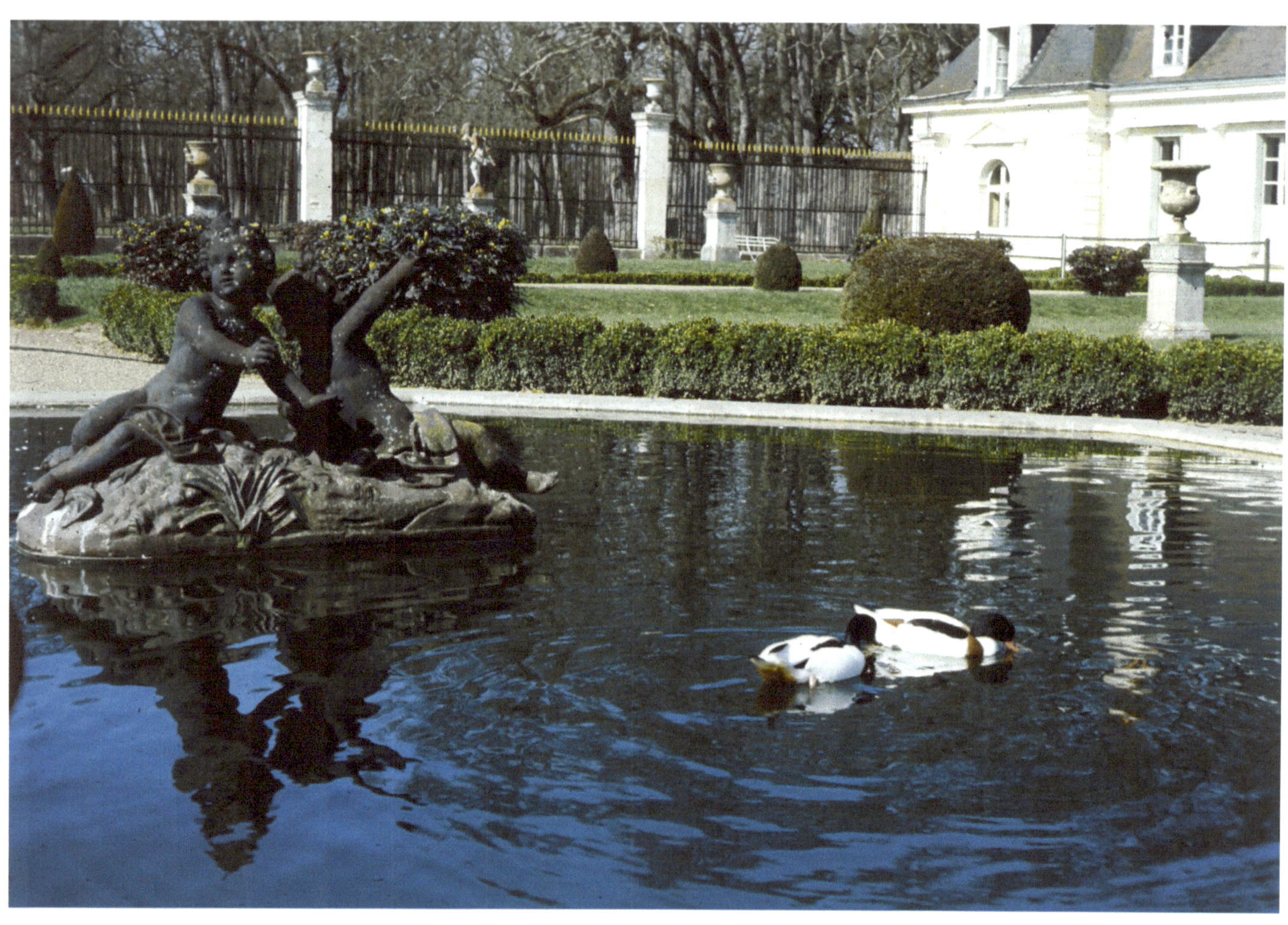

42. Valencay Parc

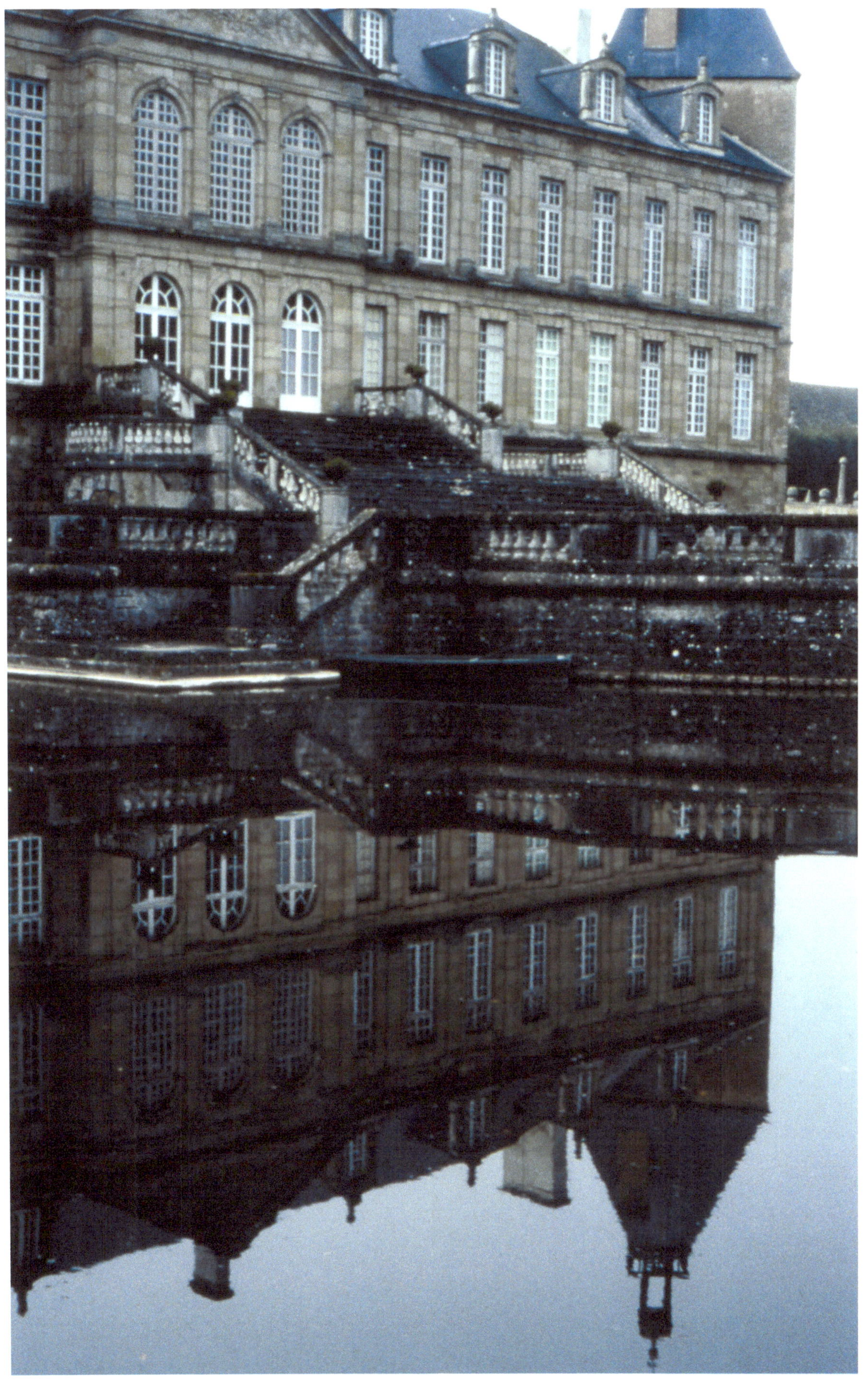

43. Chateau de Sully

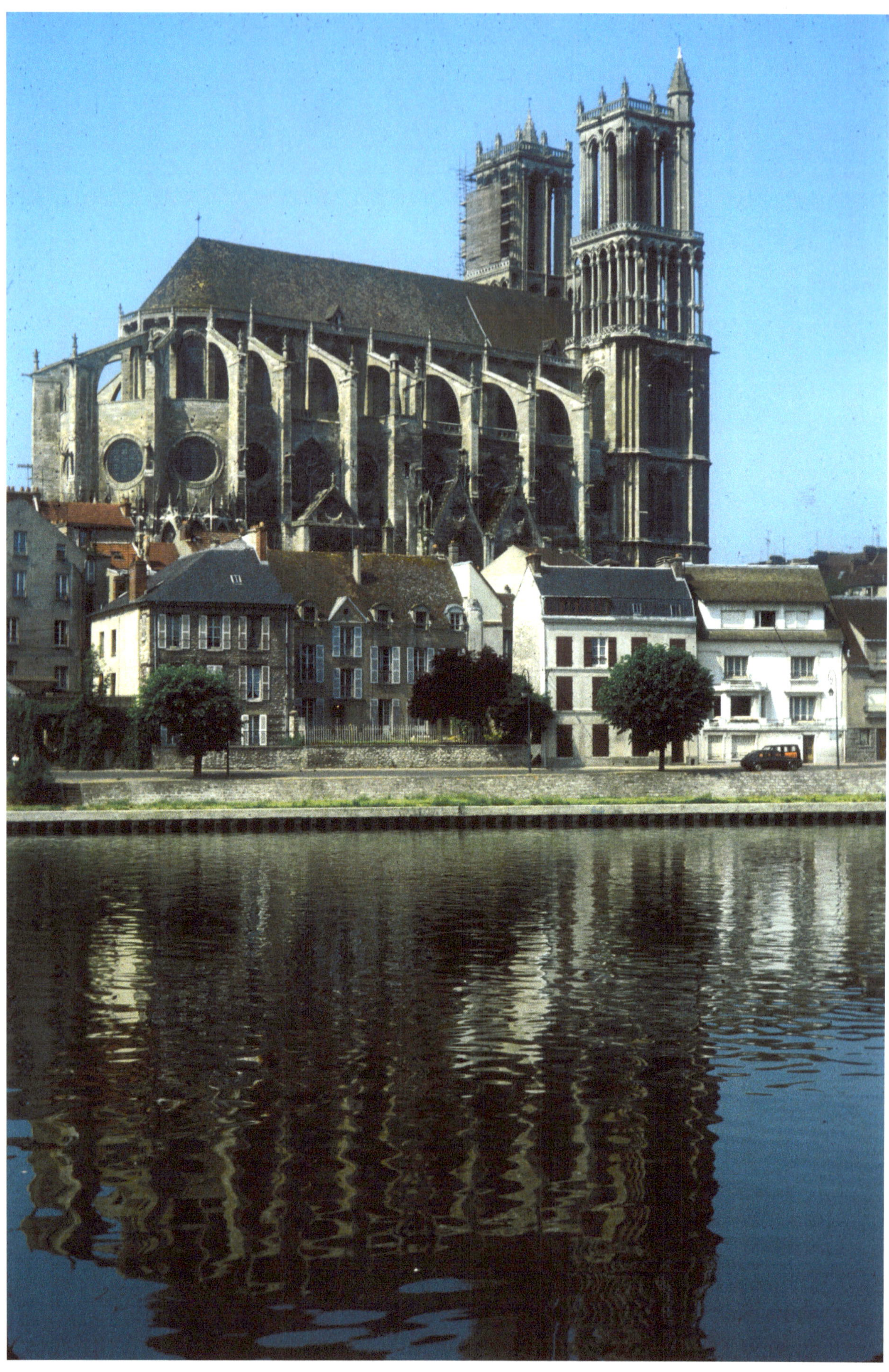

44. Mantes Notre Dame

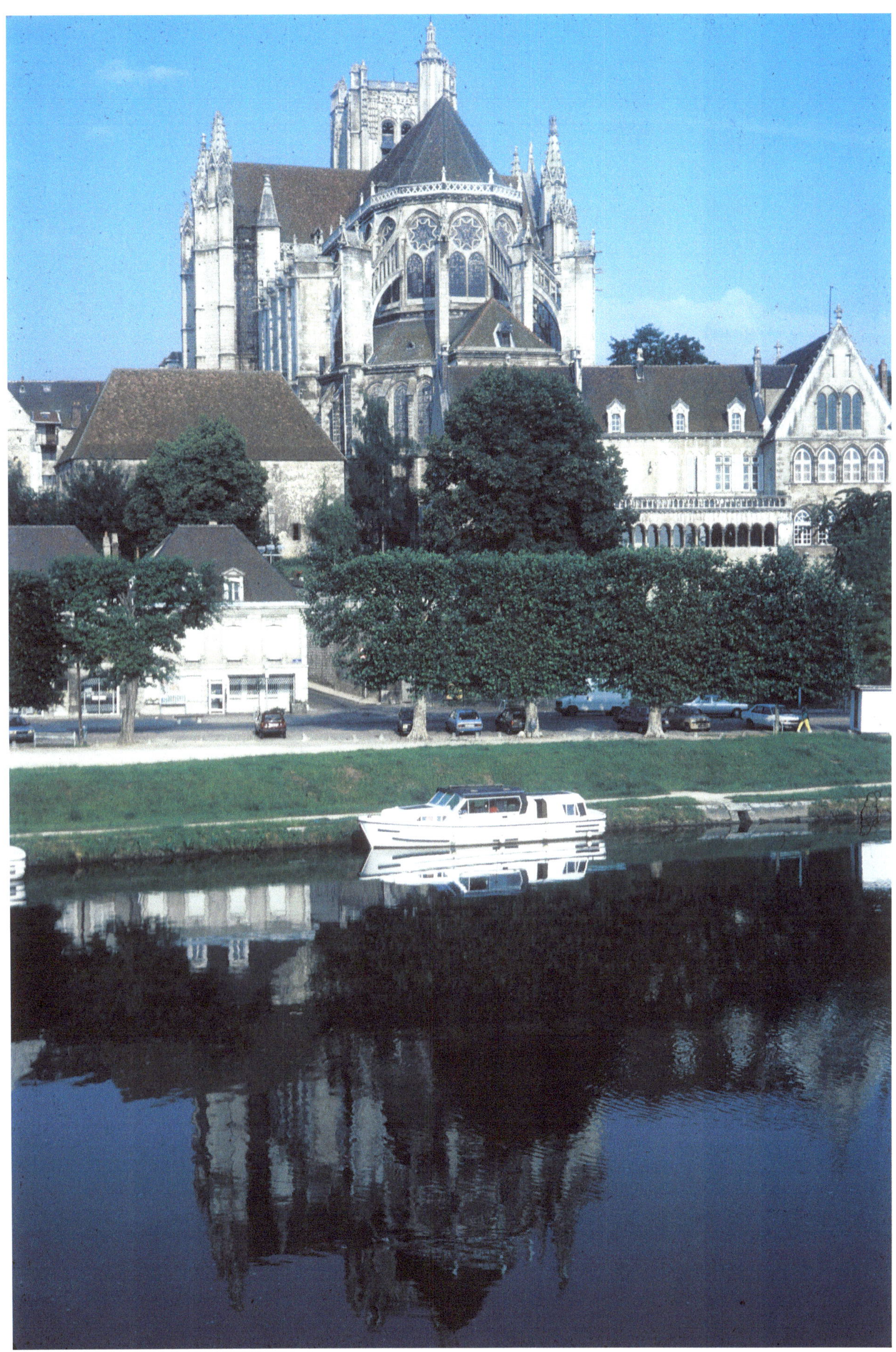

45. Auxerre Cathedral

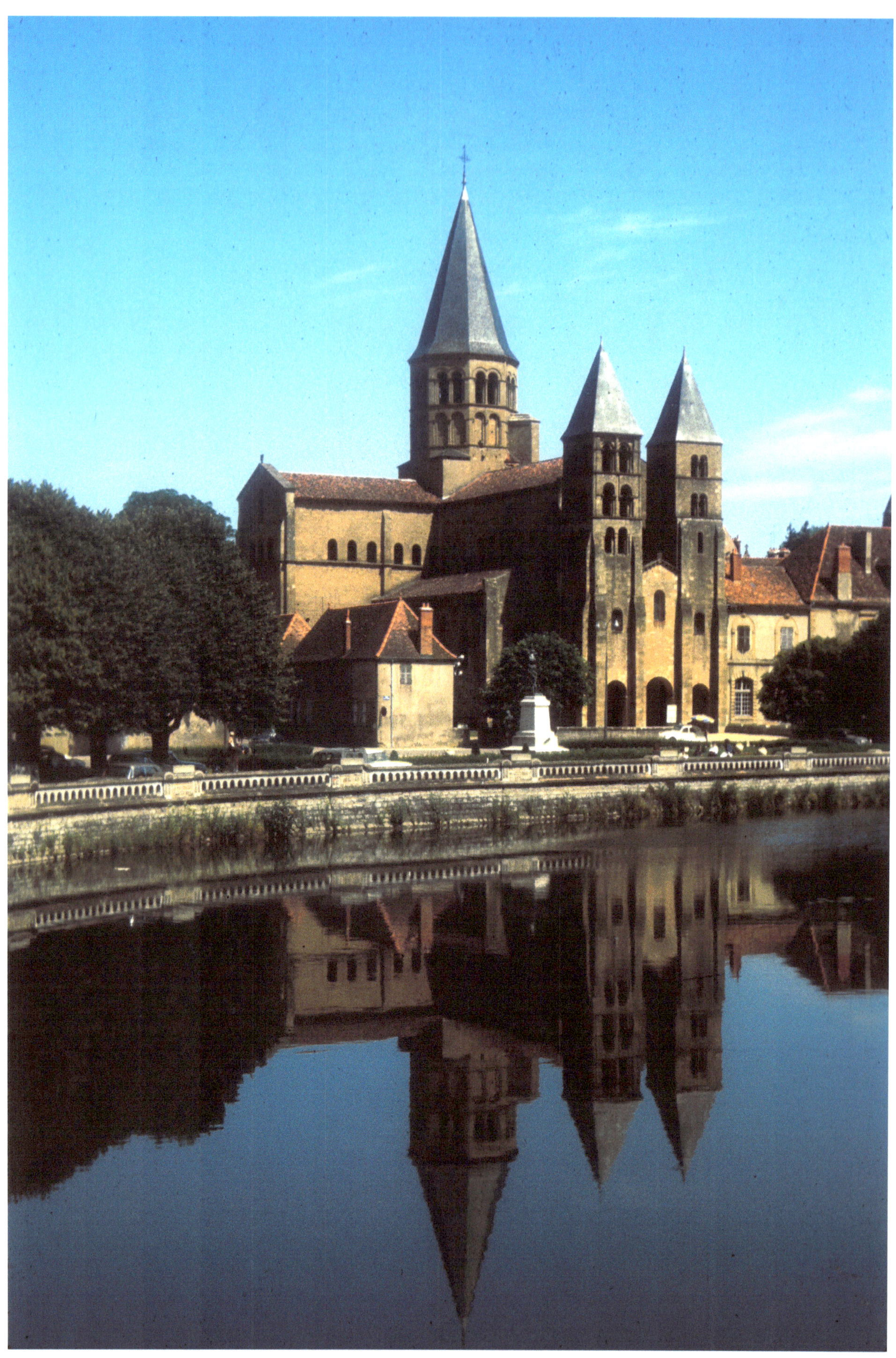

46. Paray-Le-Monial Basilique

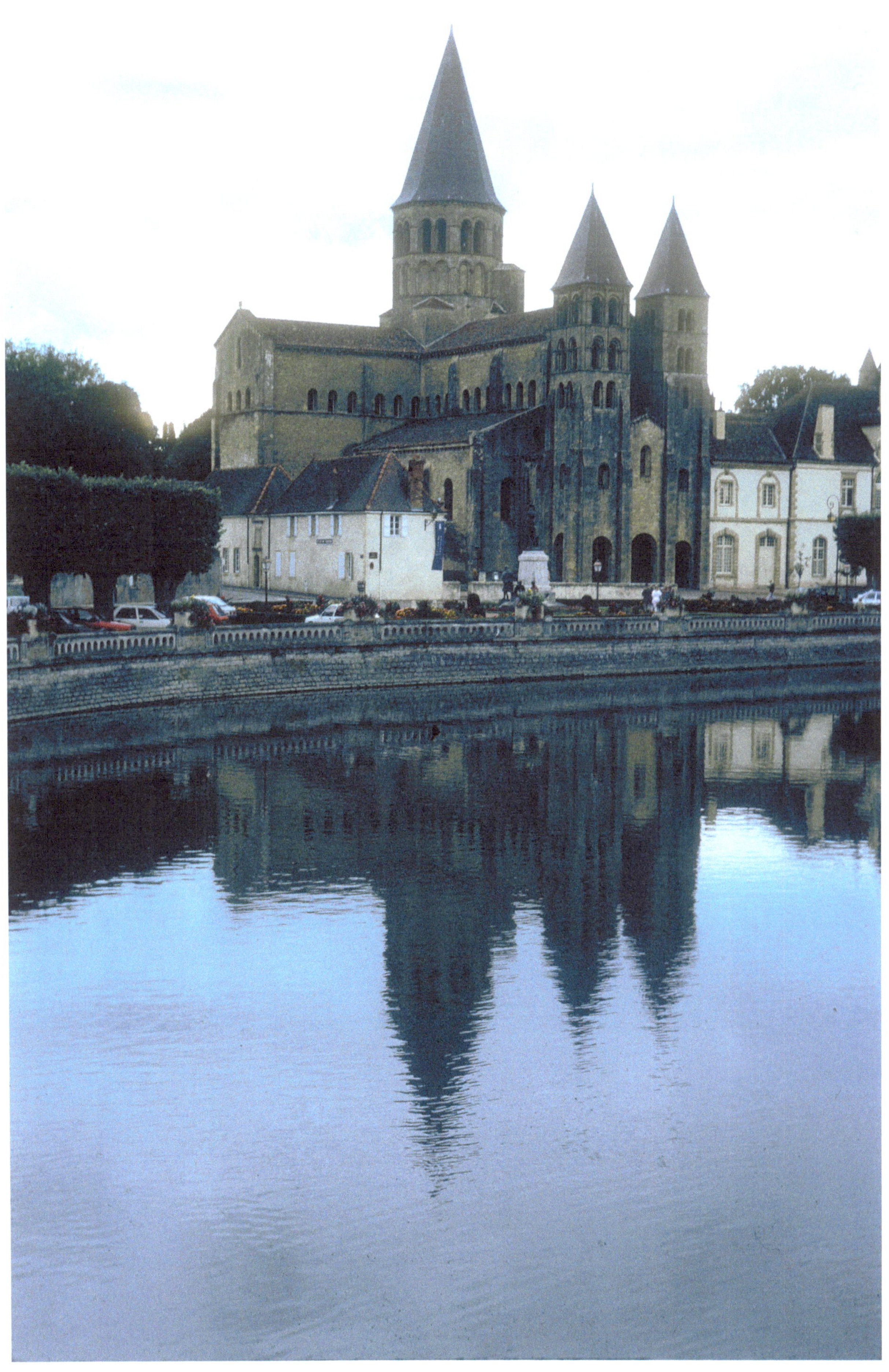

47. Paray-Le-Monal Basilique

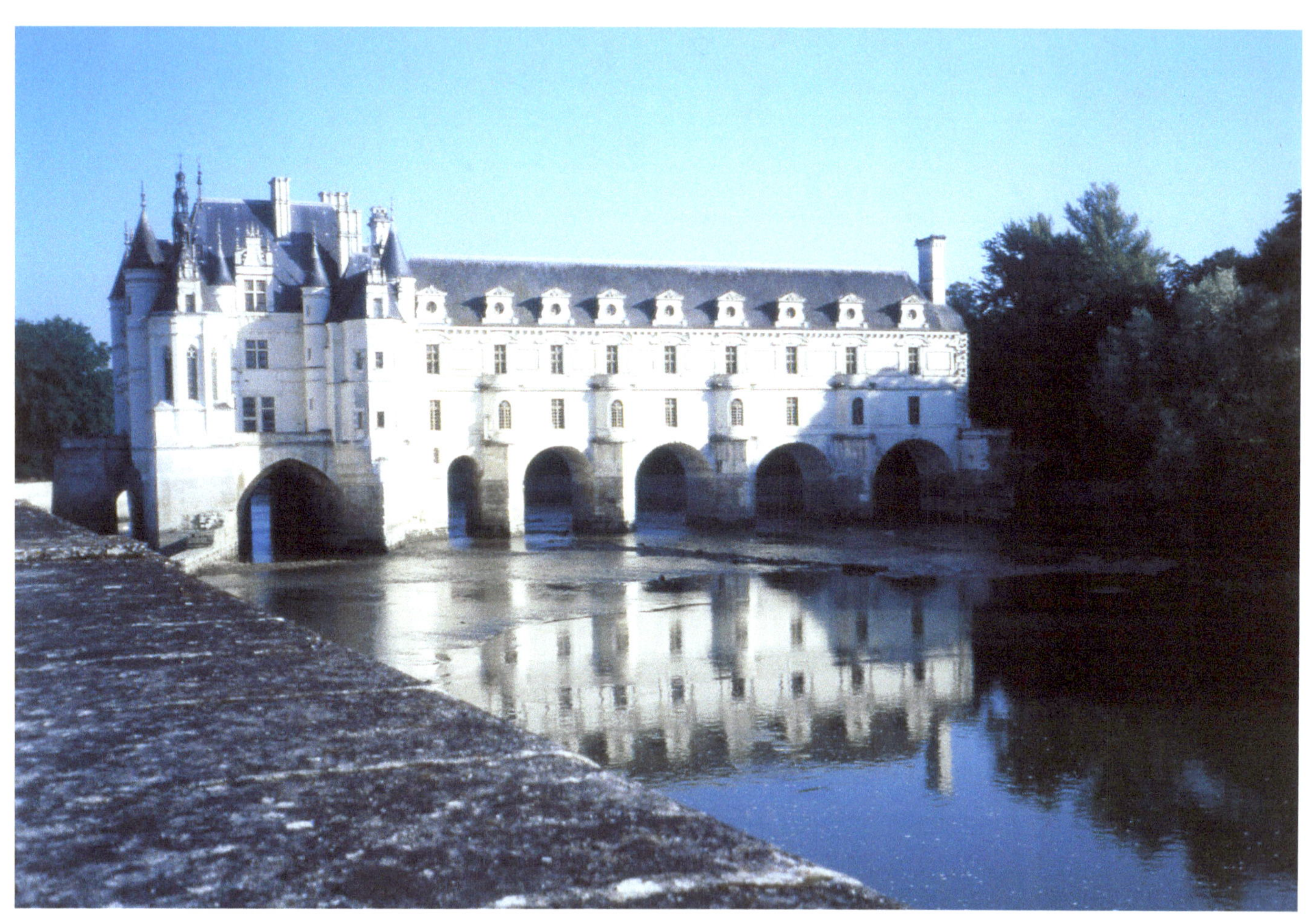

48. Chenonceau

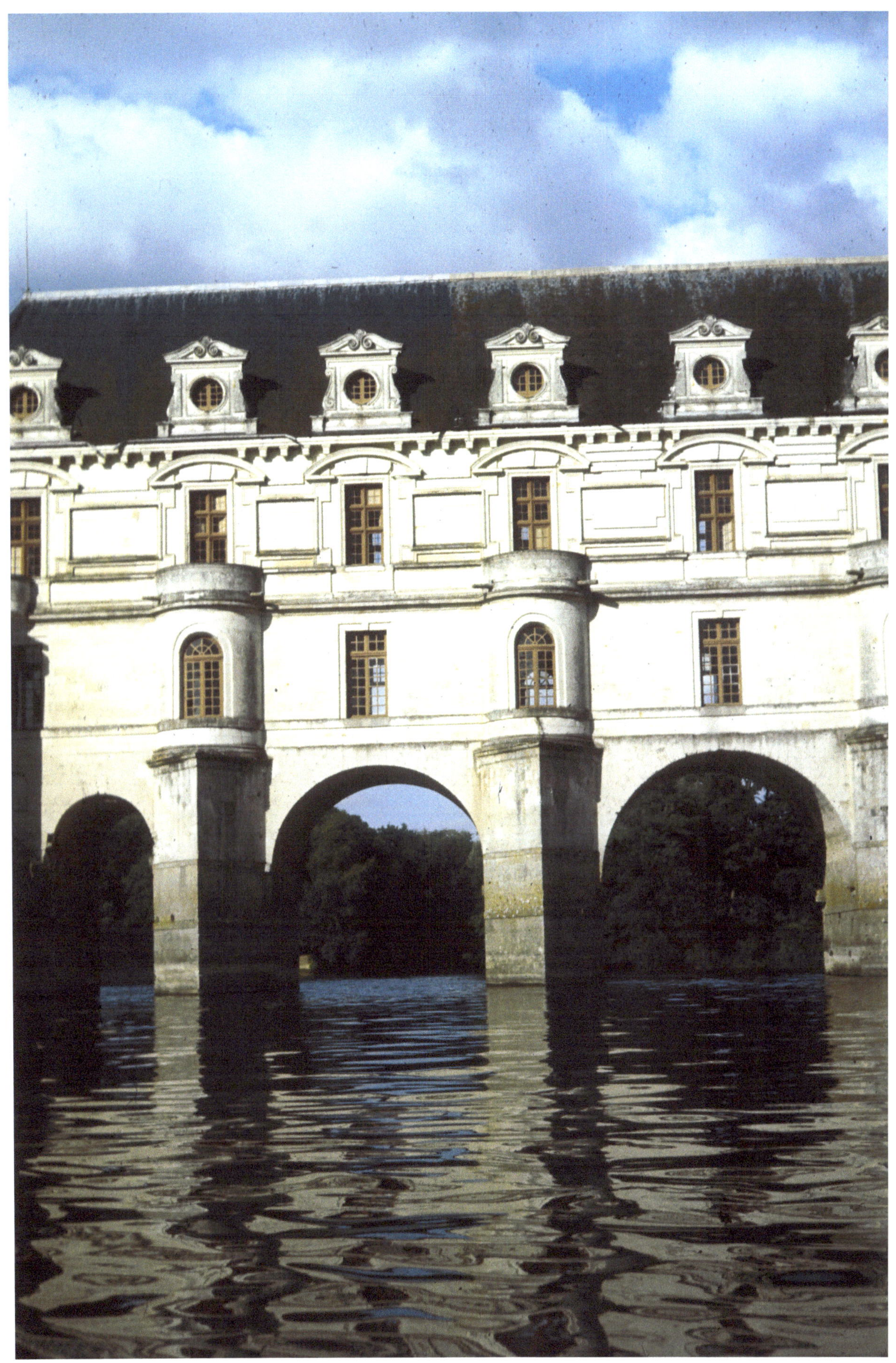

49. Chenonceau

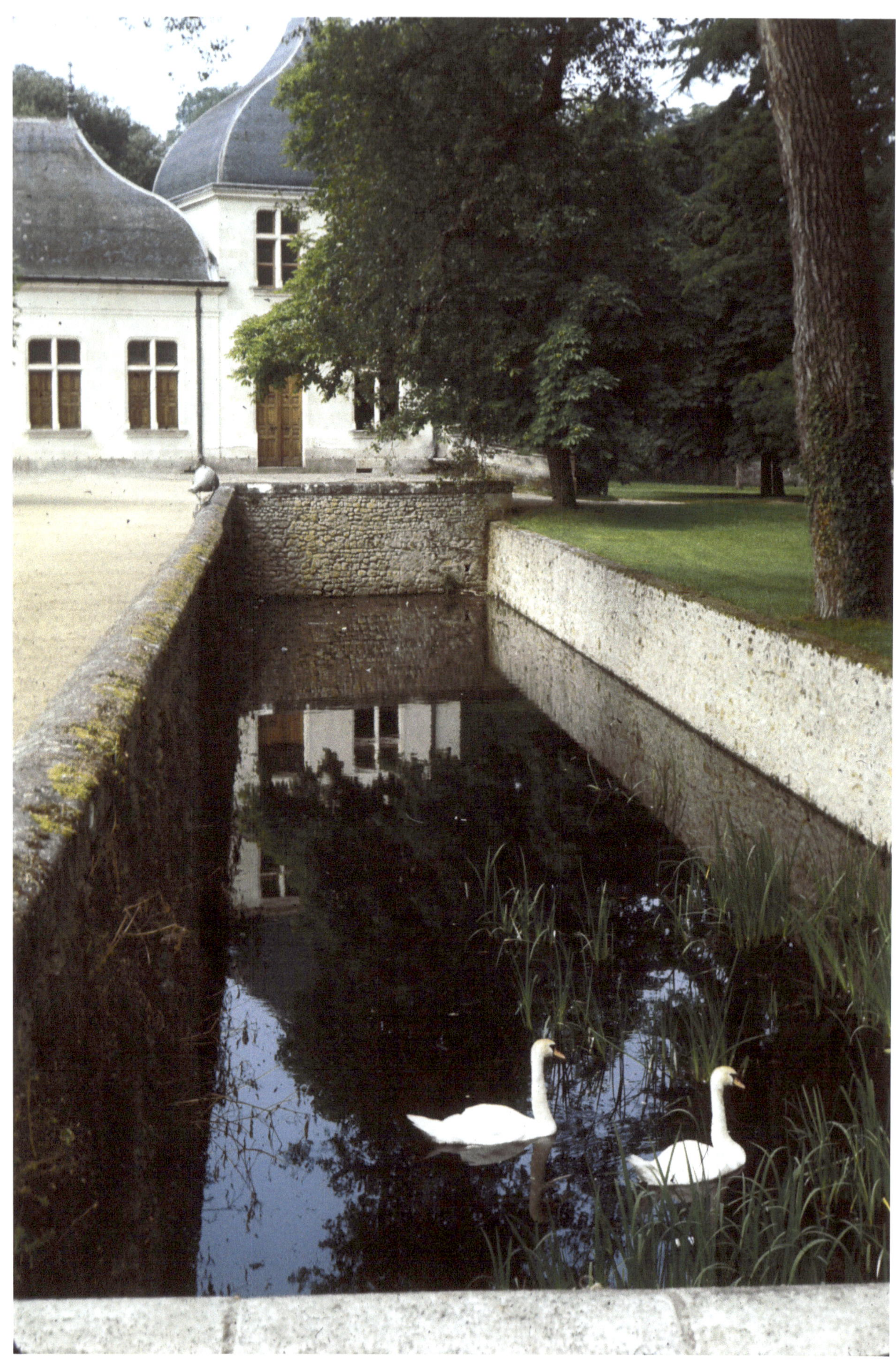

50. Chenonceau

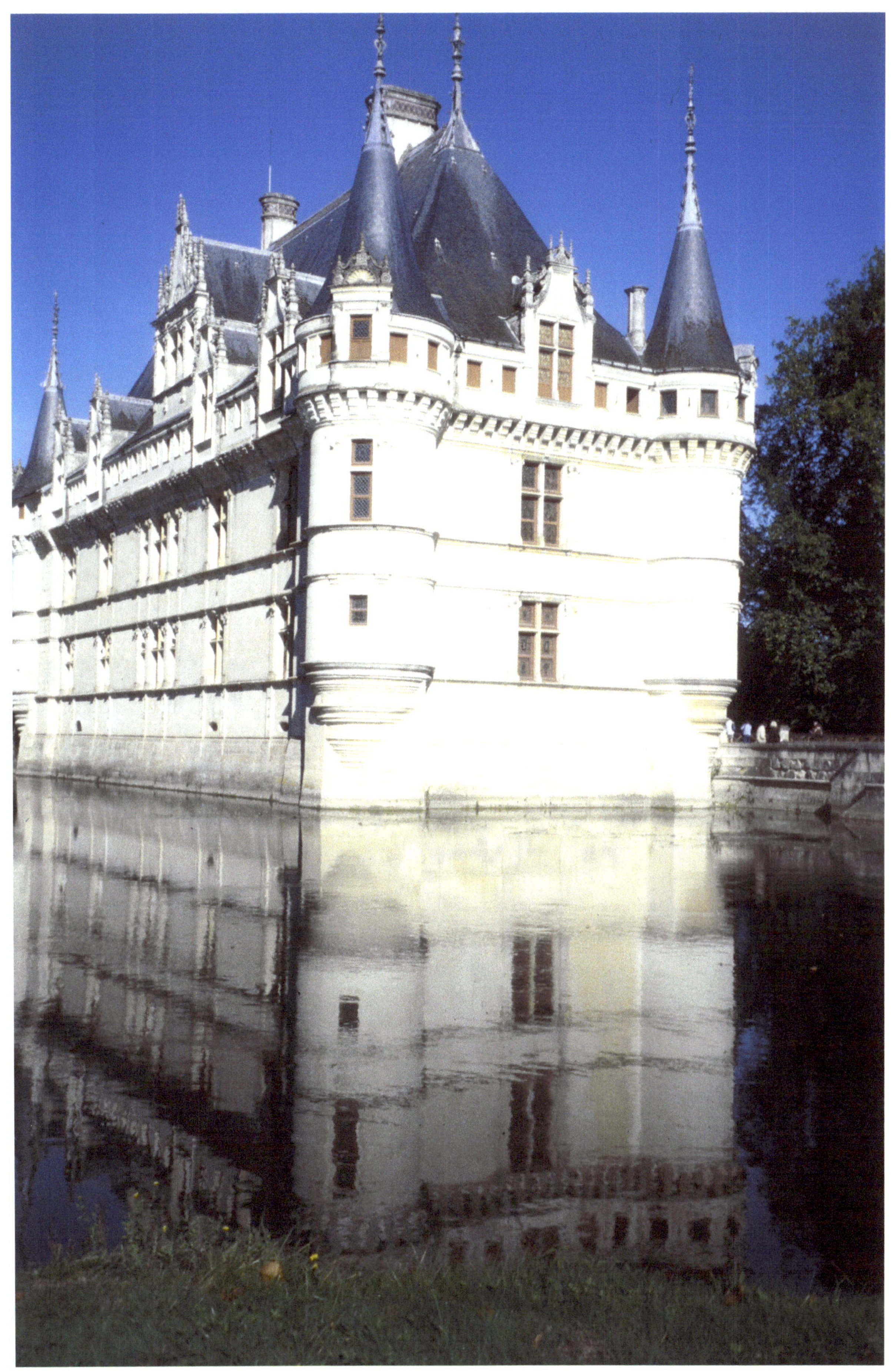

51. Azay-Le-Rideau

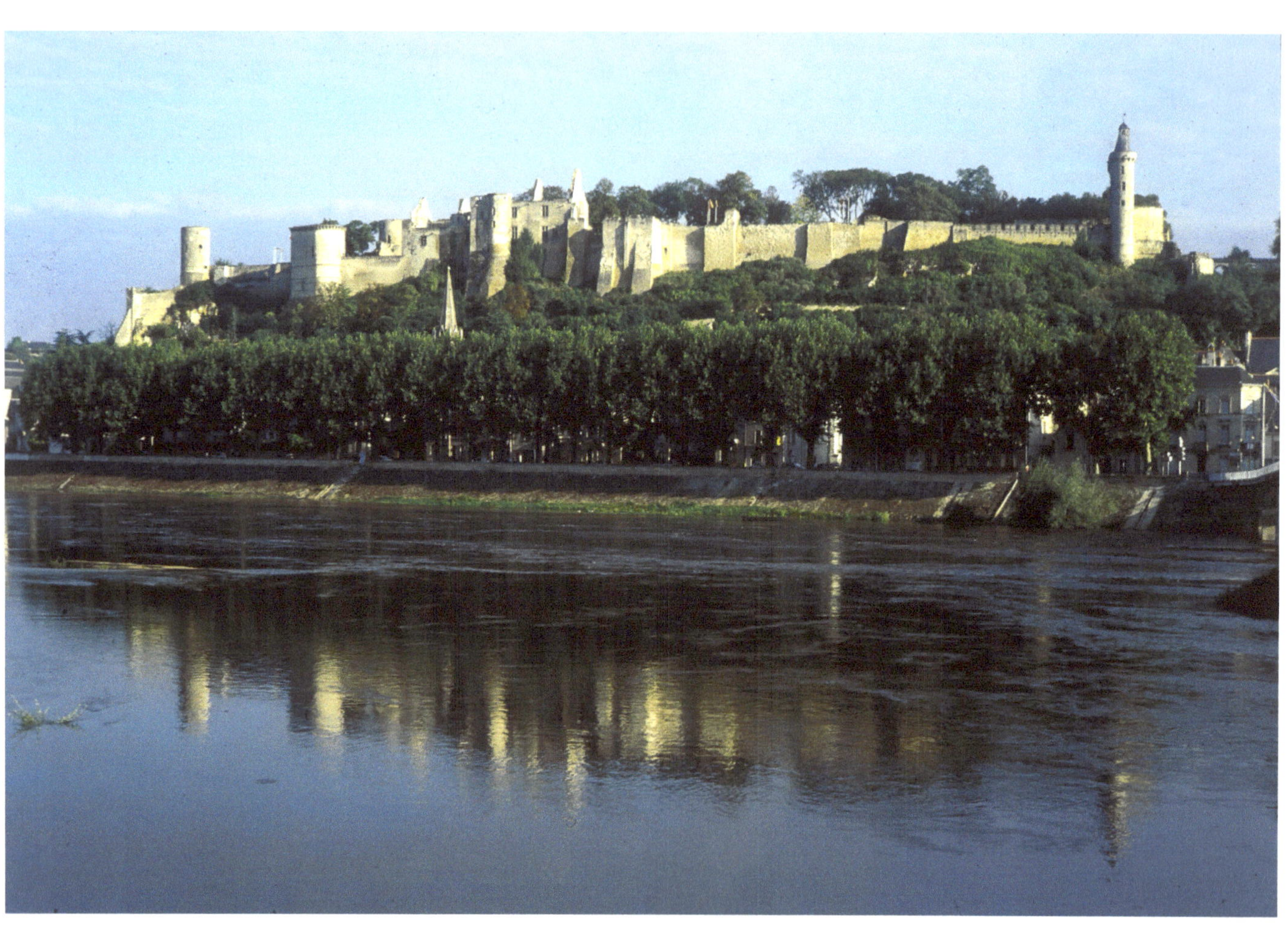

52. Chinon Chateau and Vienne River

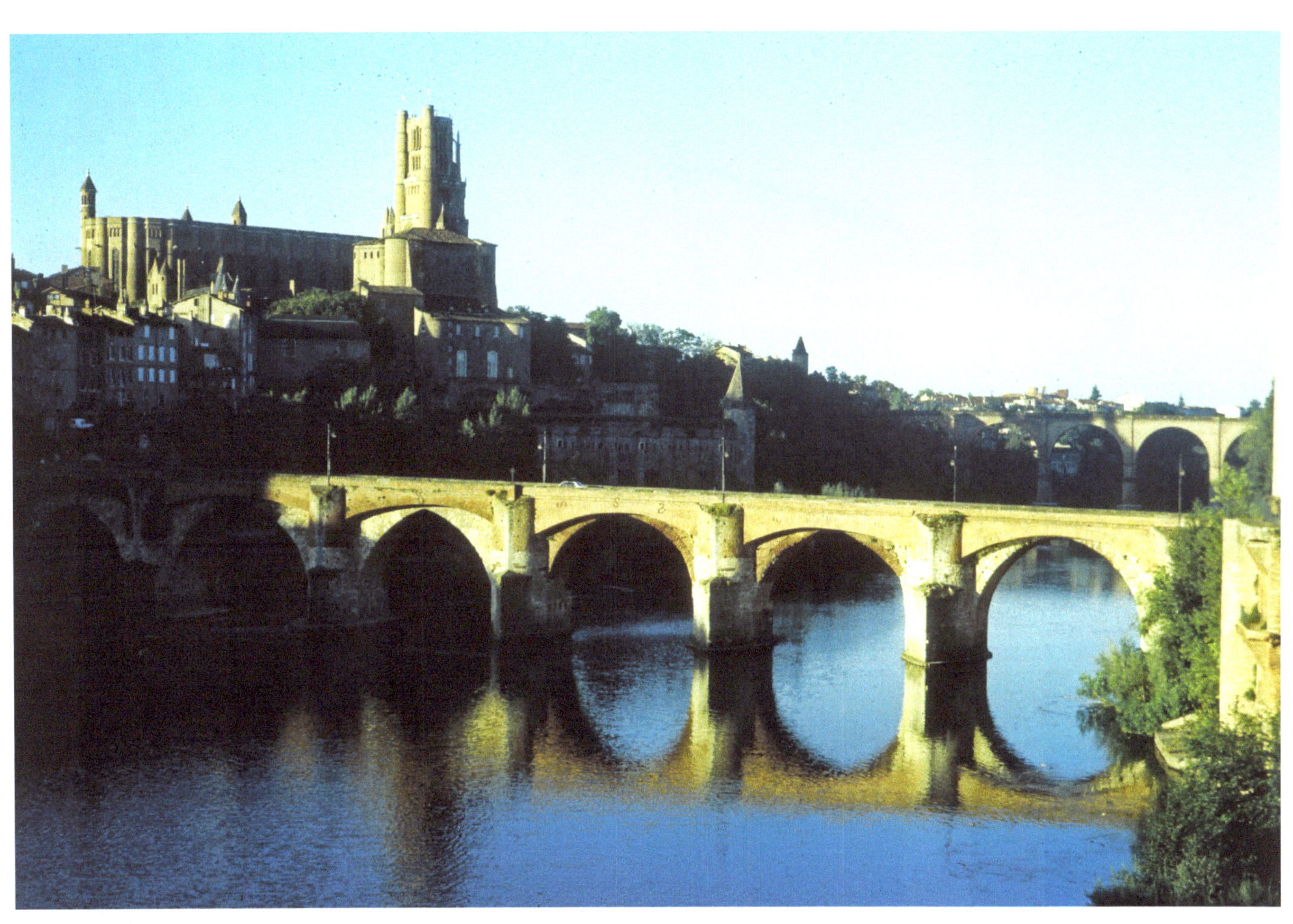

53. Albi View from Tarn River

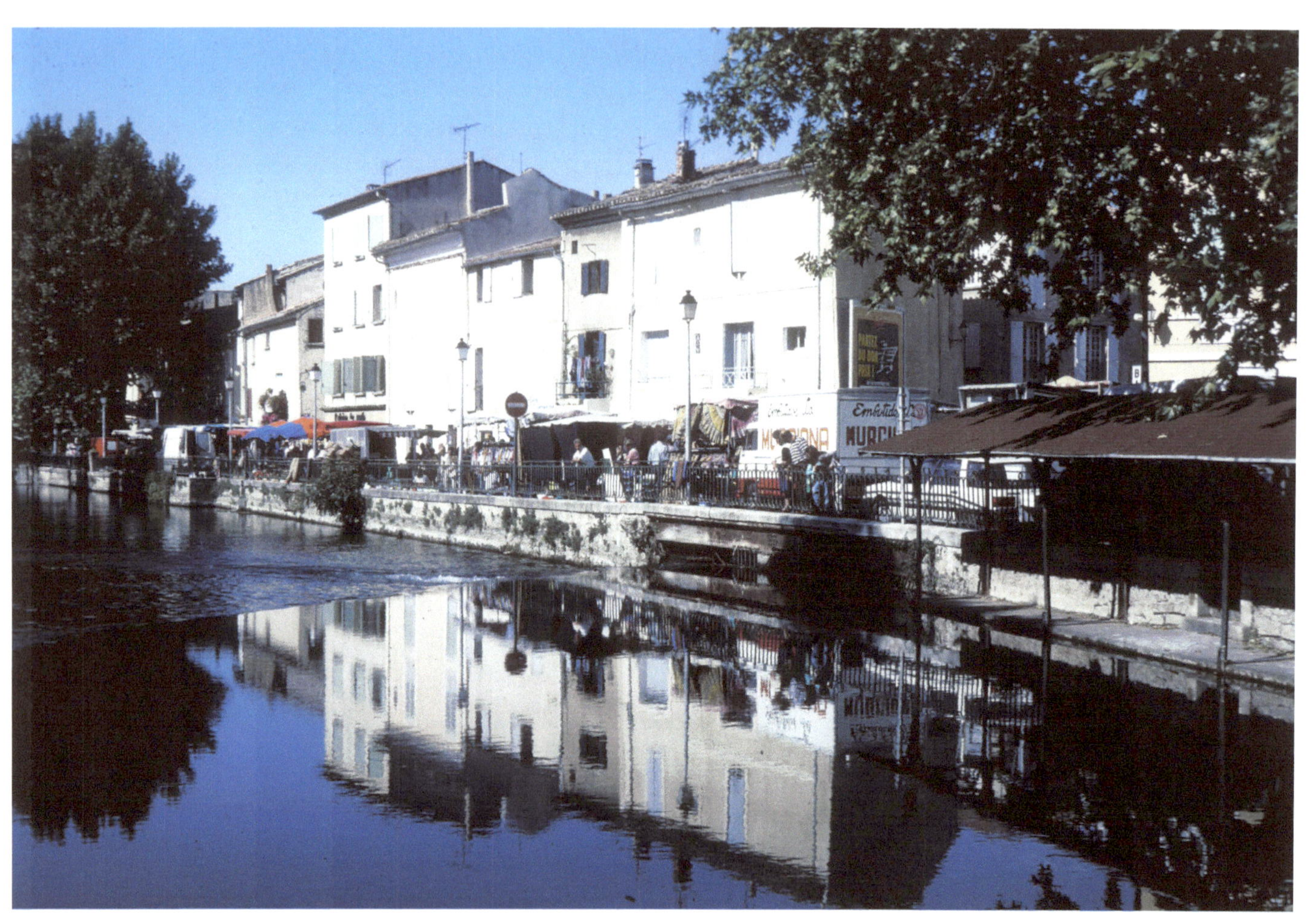

54. L'Isle-sur-La-Sorge

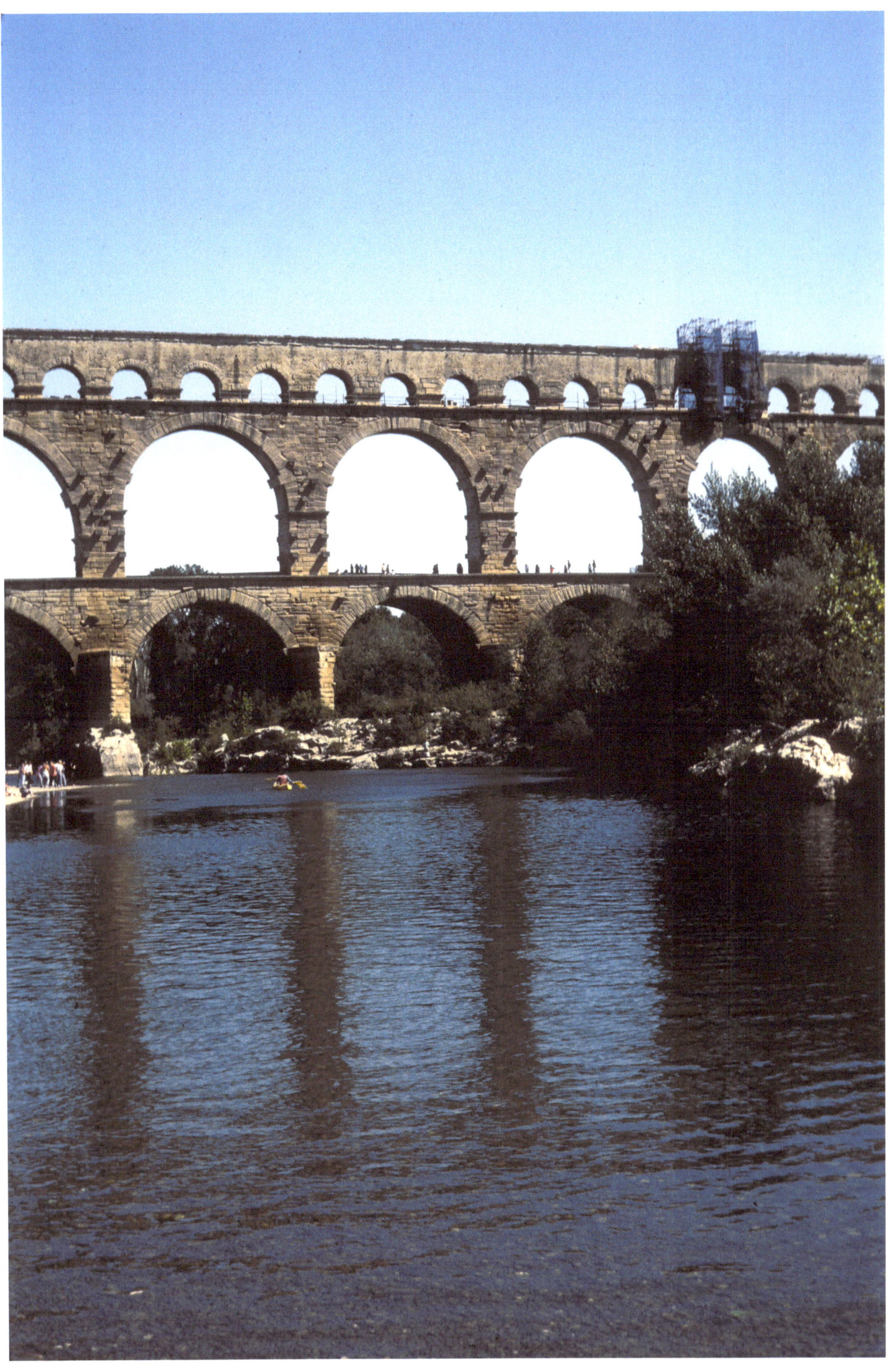

55. Pont du Gard

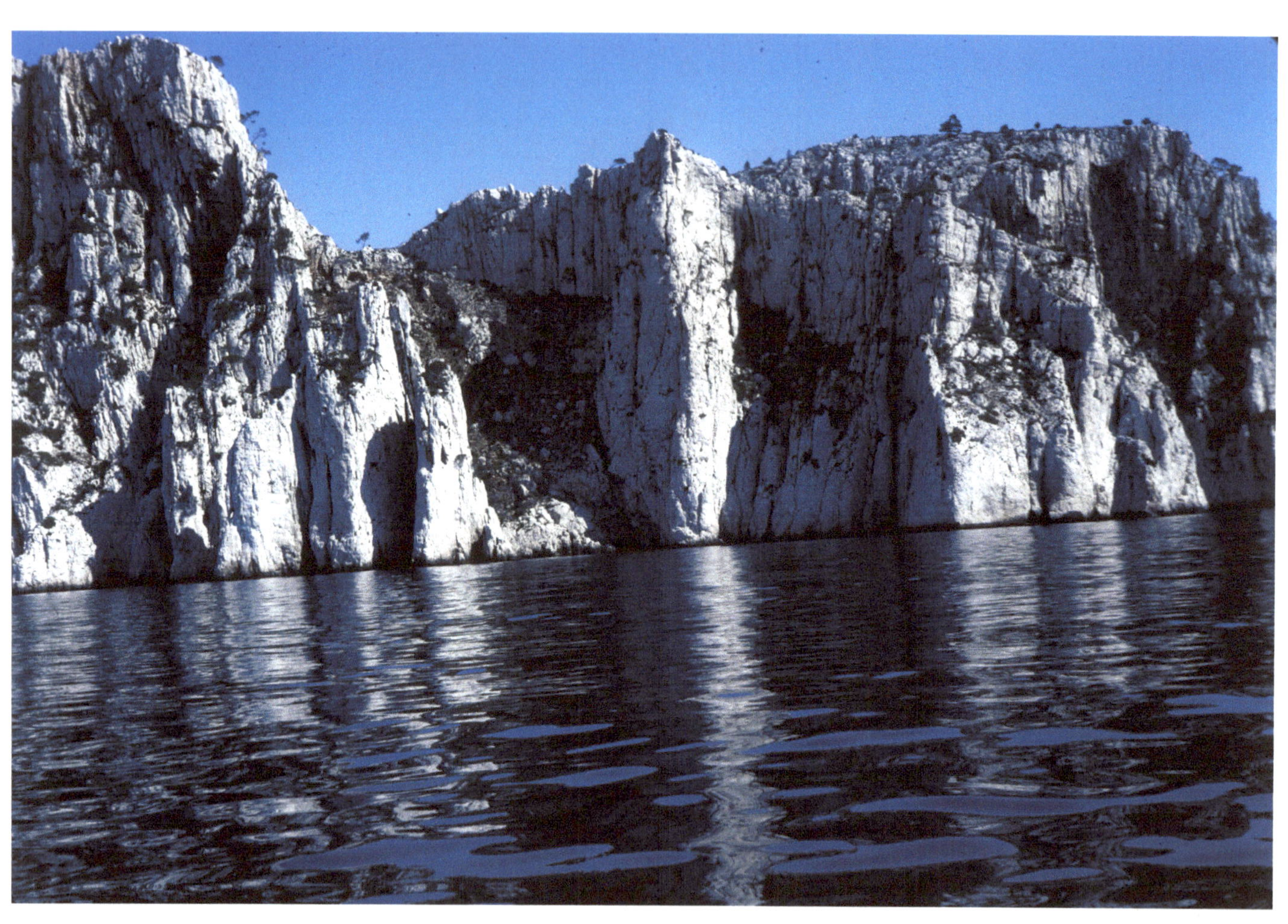

56. Near Cassis Les Calanques

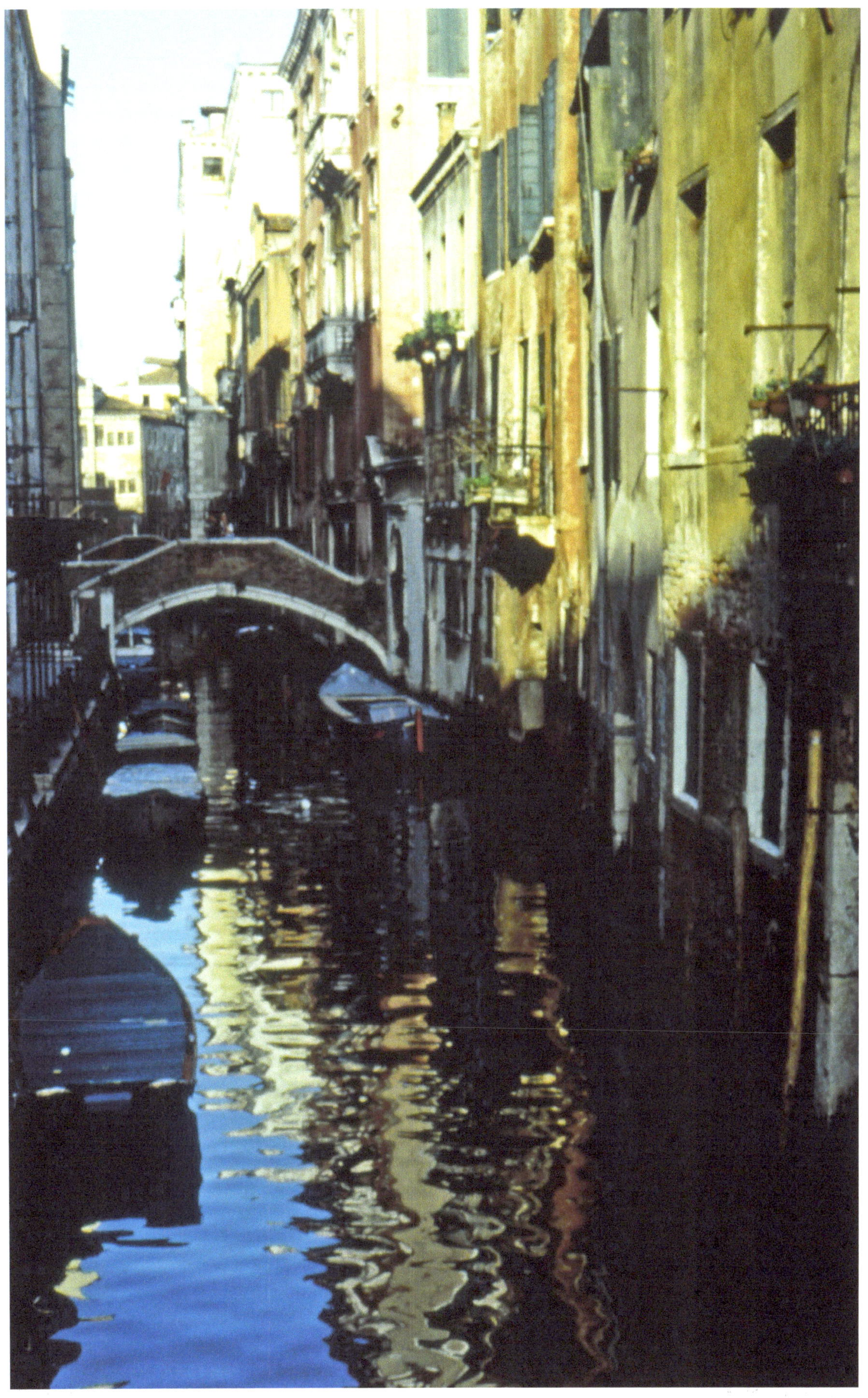

57. Venice A canal

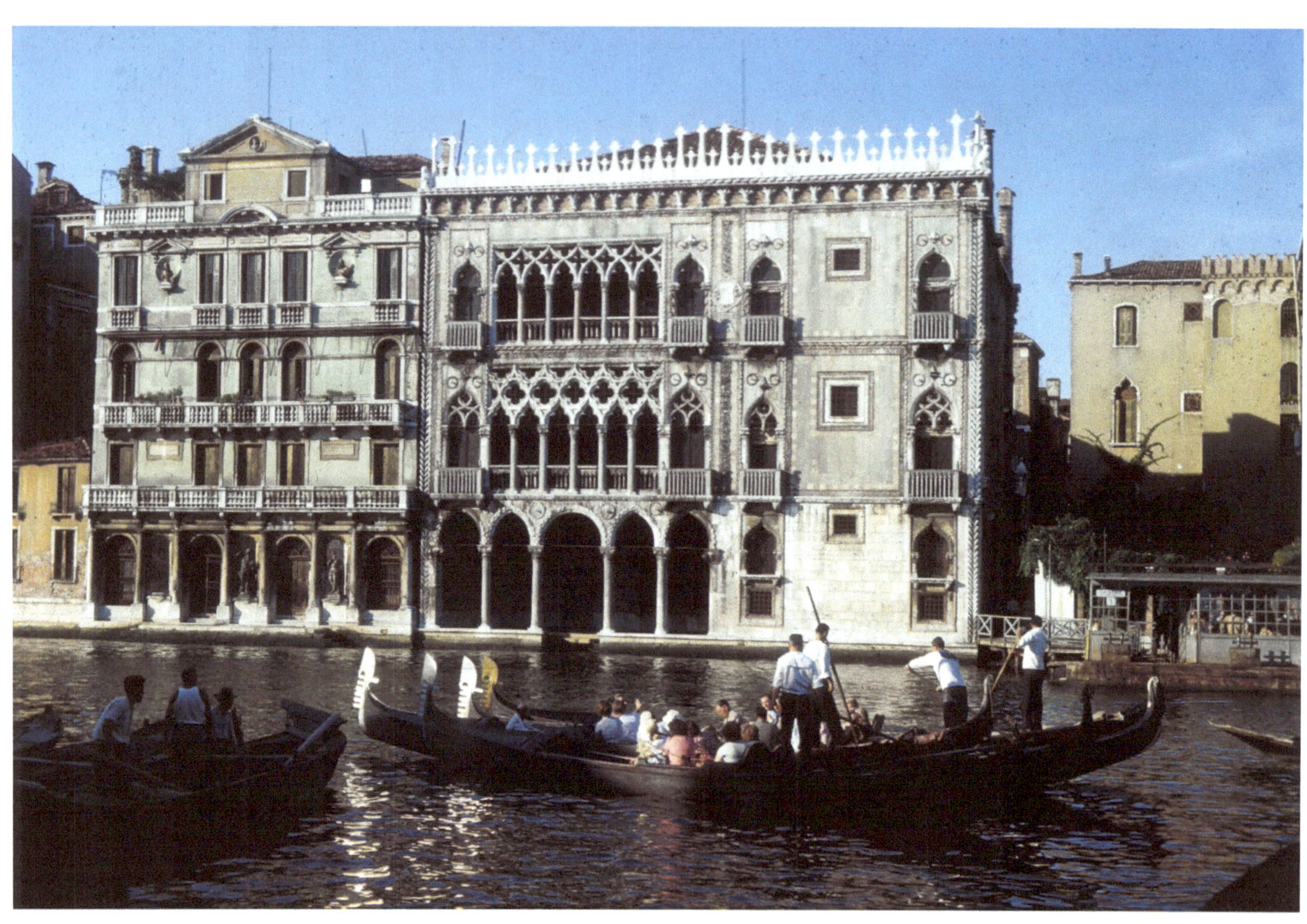

58. Venice Cà d'Oro

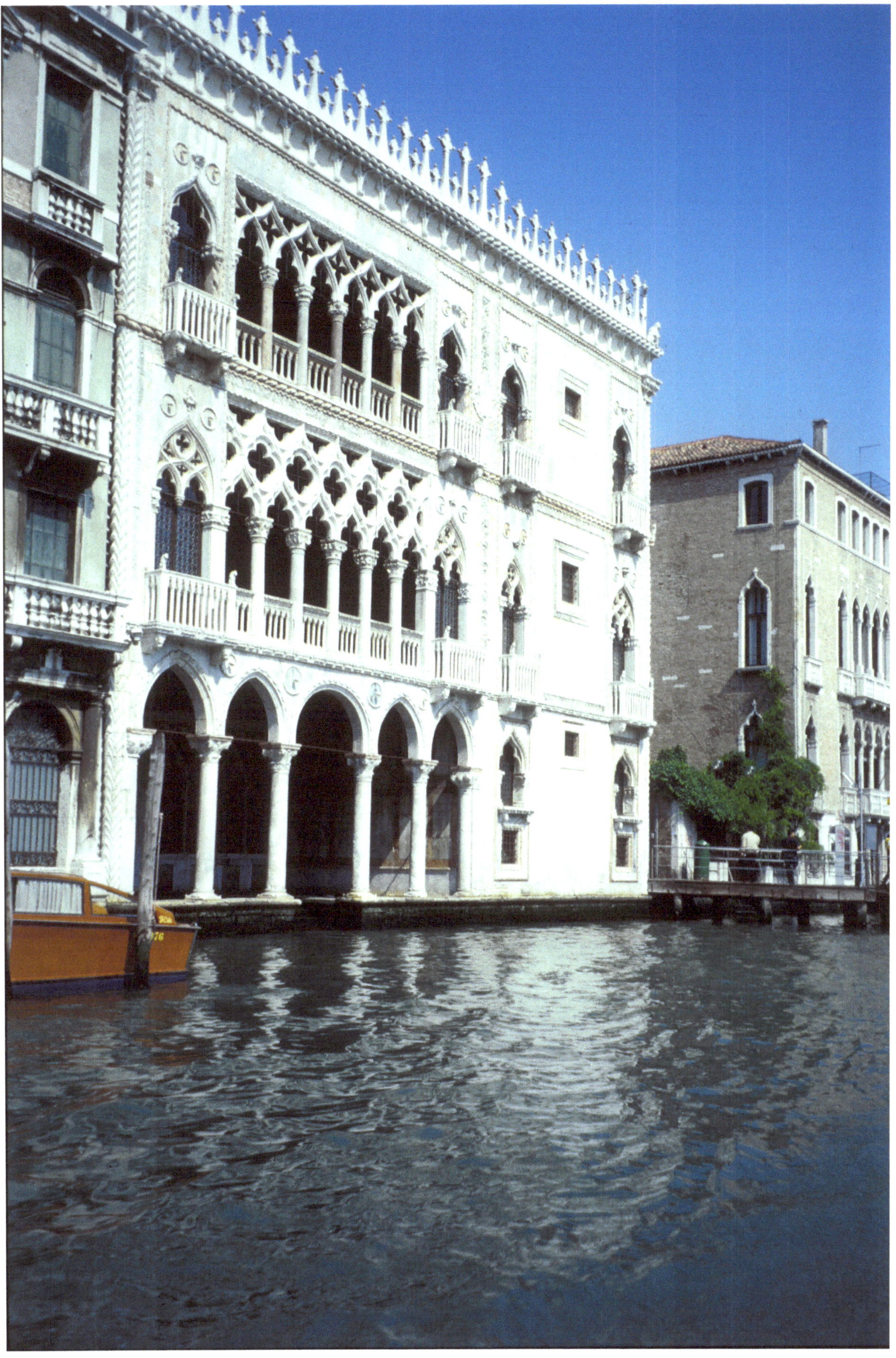

59. Venice Cà d'Oro

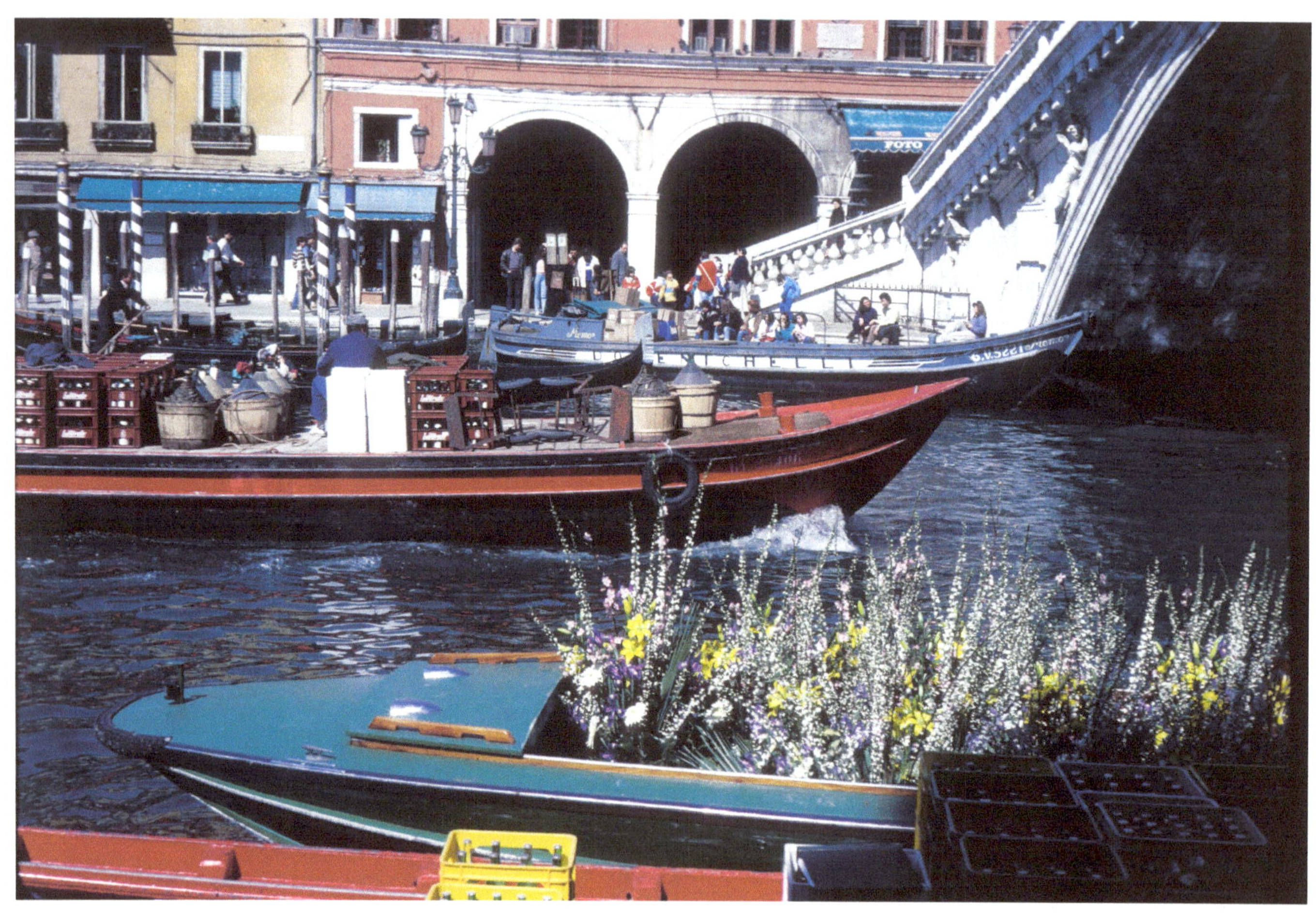

60. <u>Venice</u> Near Rialto

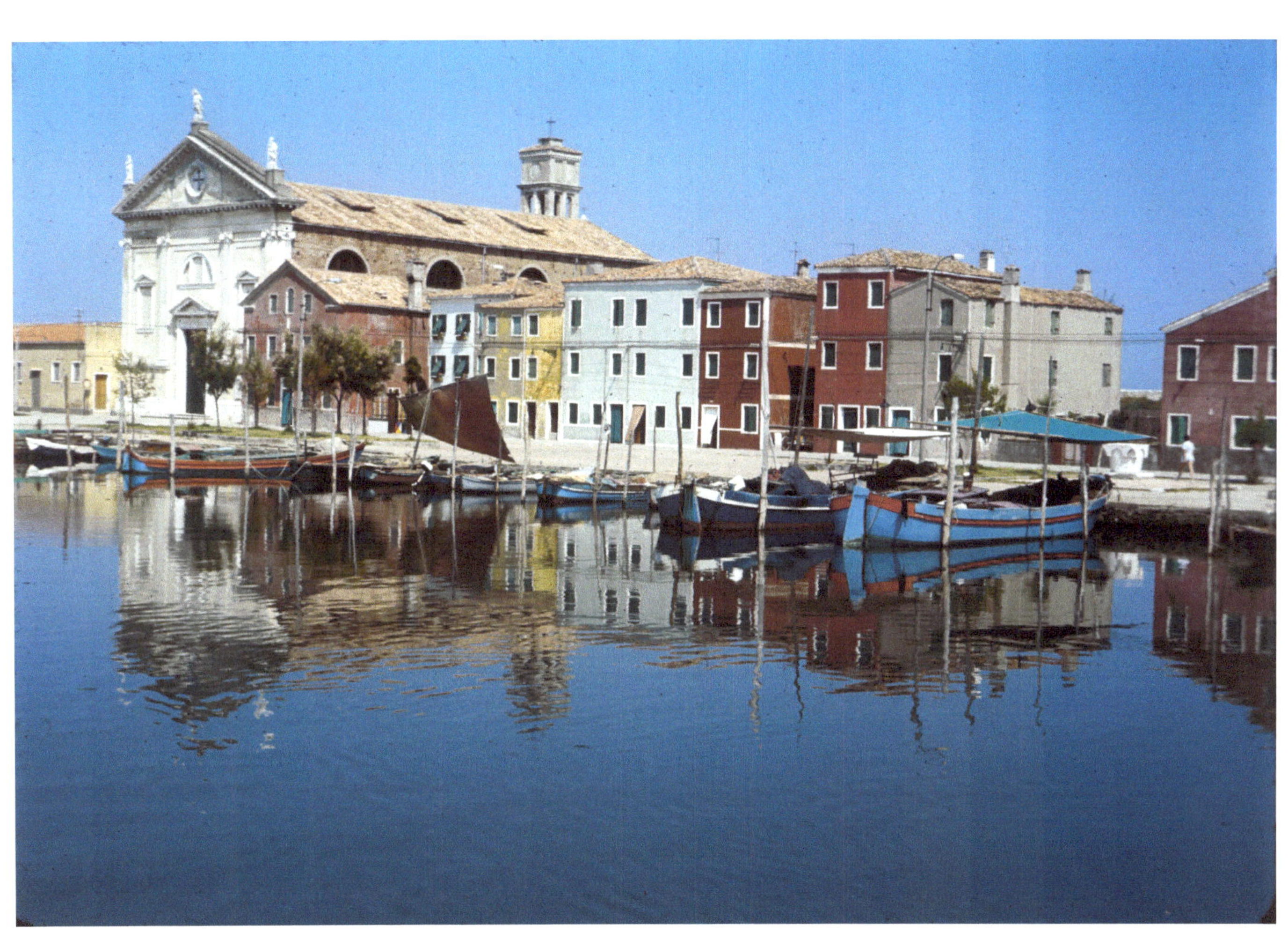

61. Venice Toward Chioggia

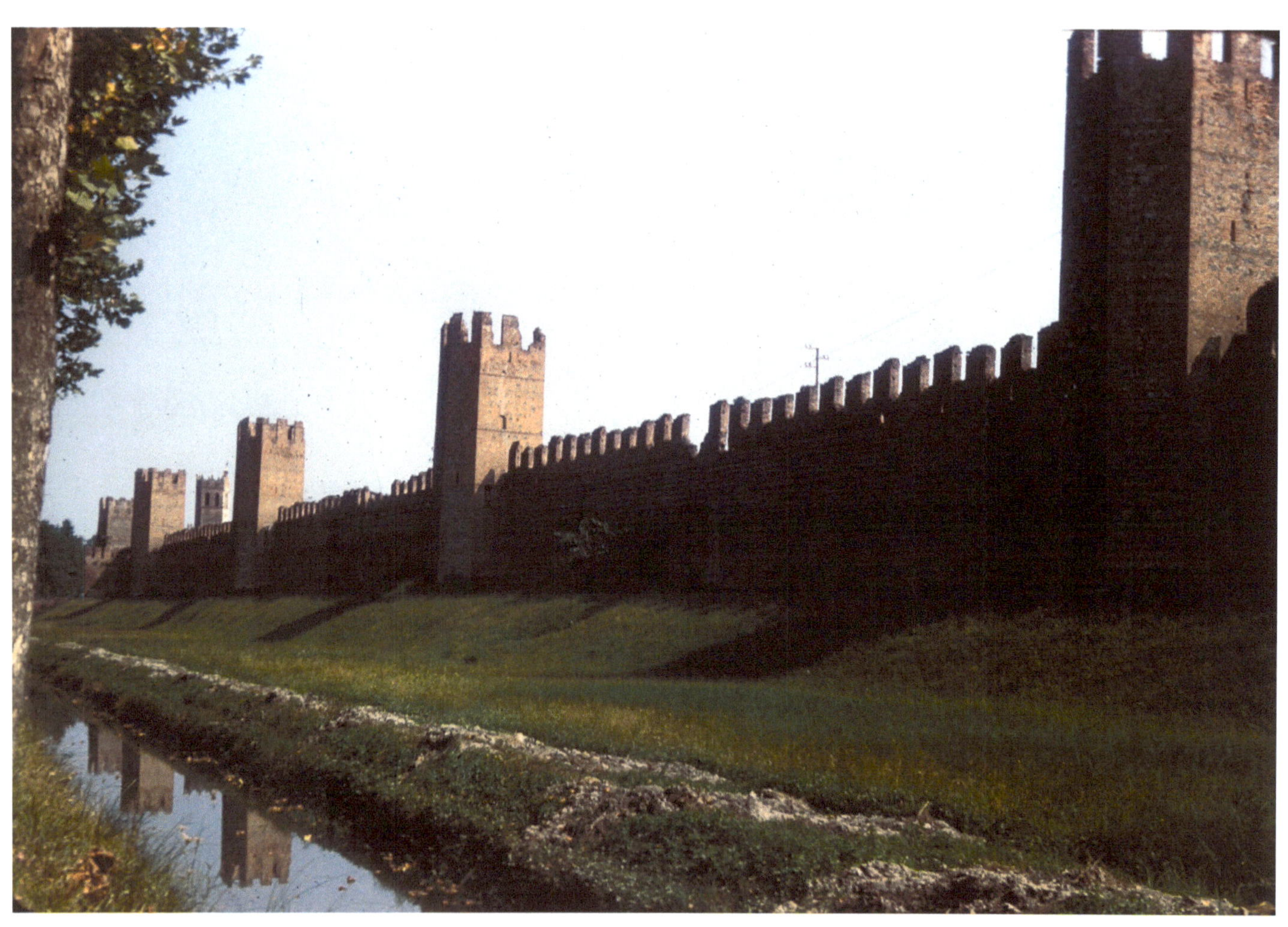

62. Montagnana

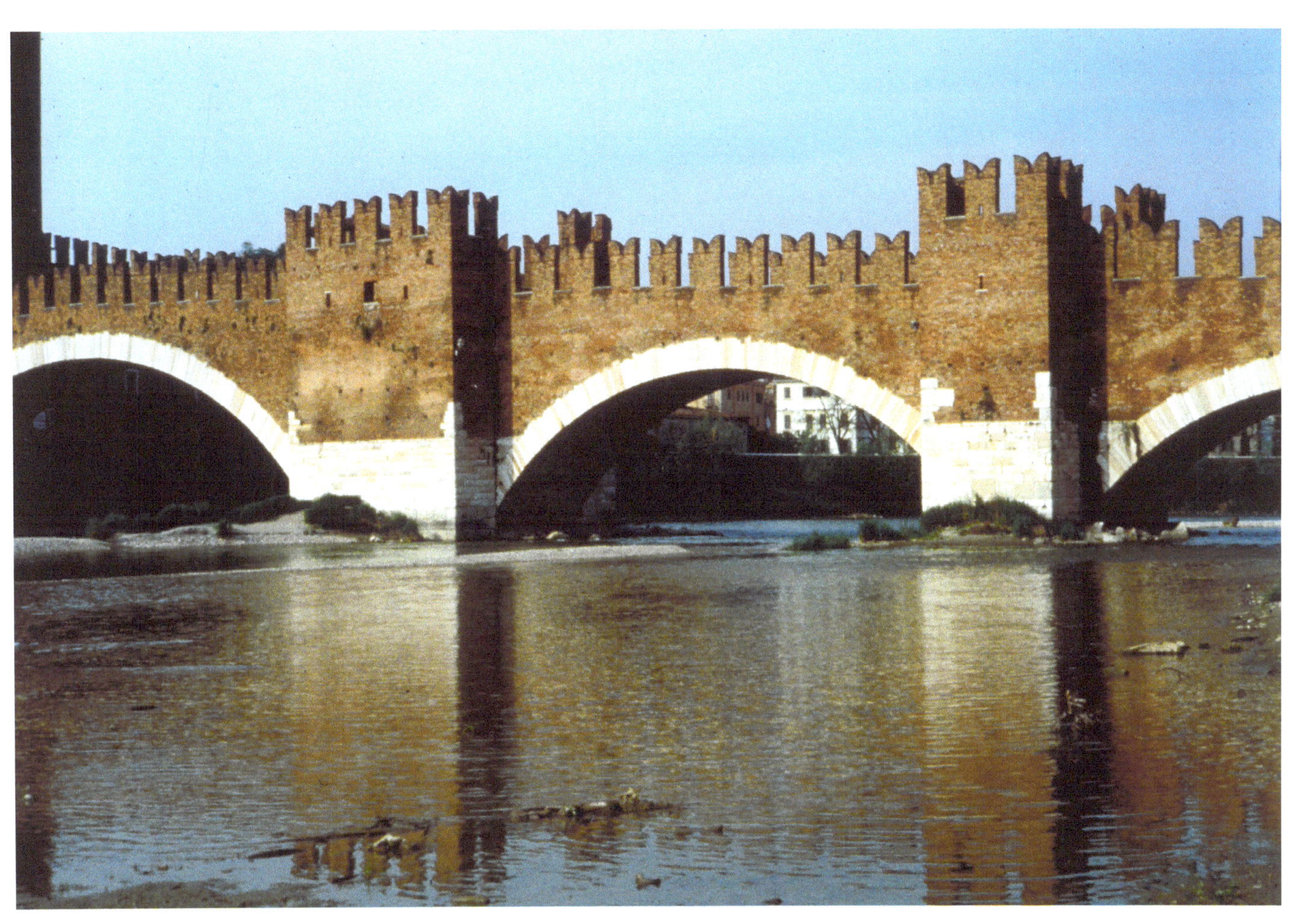

63. Verona Bridge over Adige

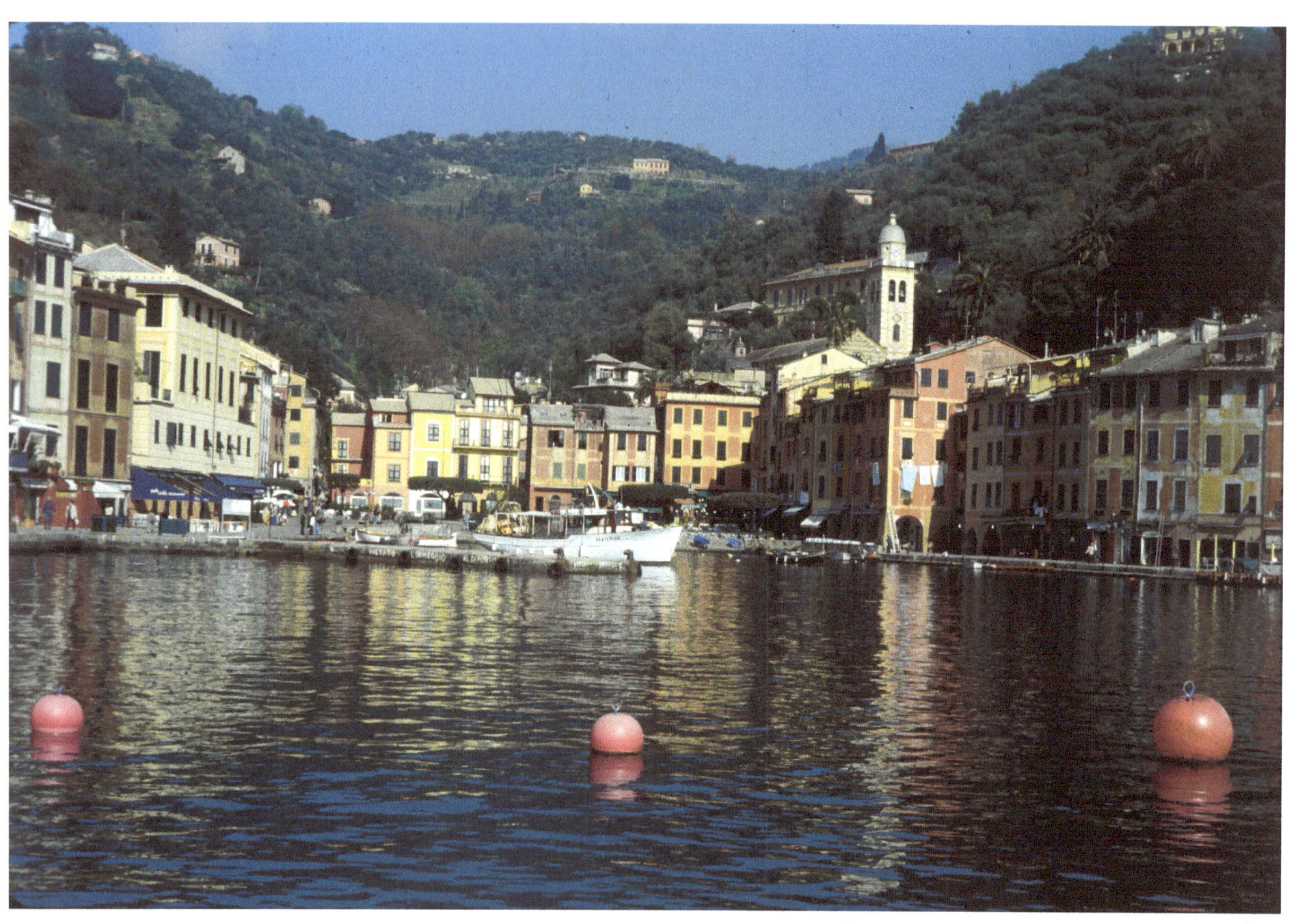

64. Portofino

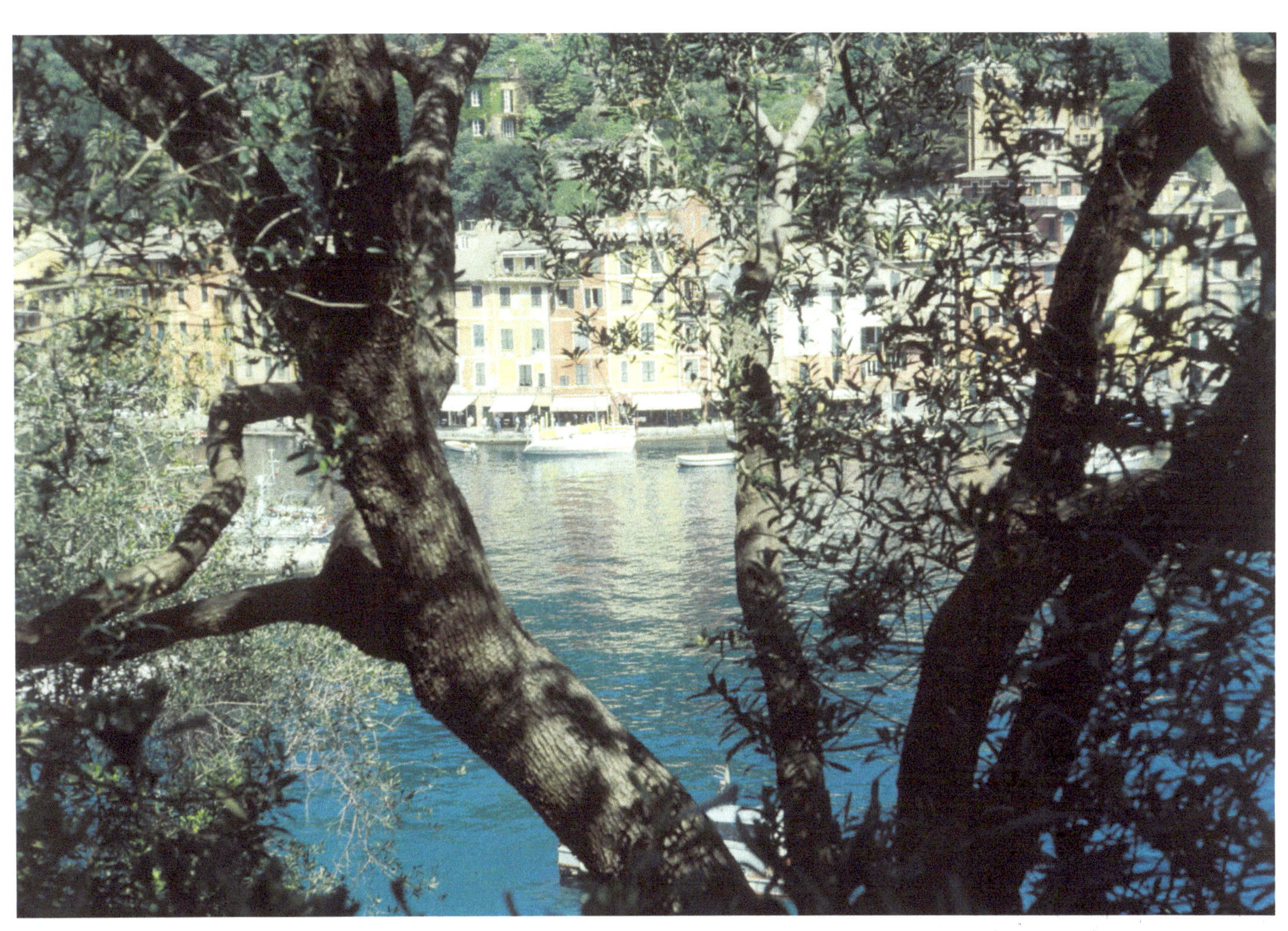

65. Portofino

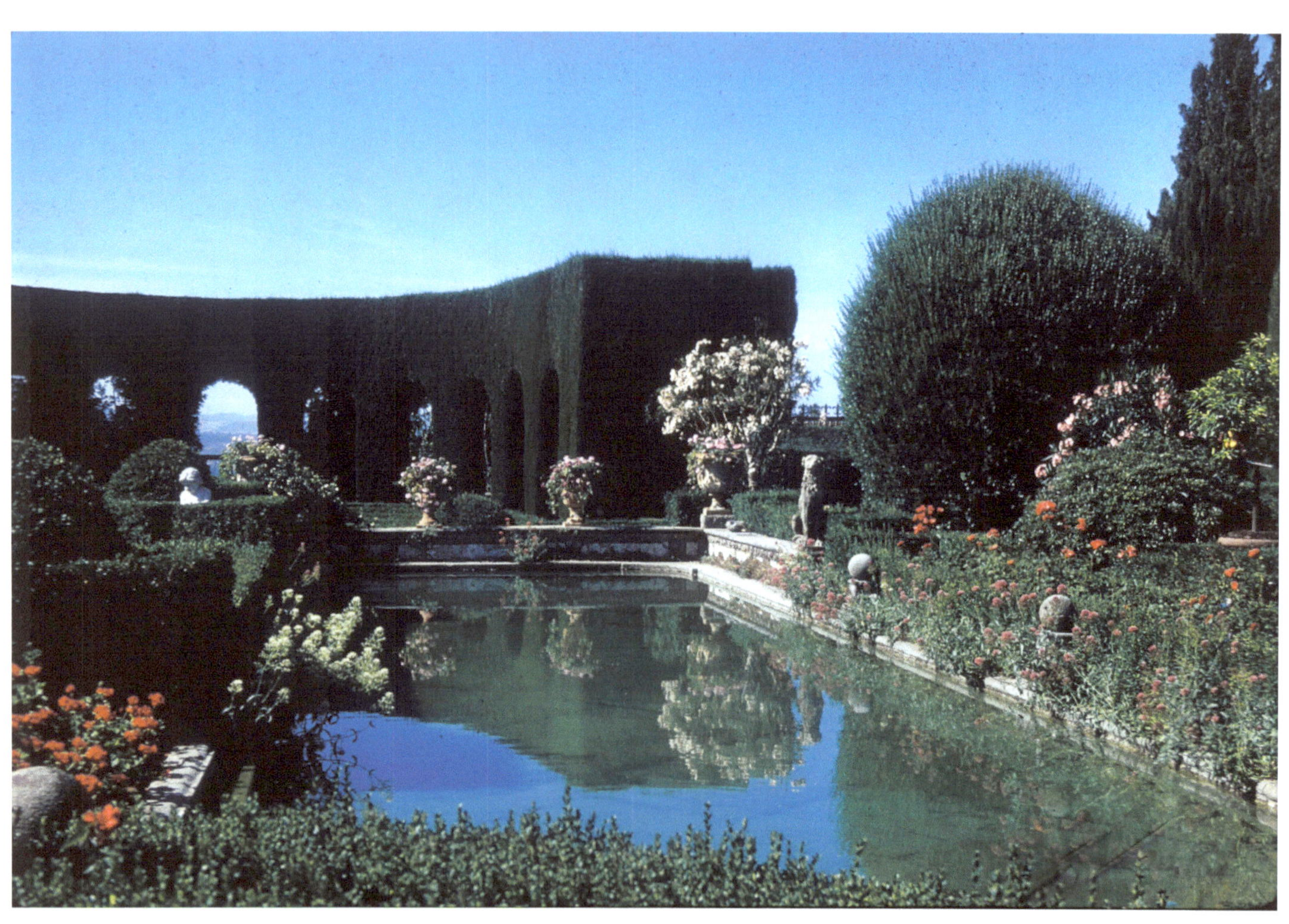

66. Settignano Garden of Villa Gamberaia

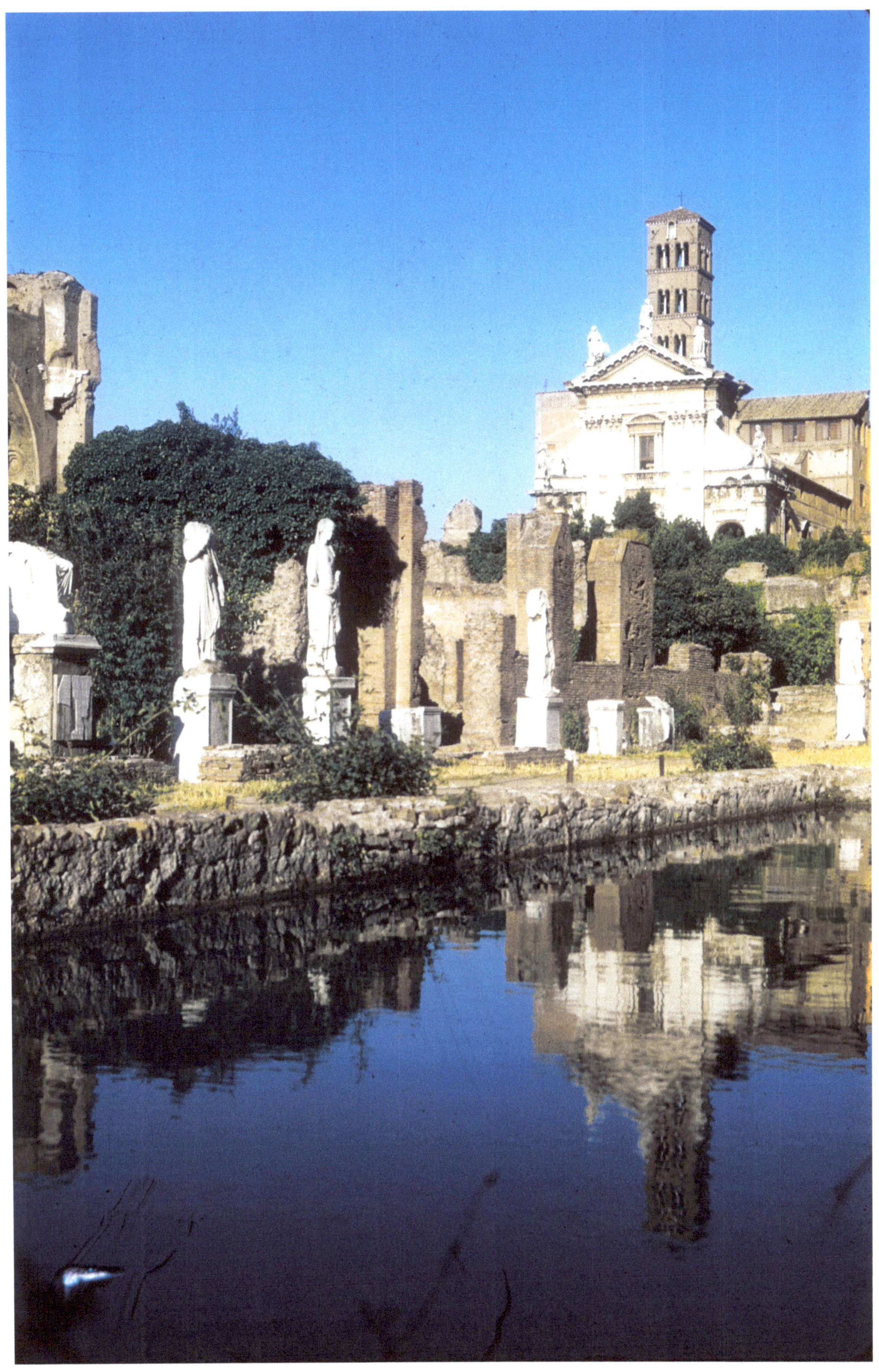

67. Roma Foro Romano

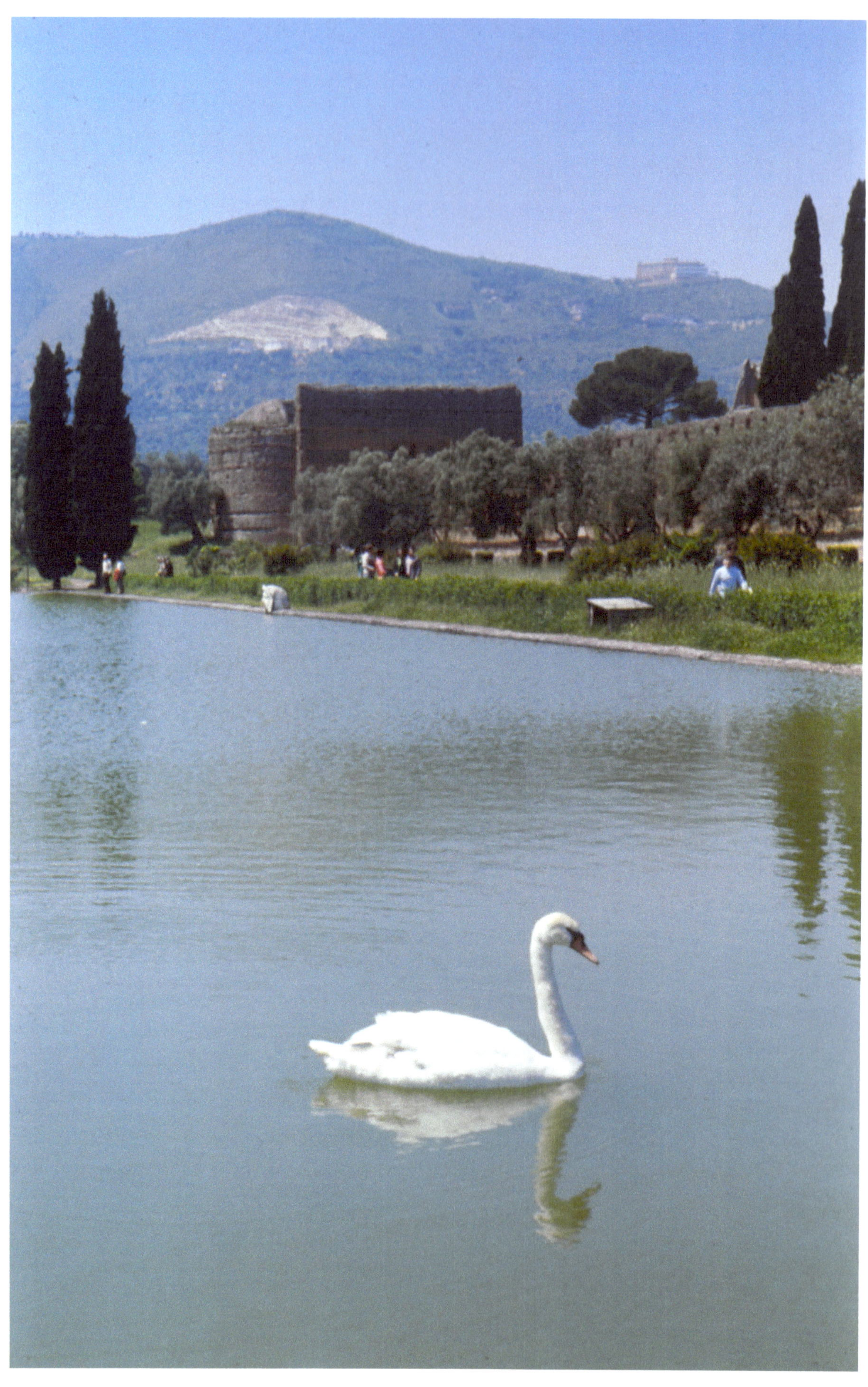

68. Villa Adriana (Hadrian's Villa)

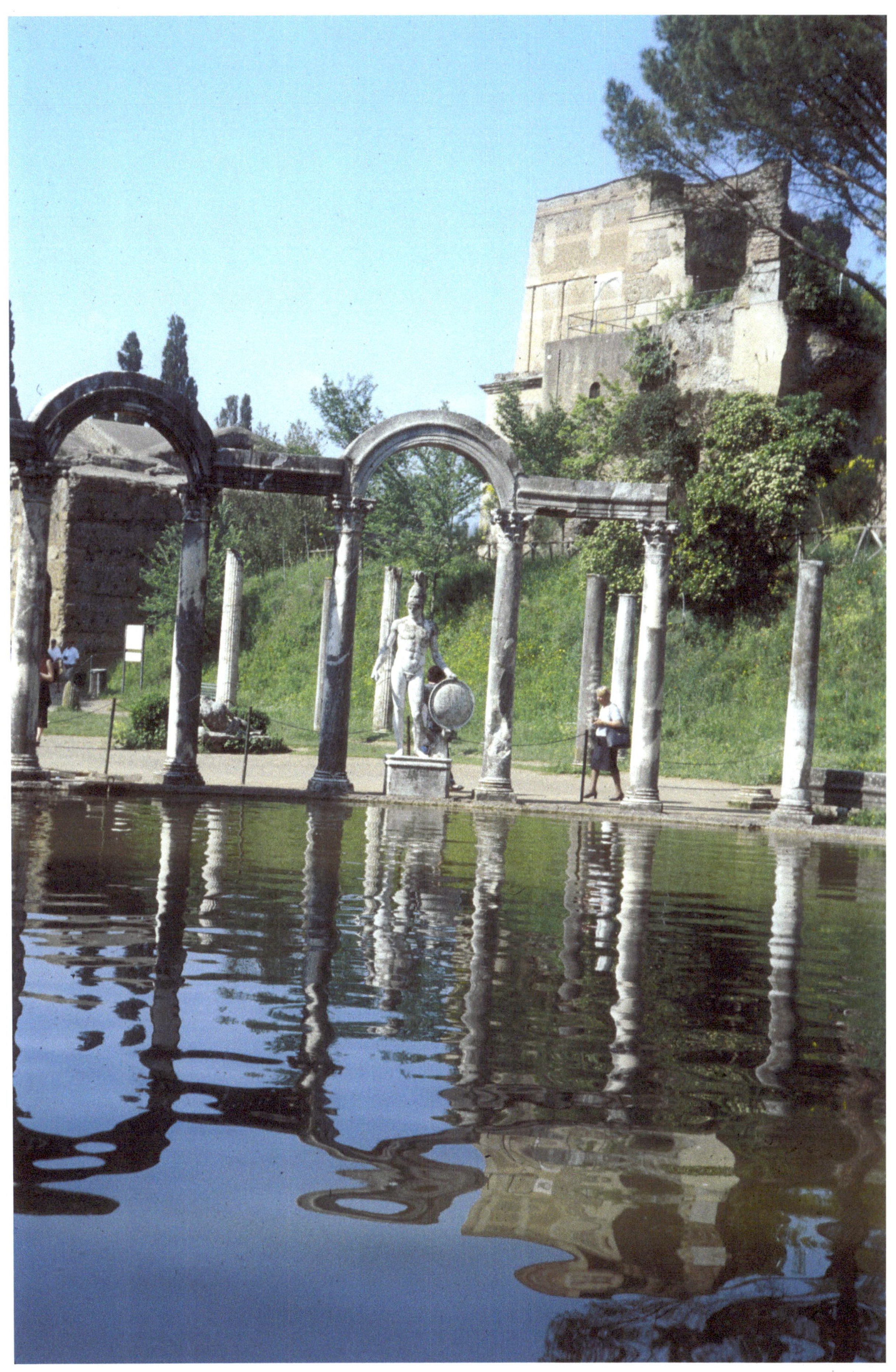

69. Villa Adriana (Hadrian's Villa)

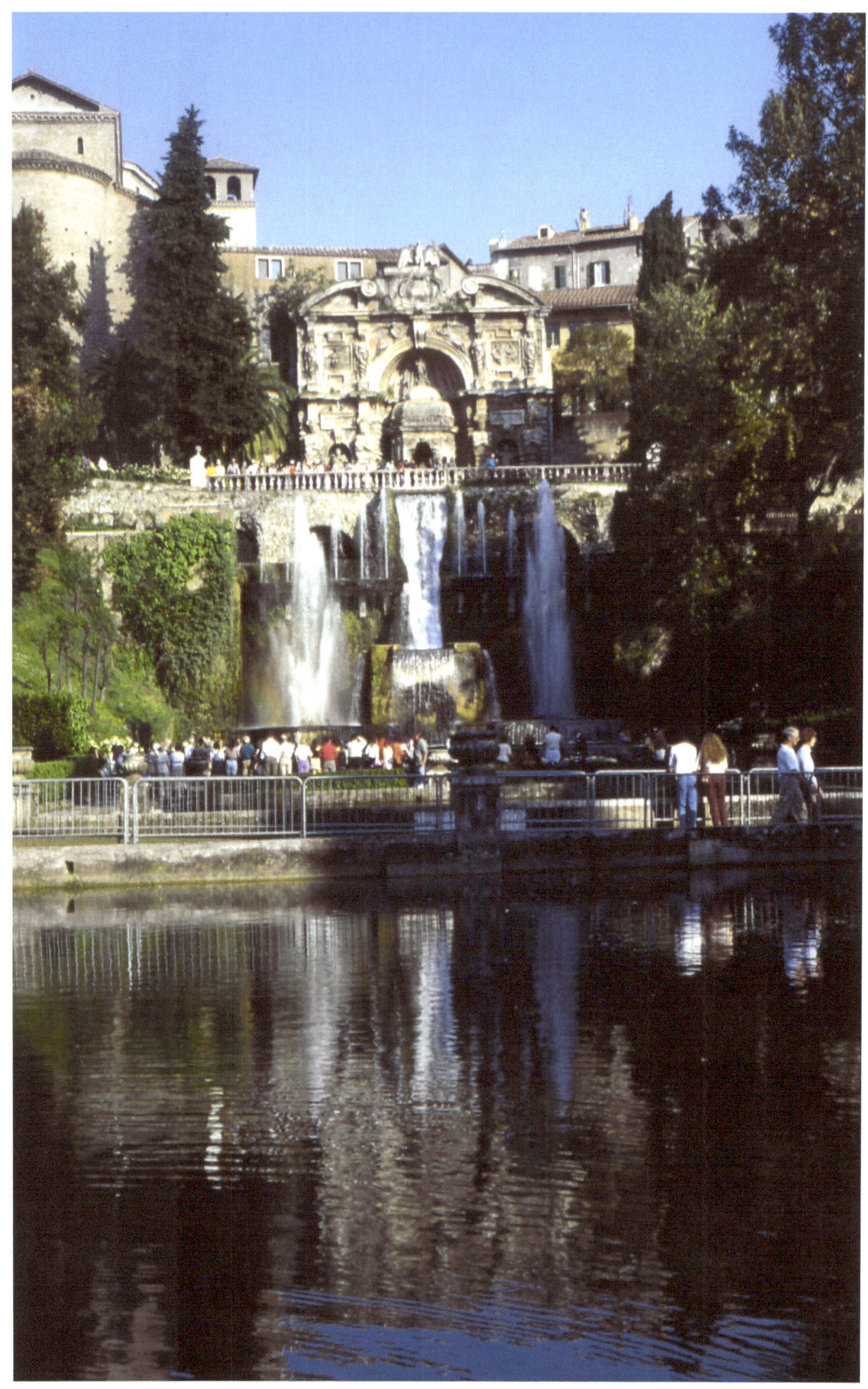

70. Tivoli Villa d'Este

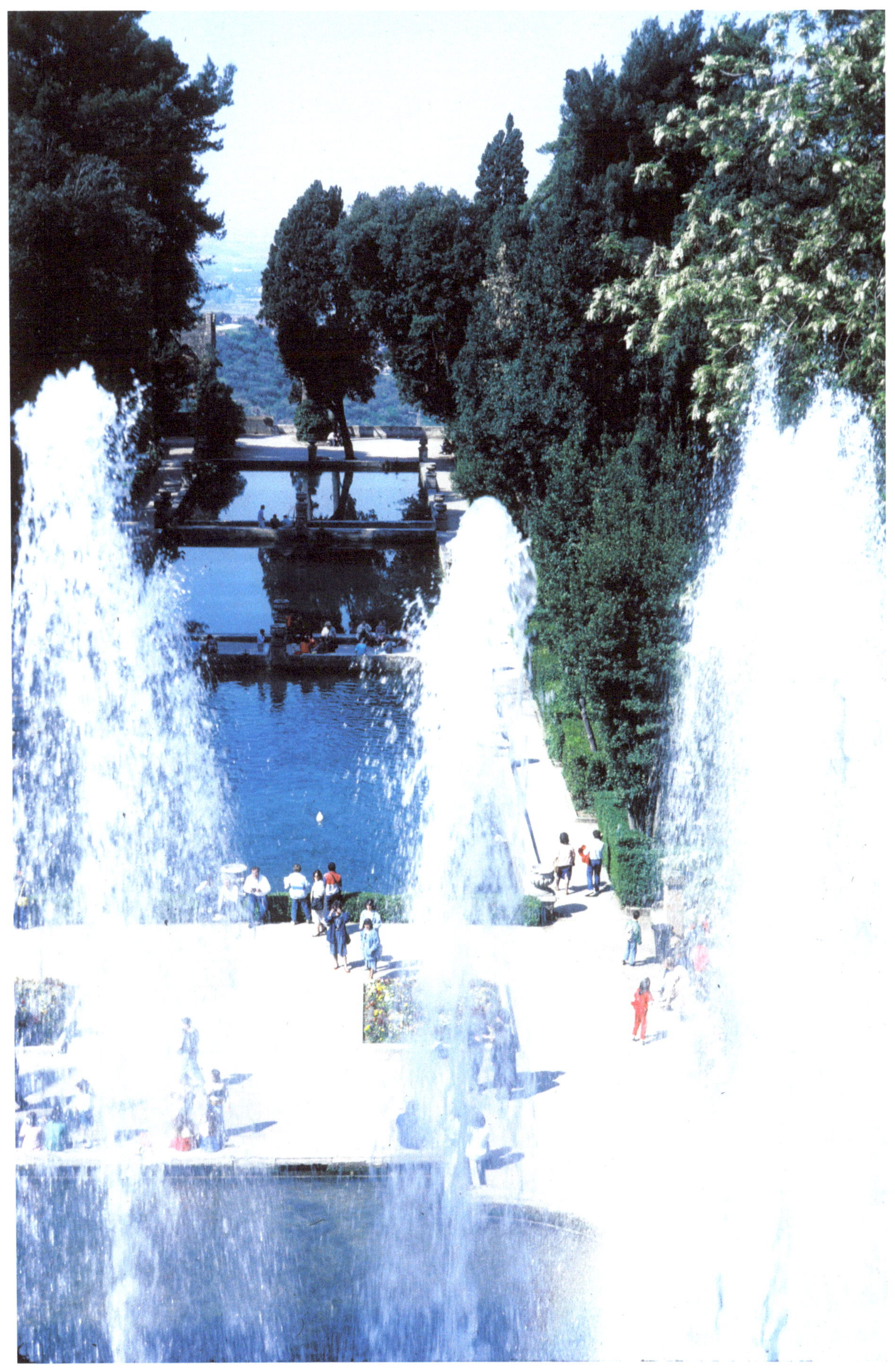

71. Tivoli Villa d'Este

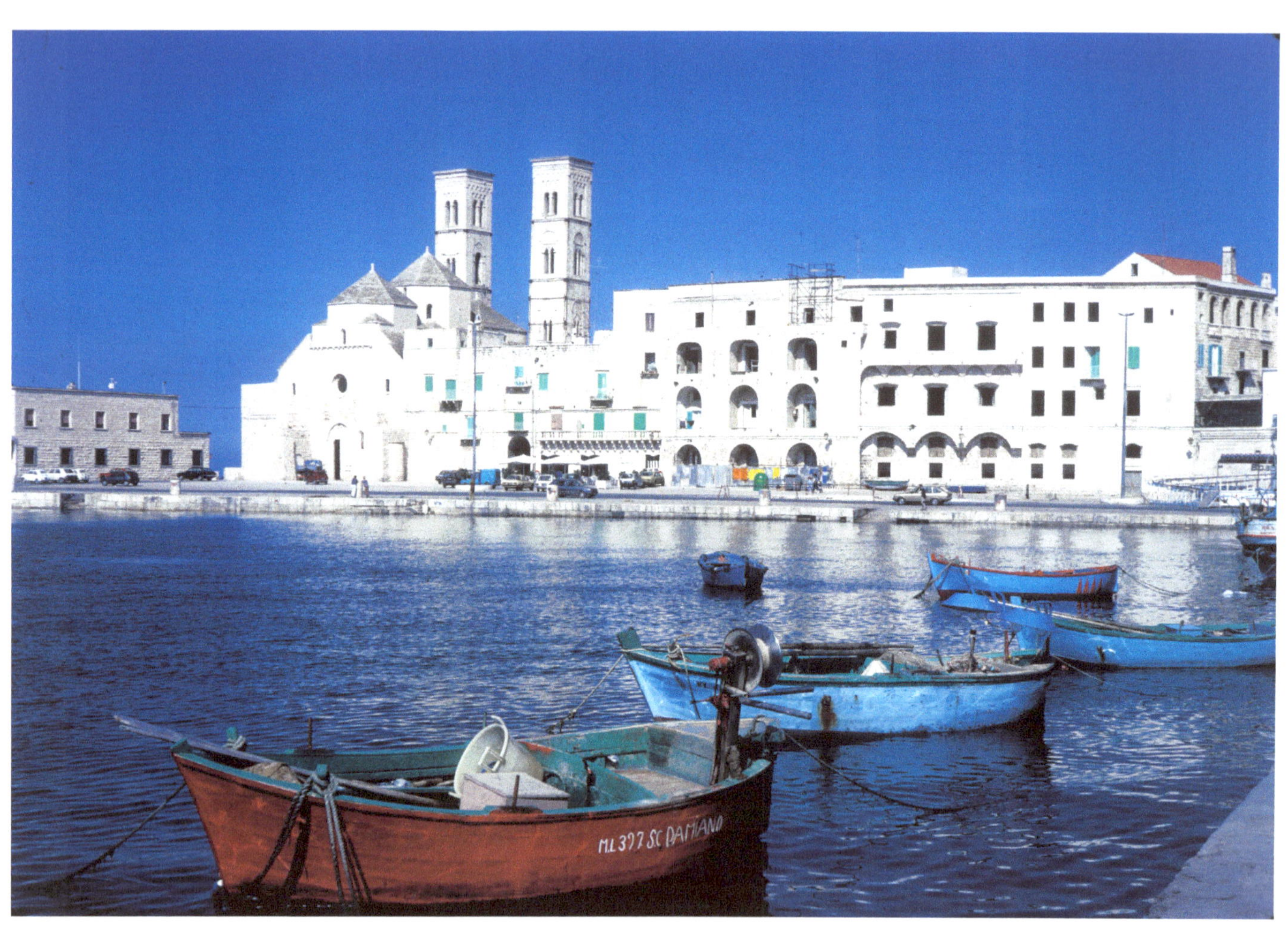

72. Molfetta

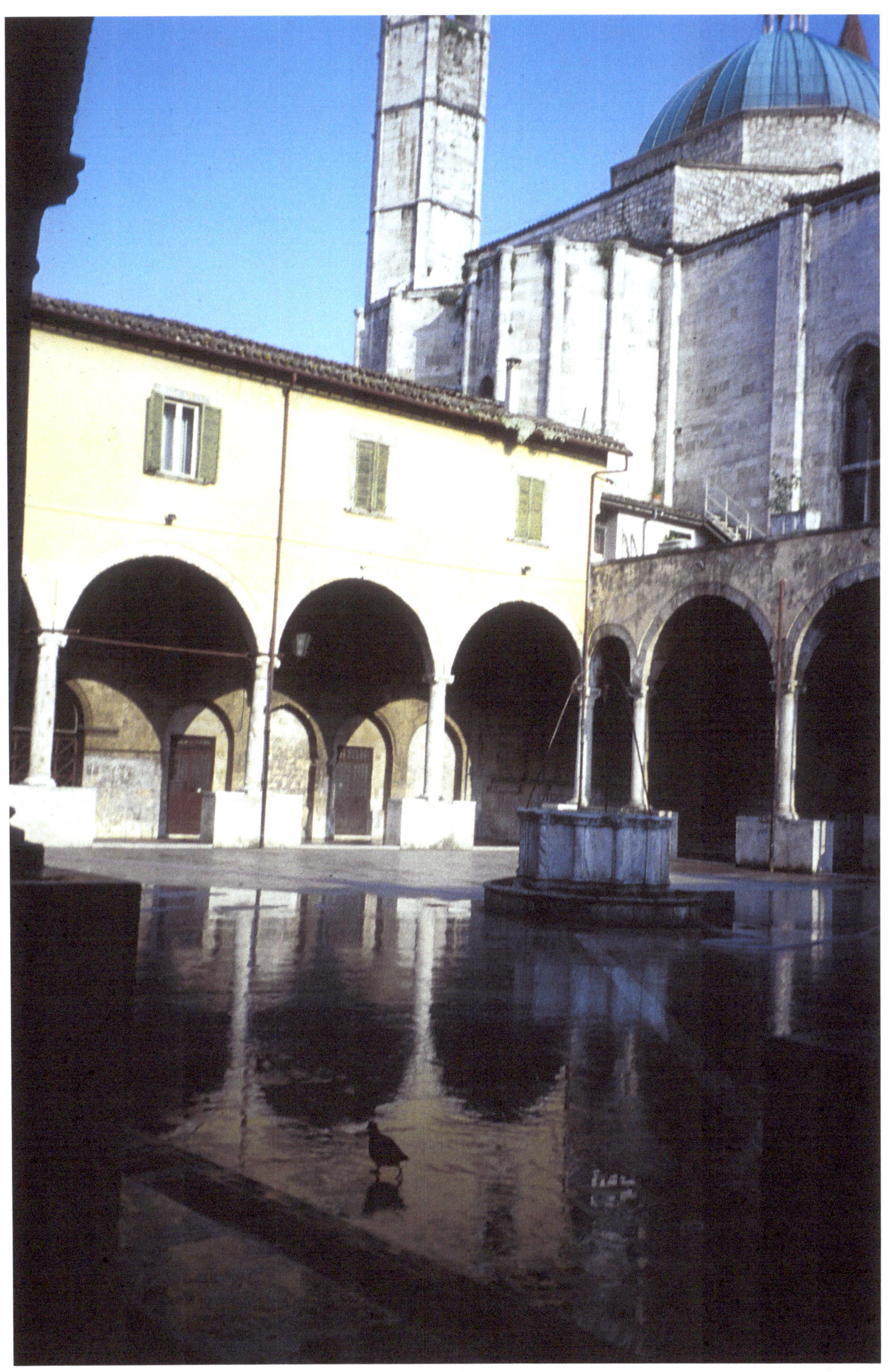

73. Ascoli Piceno Duomo

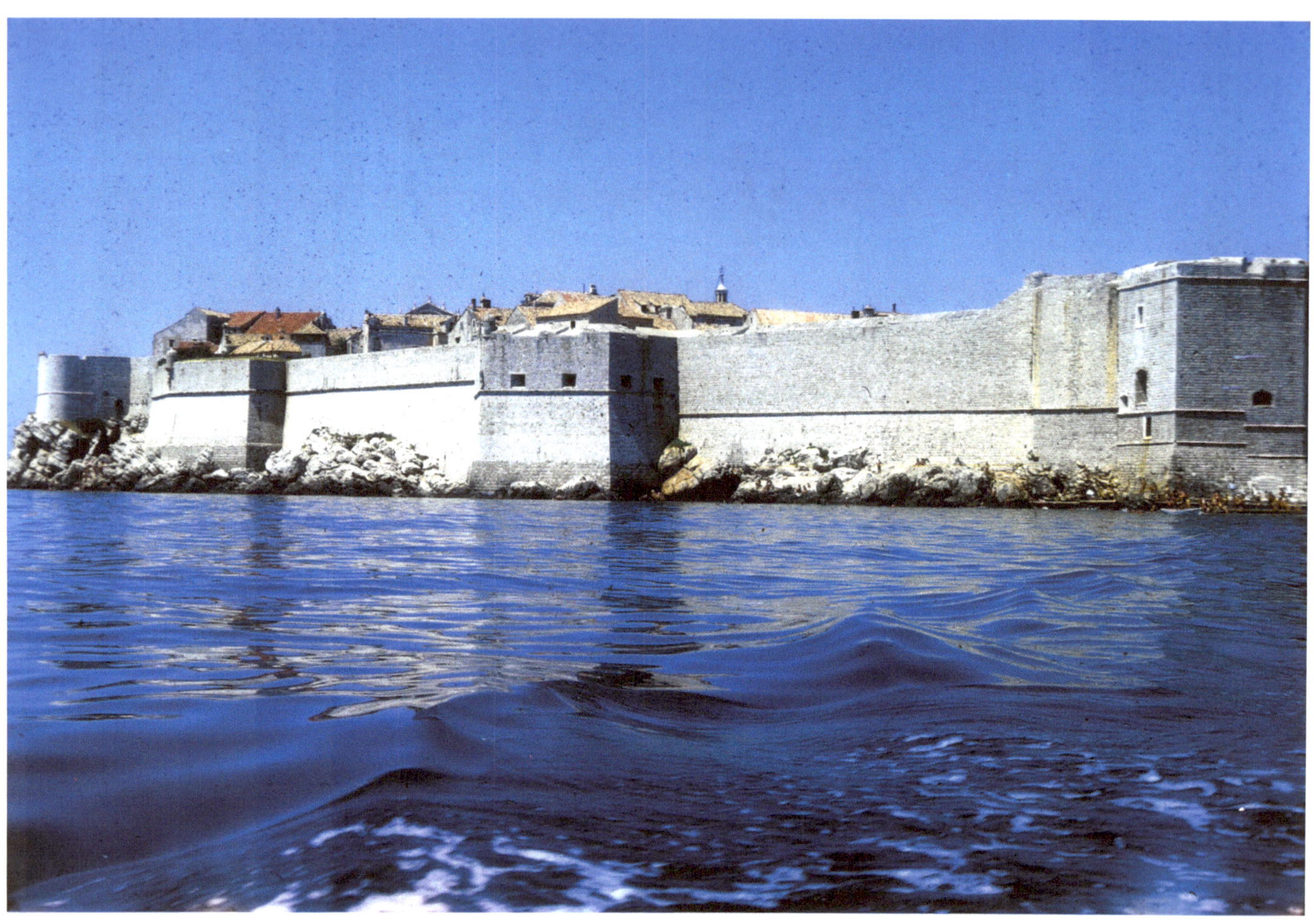

74. Dubrovnik

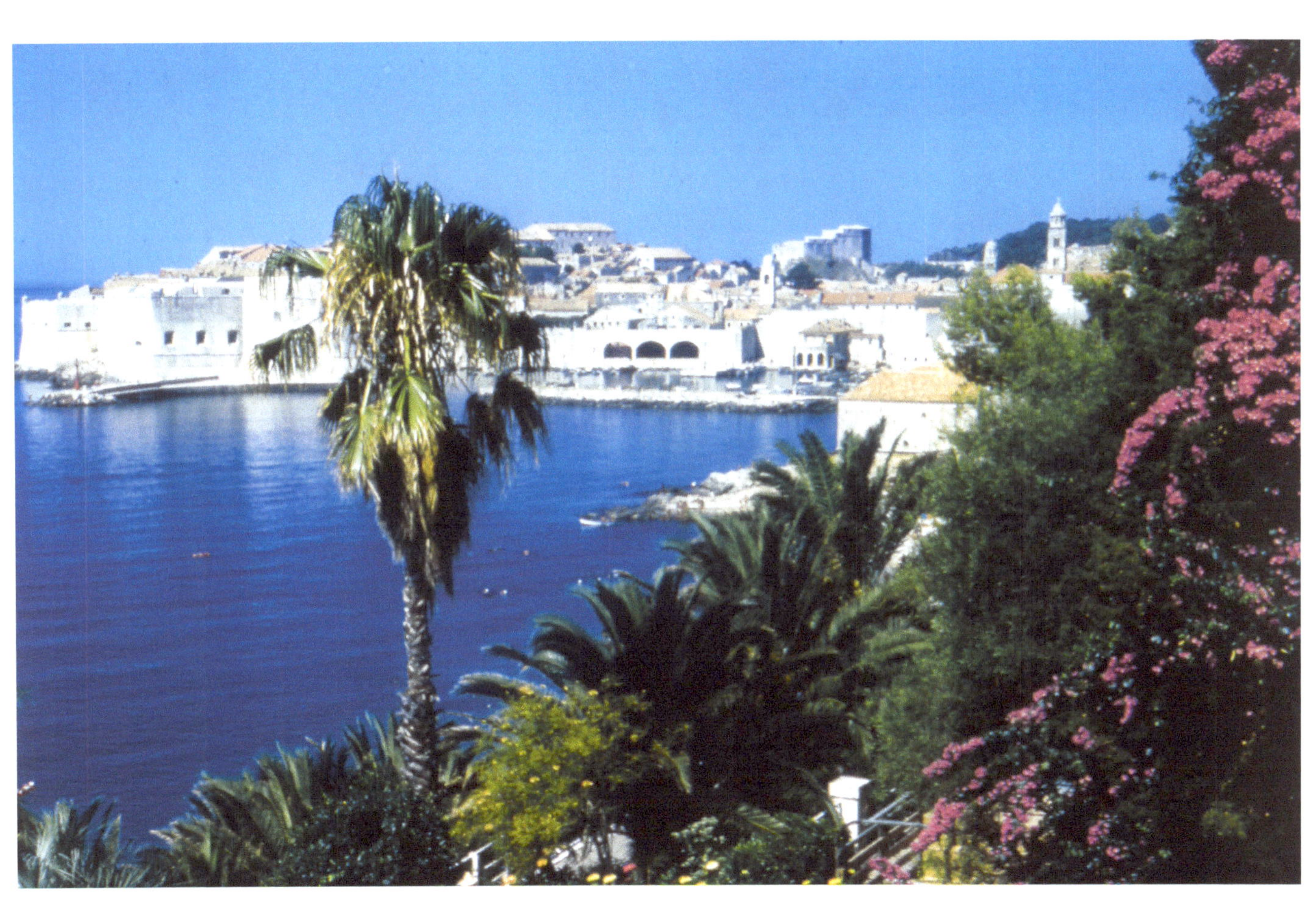

75. Dubrovnik

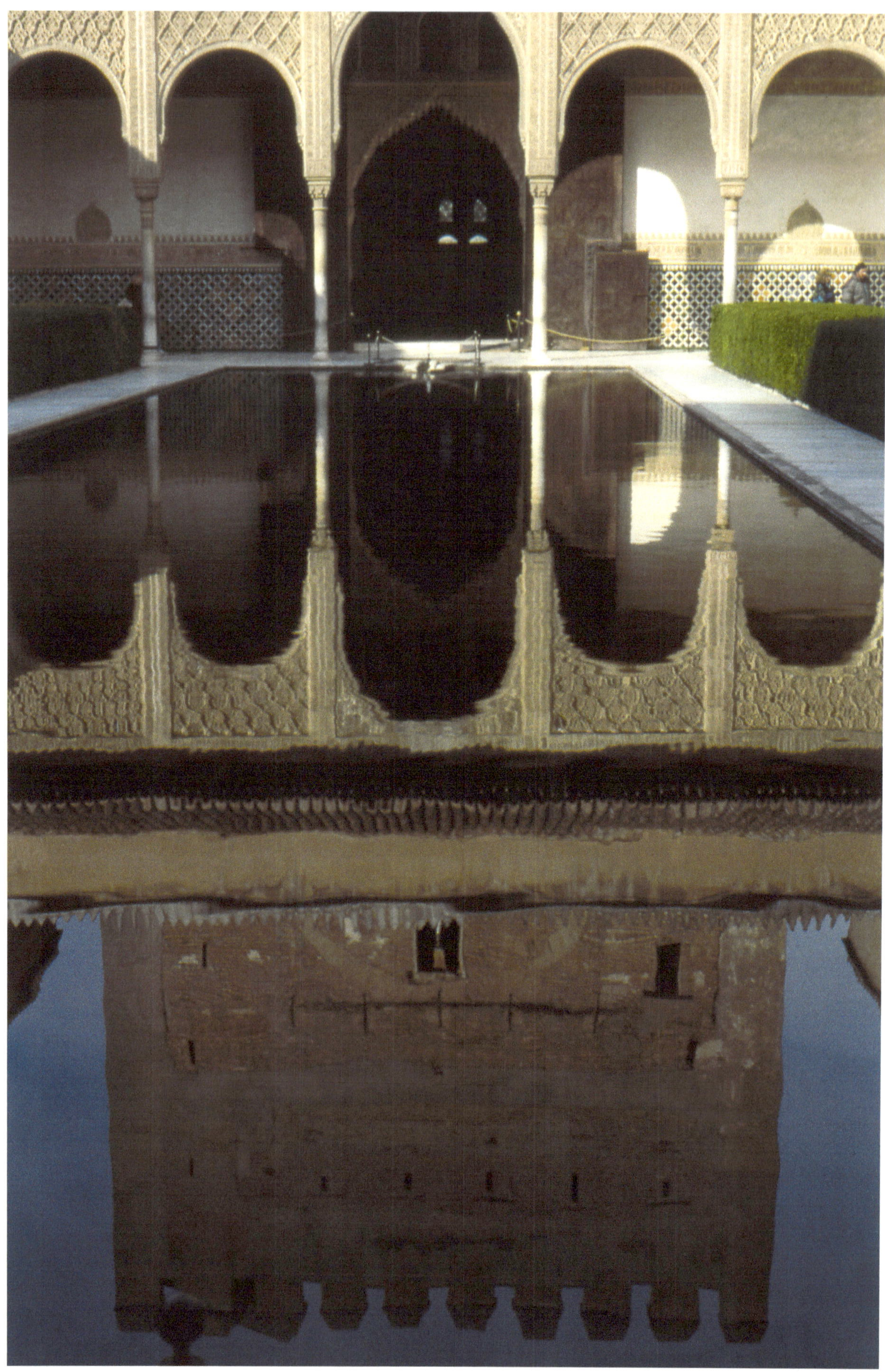

76. Granada Alhambra

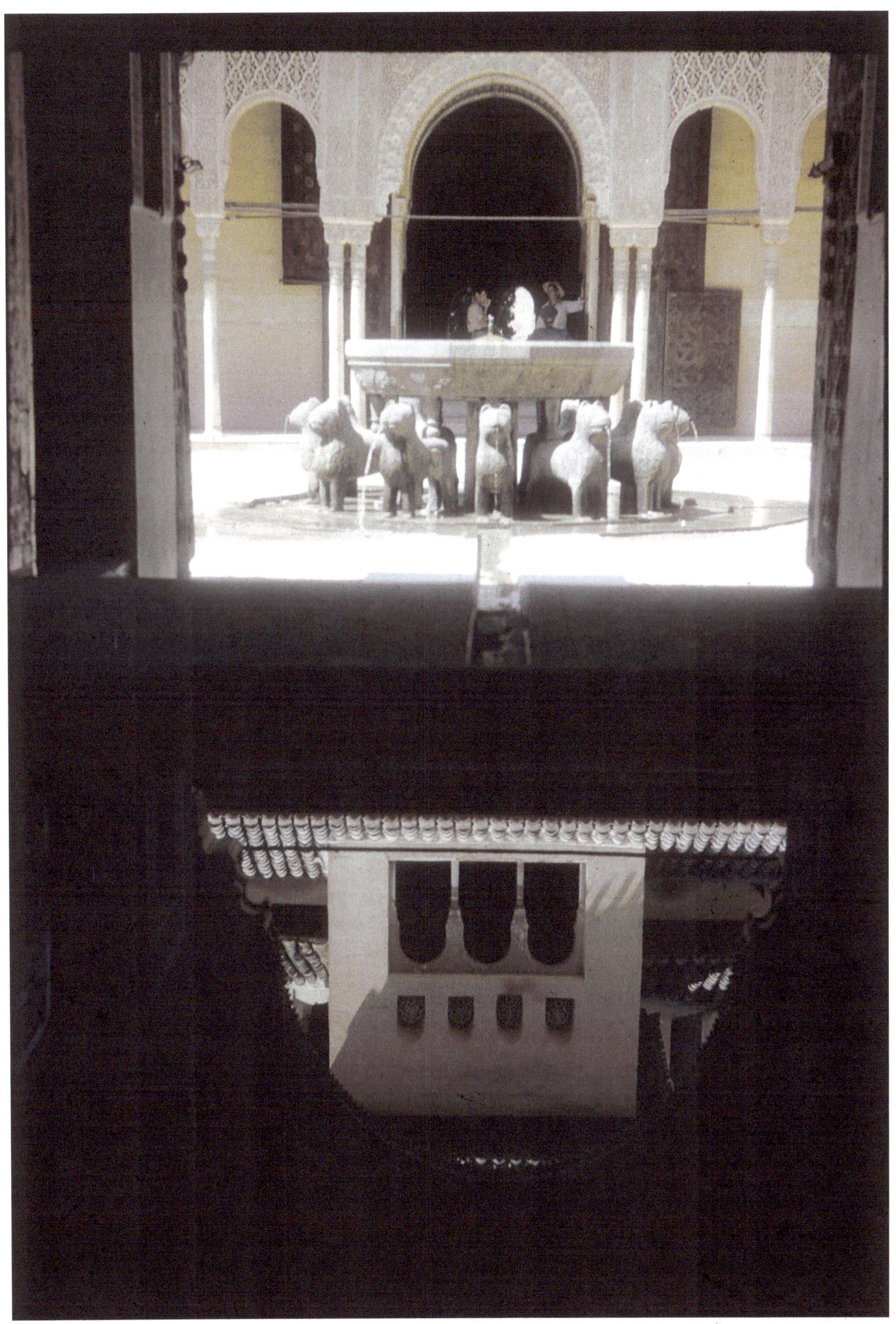

77. Granada Alhambra

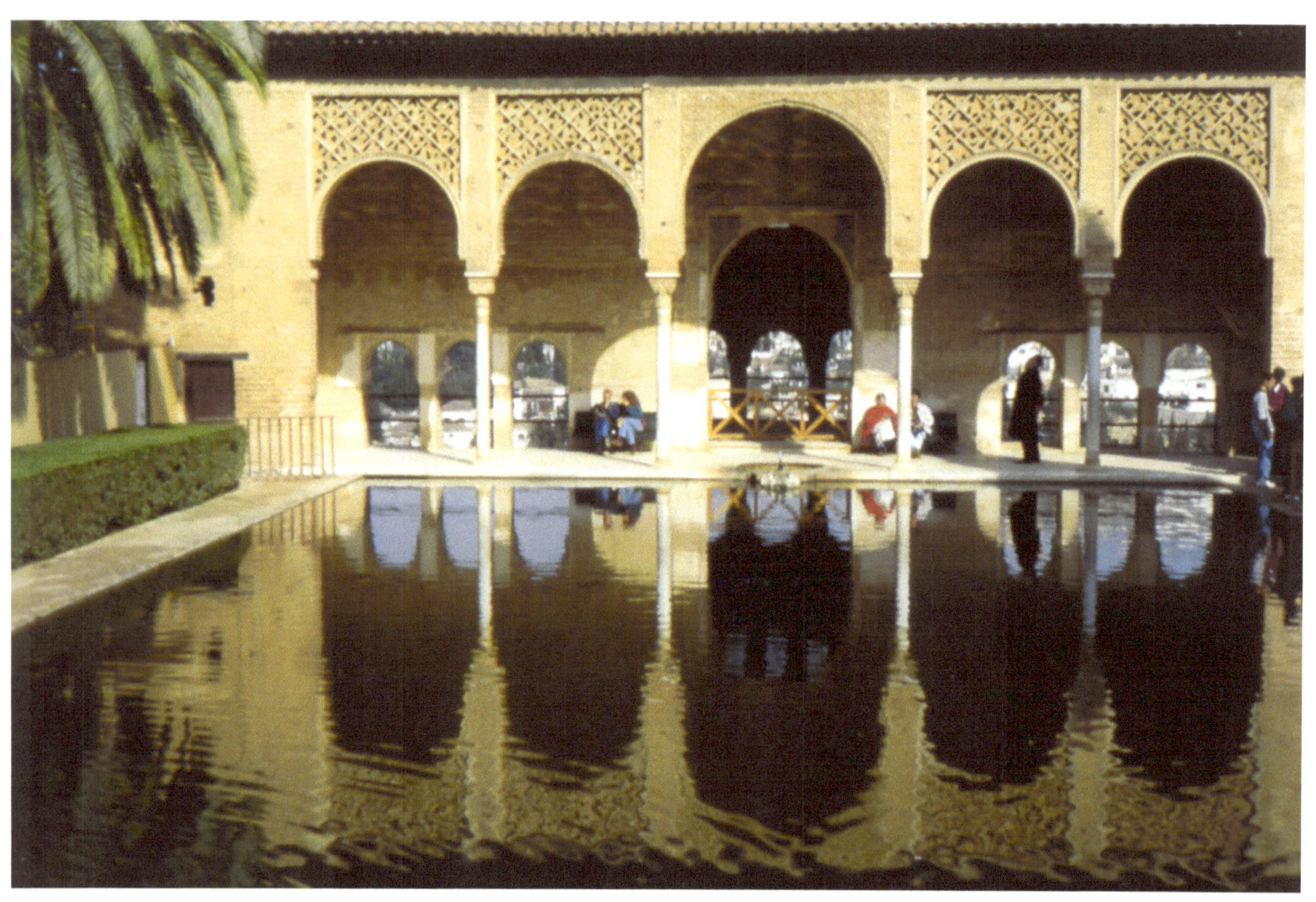

78. Granada Alhambra

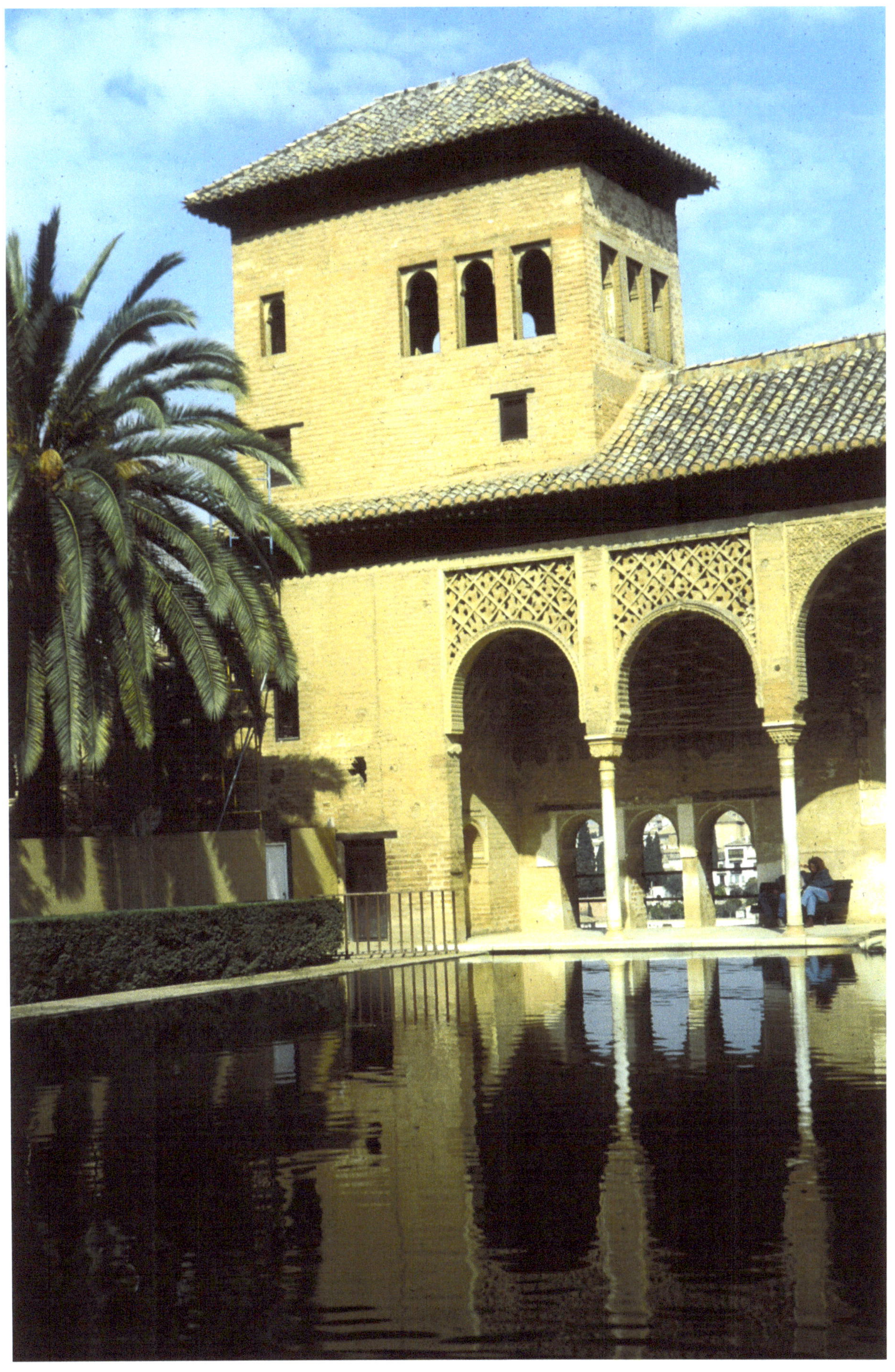

79. Granada Alhambra

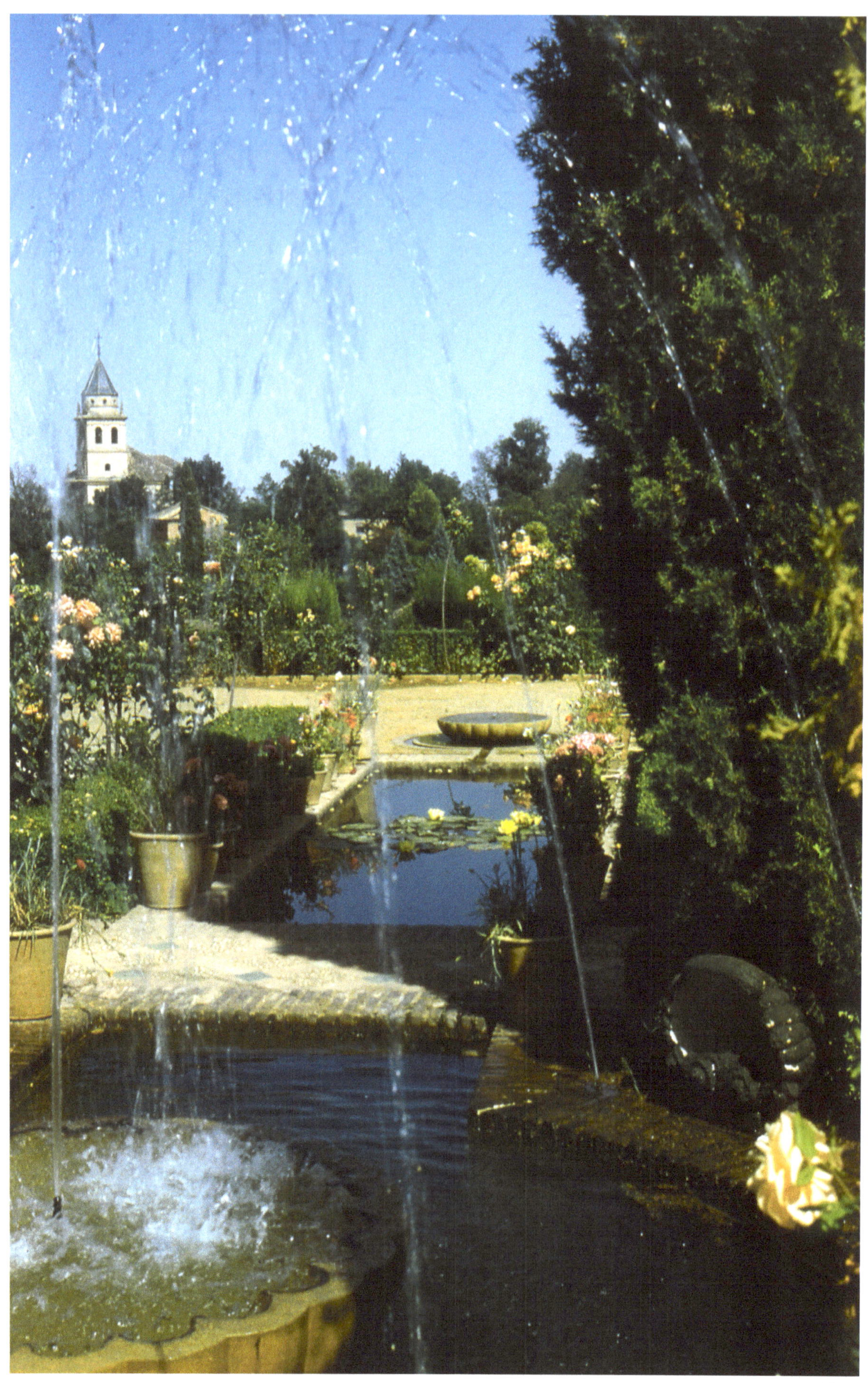

80. Granada Alhambra

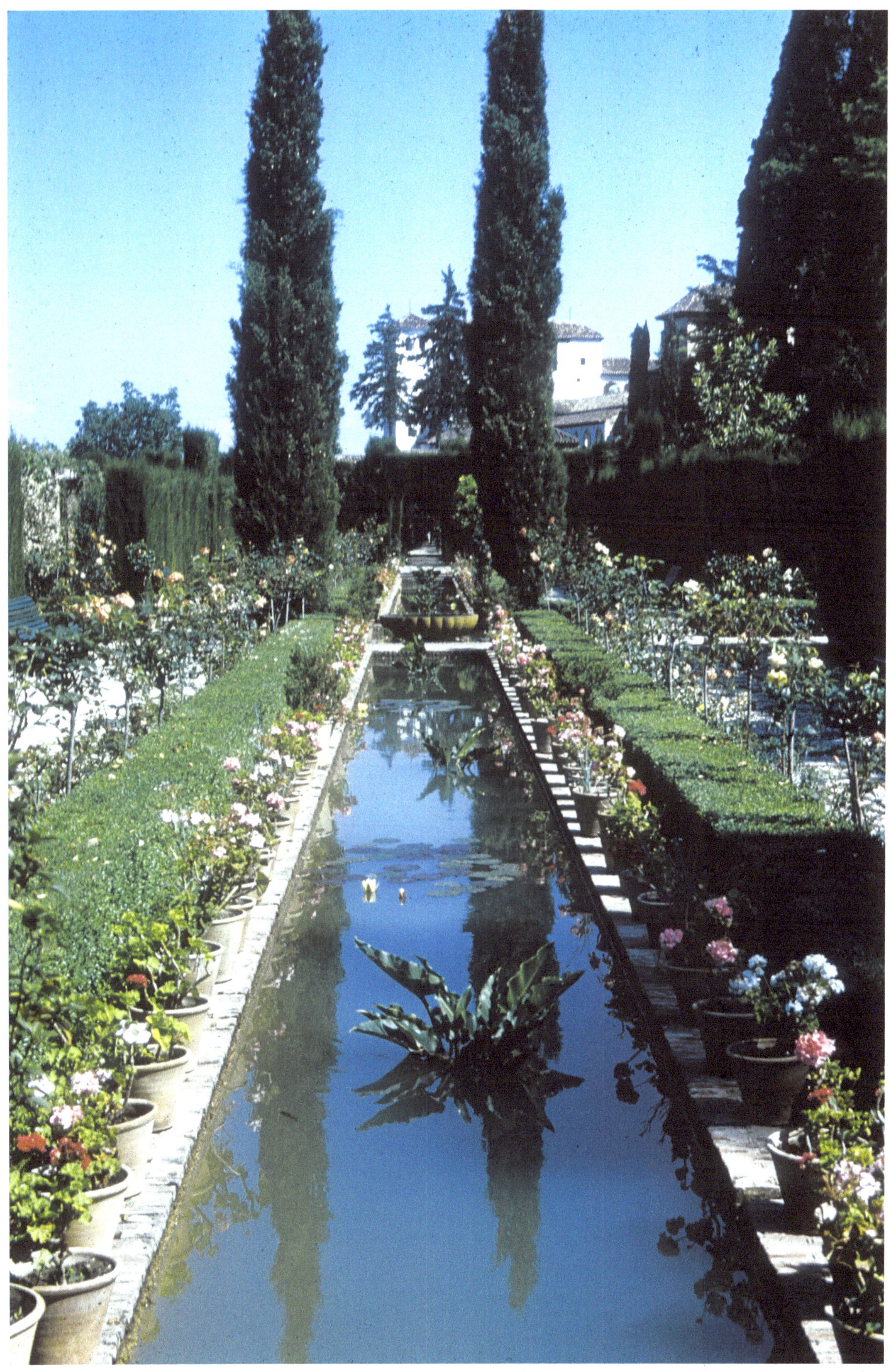

81. Granada Generalife

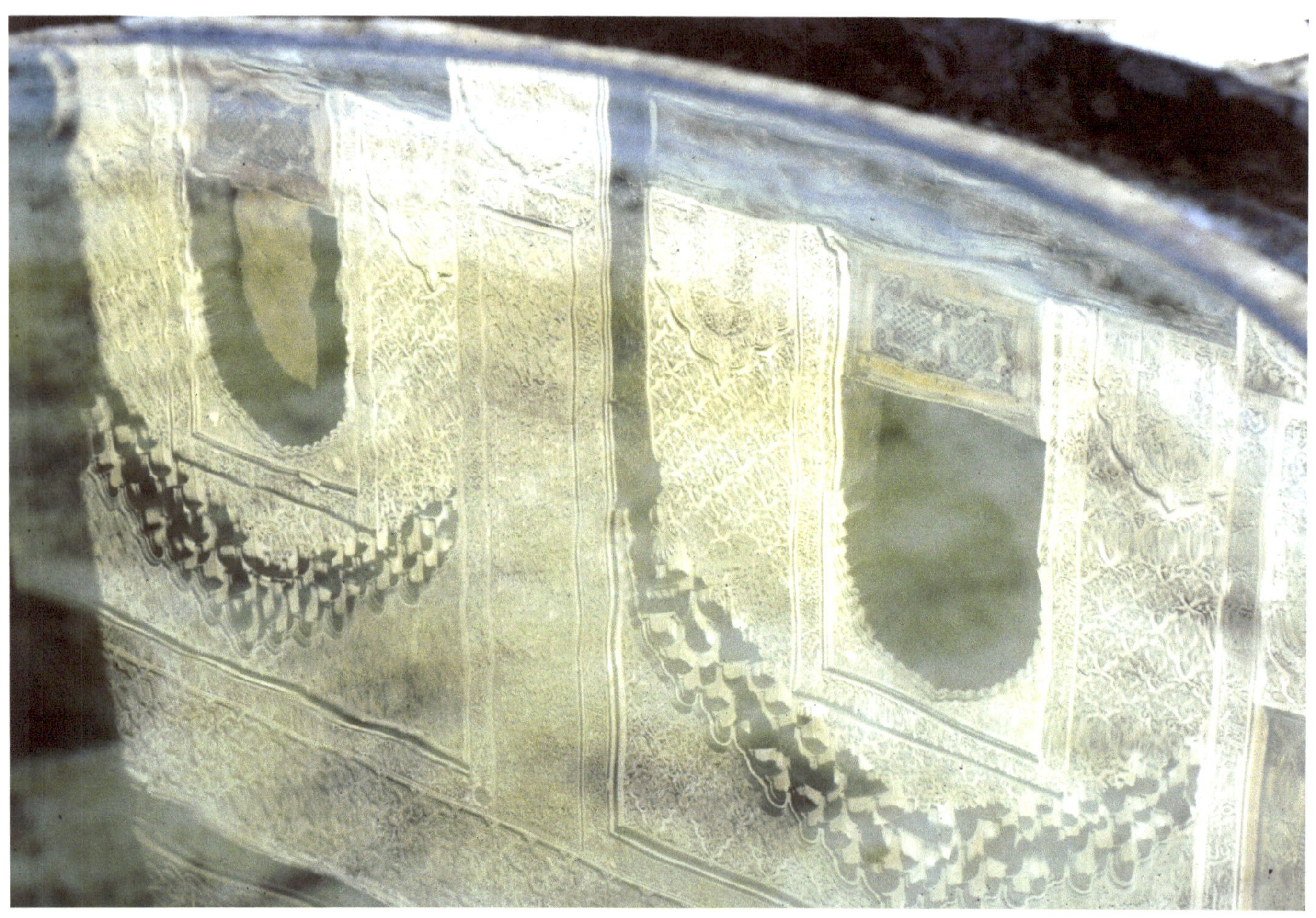

82. Fes Medersa Bou Inania

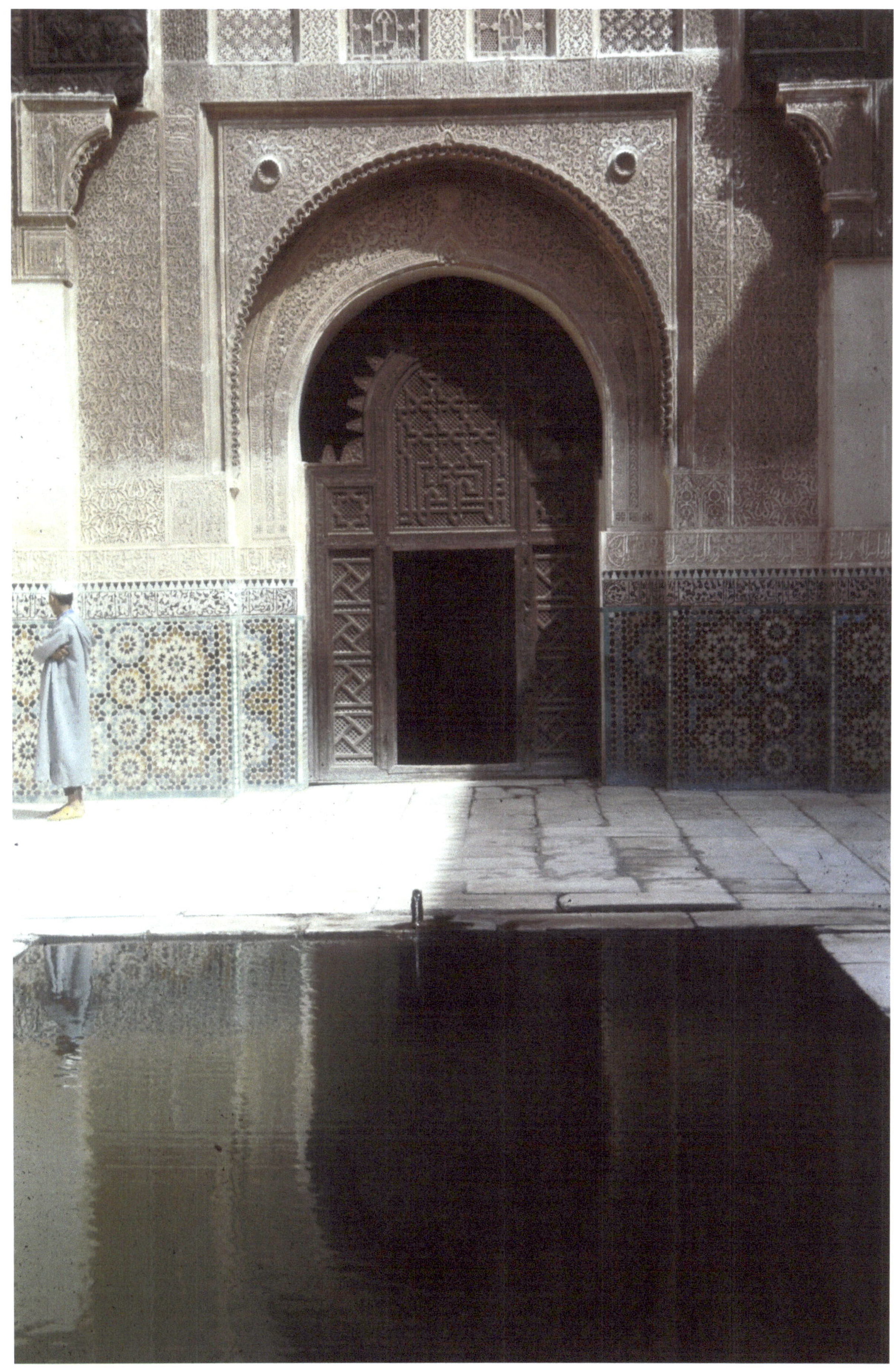

83. Marrakech Medersa Ben Youssef

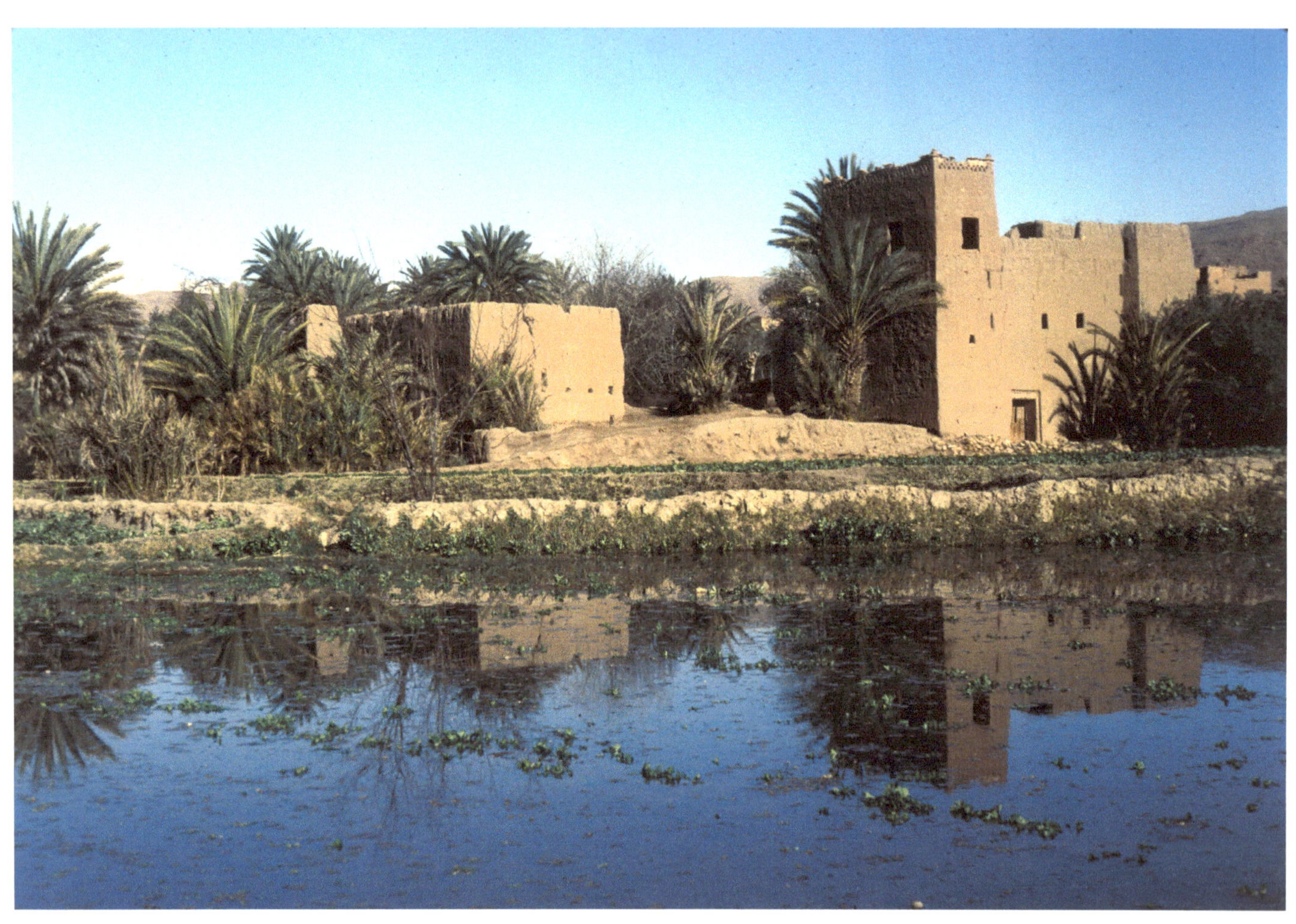

84. Tinghir

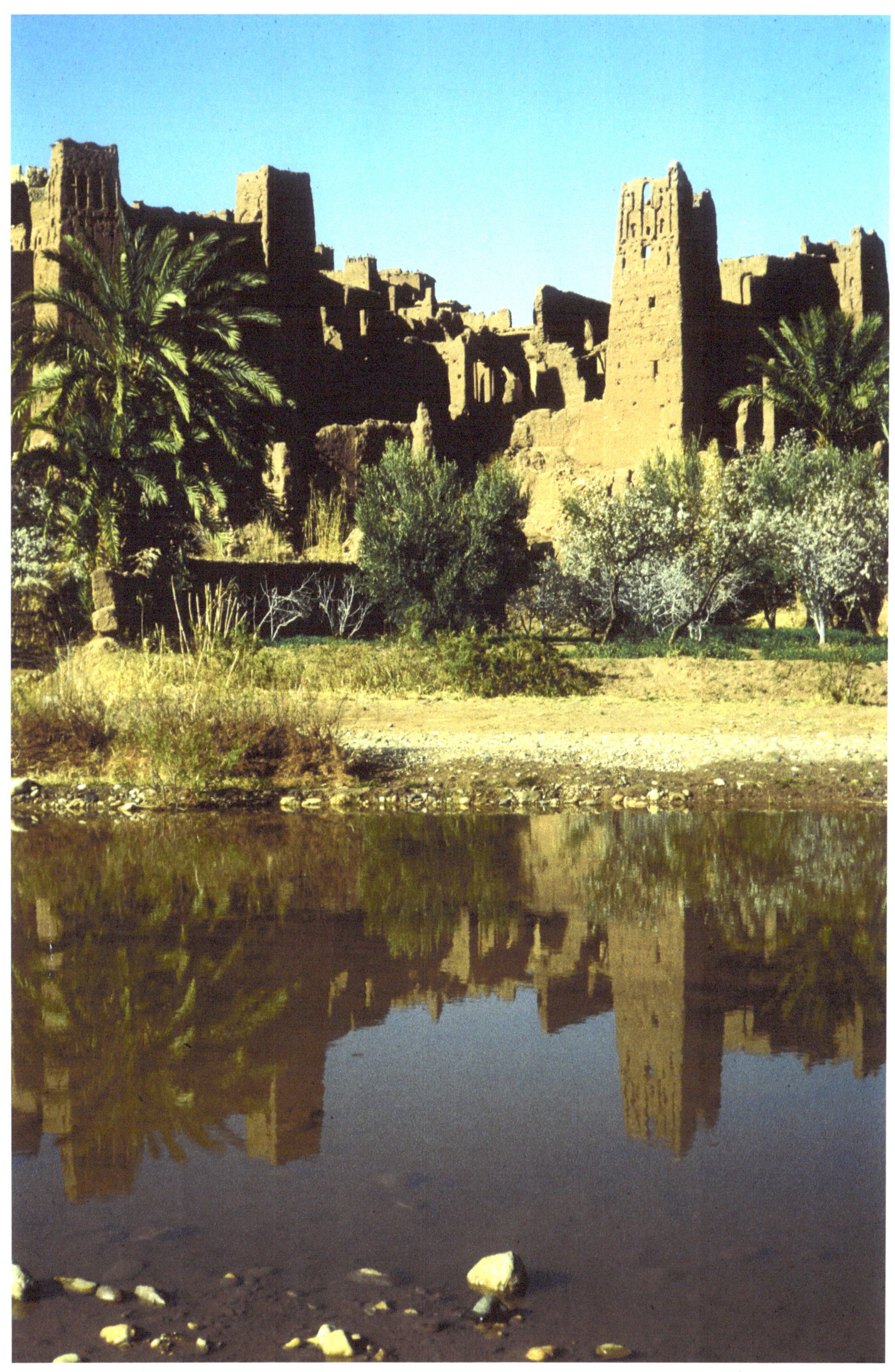

85. Ait-Benhaddou Near Quarzazate

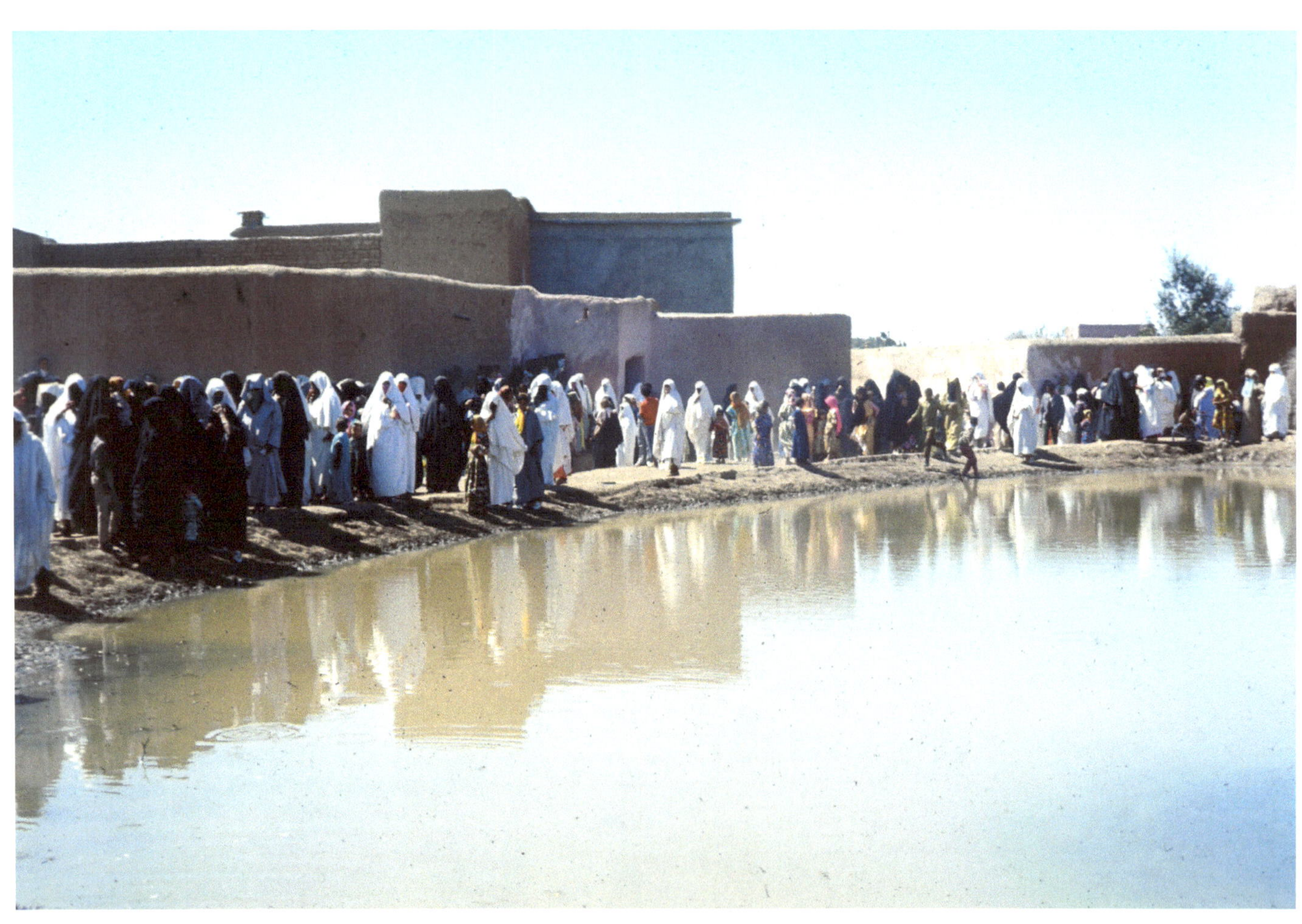

86. Taroudant Village near town

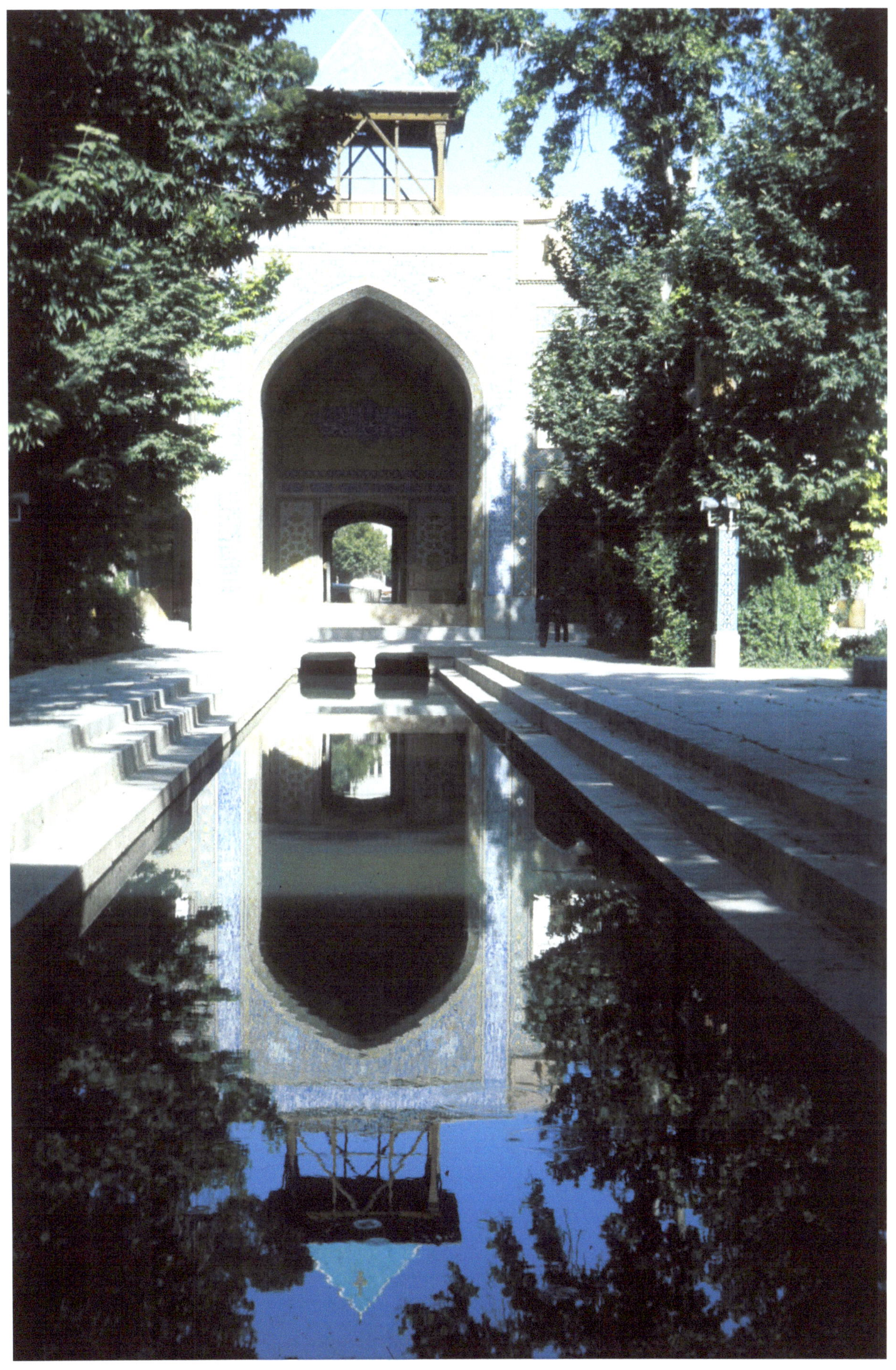

87. Isfahan Mosque Mother of Shah

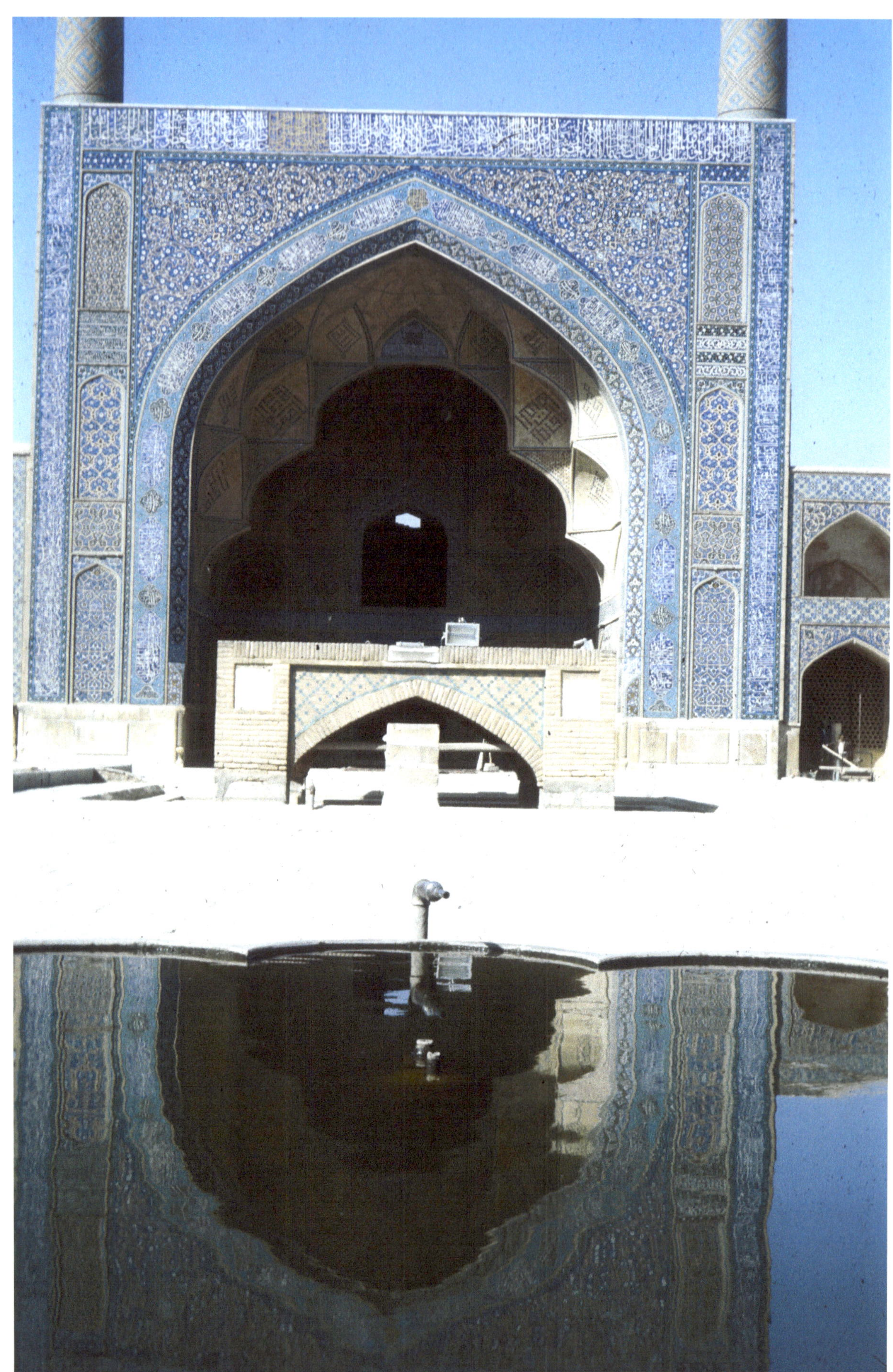

88. Isfahan Friday Mosque

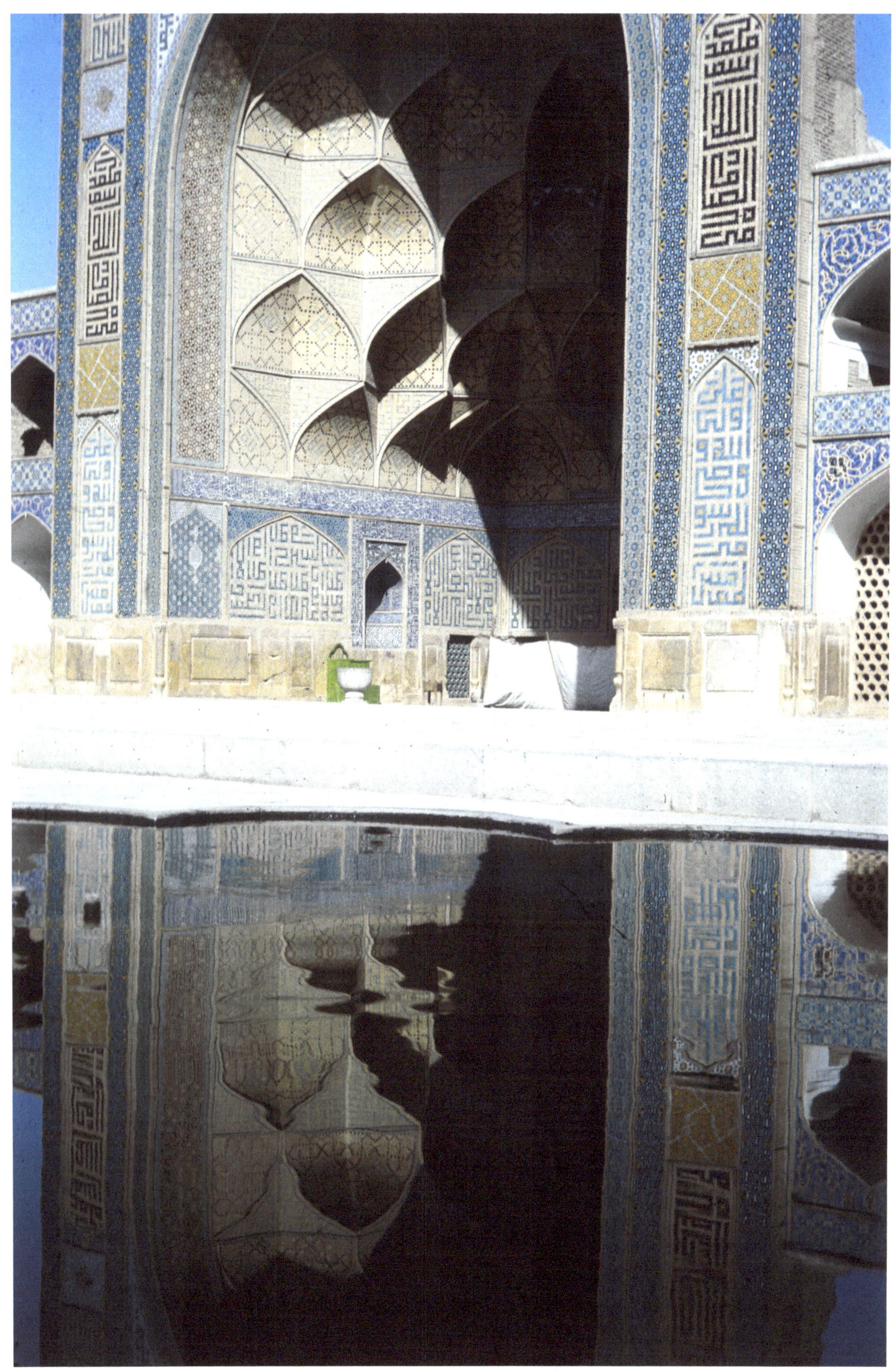

89. Isfahan Friday Mosque

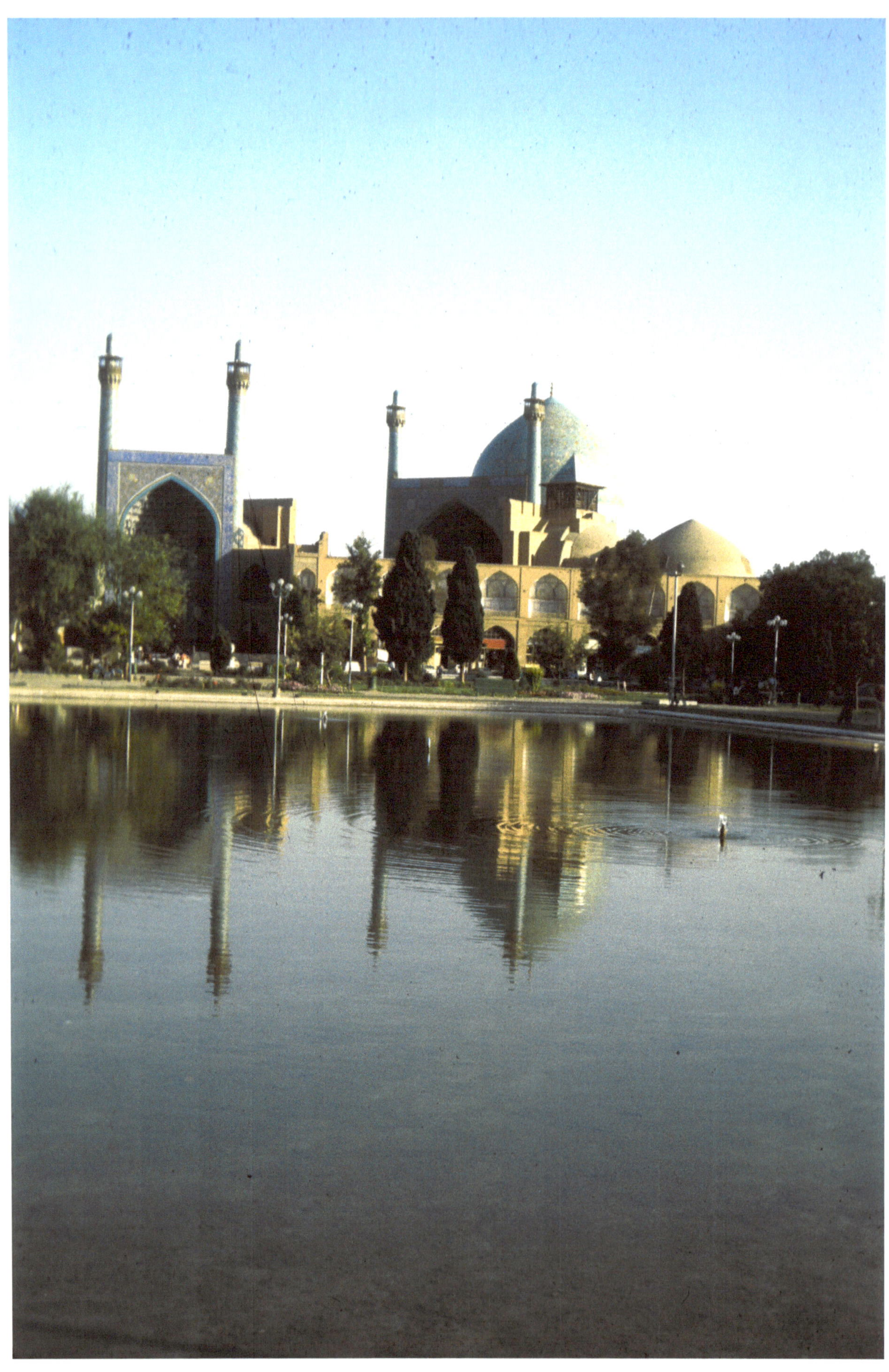

90 Isfahan Mosque of Shah Abbas

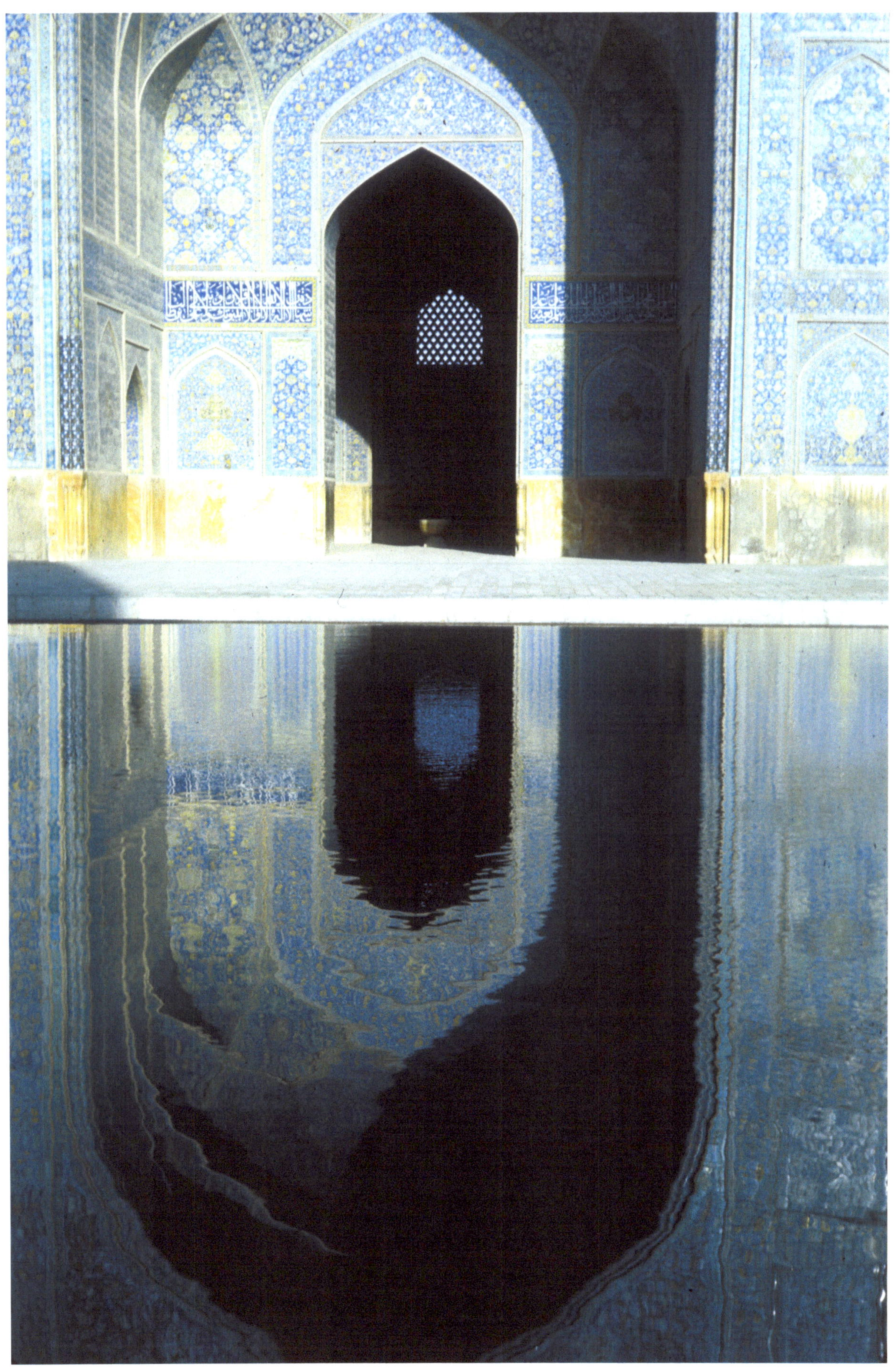

91. Isfahan Mosque of Shah Abbas

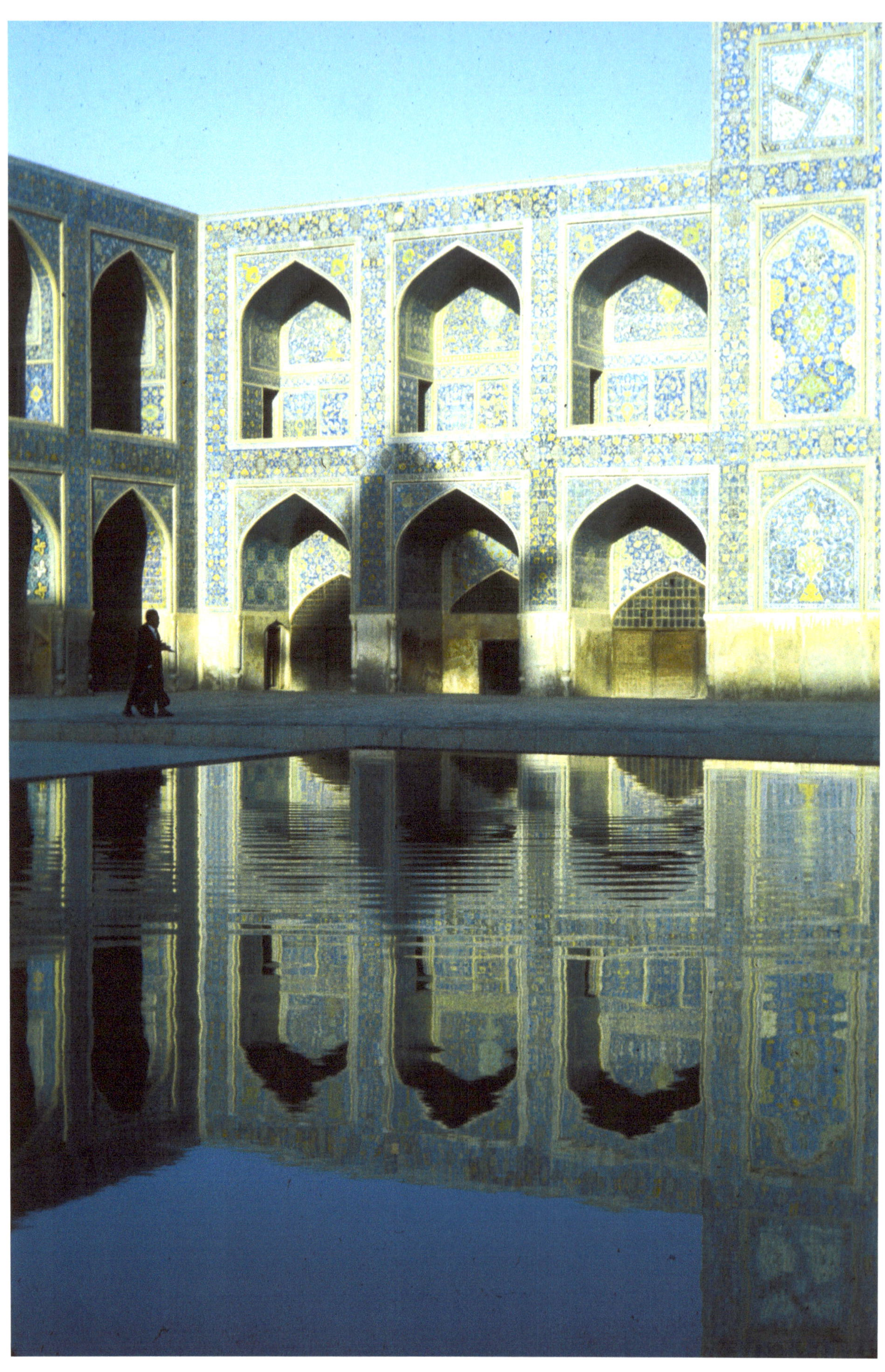

92. Isfahan Mosque of Shah Abbas

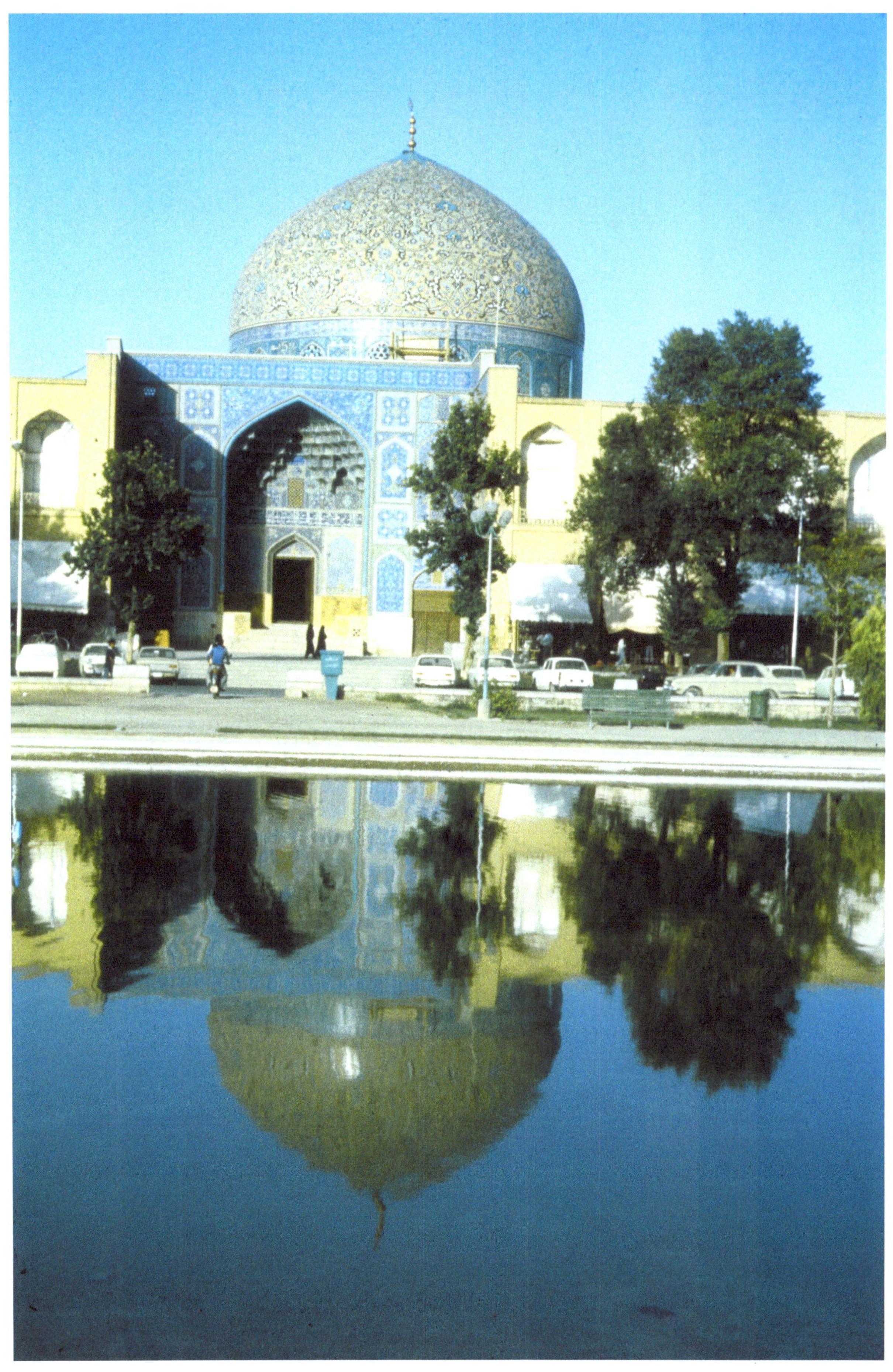

93. Isfahan Mosque of Sheikh Lutfallah

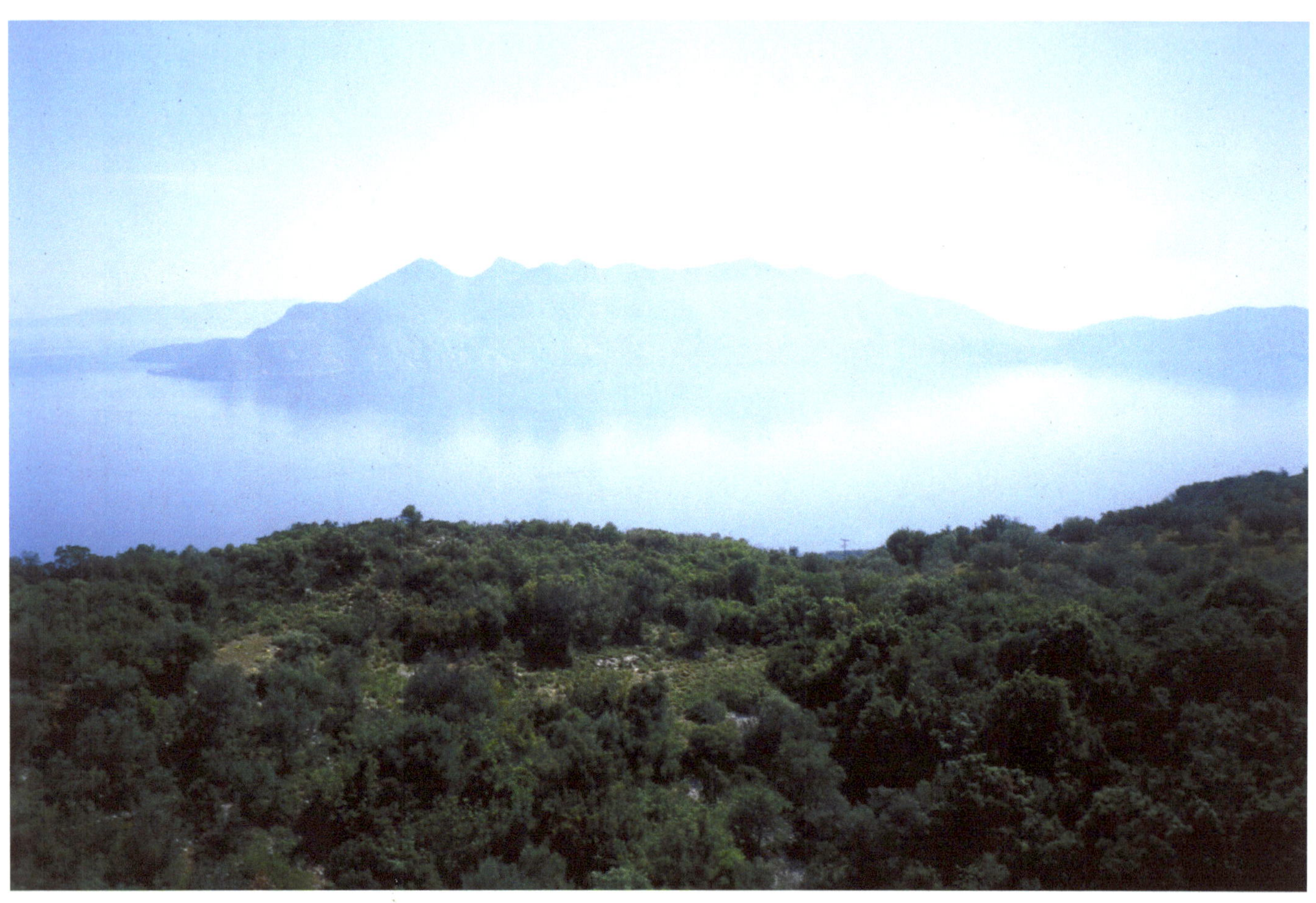

94. Methana View fom Peloponnese

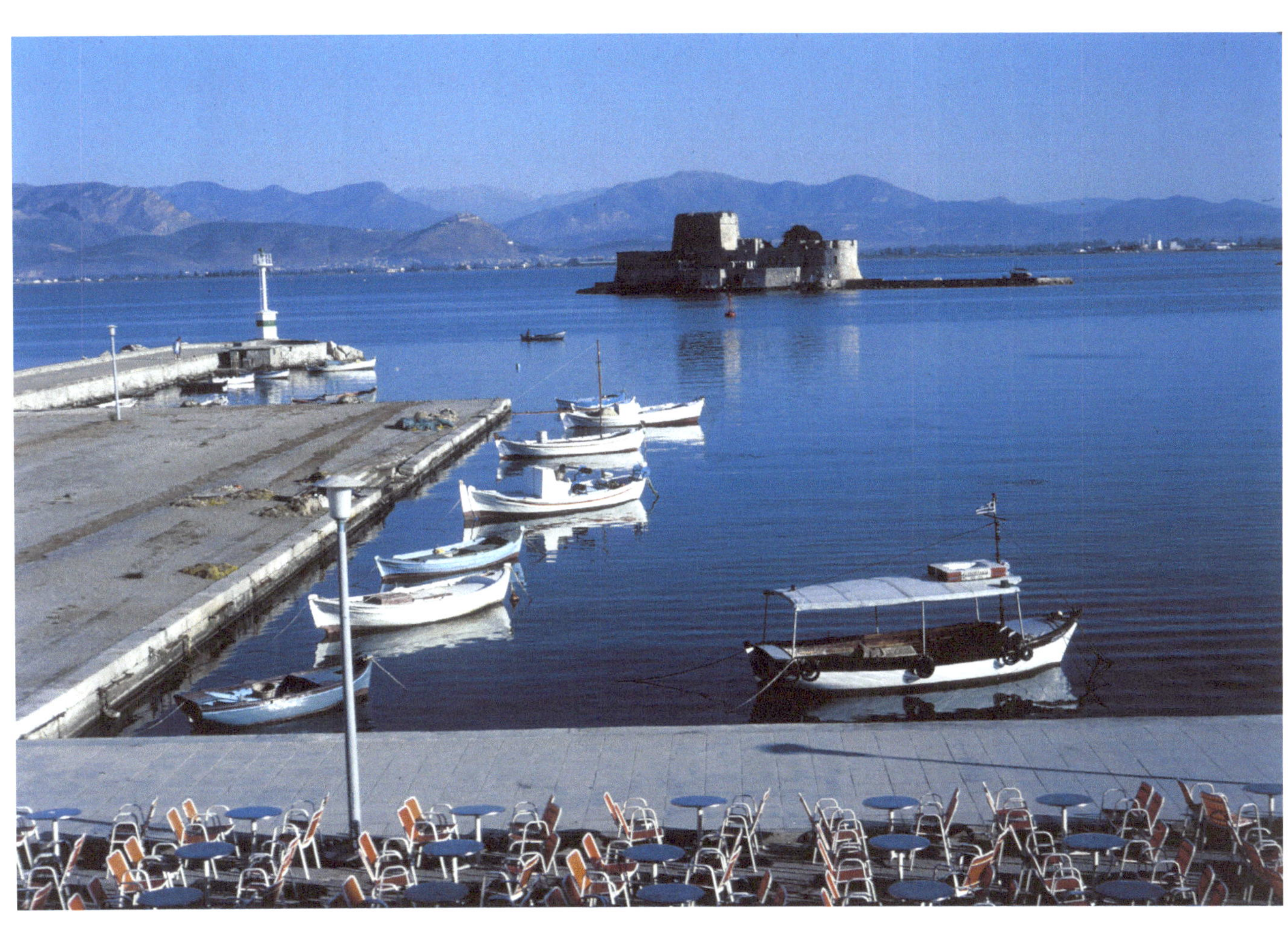

95. Nafplion

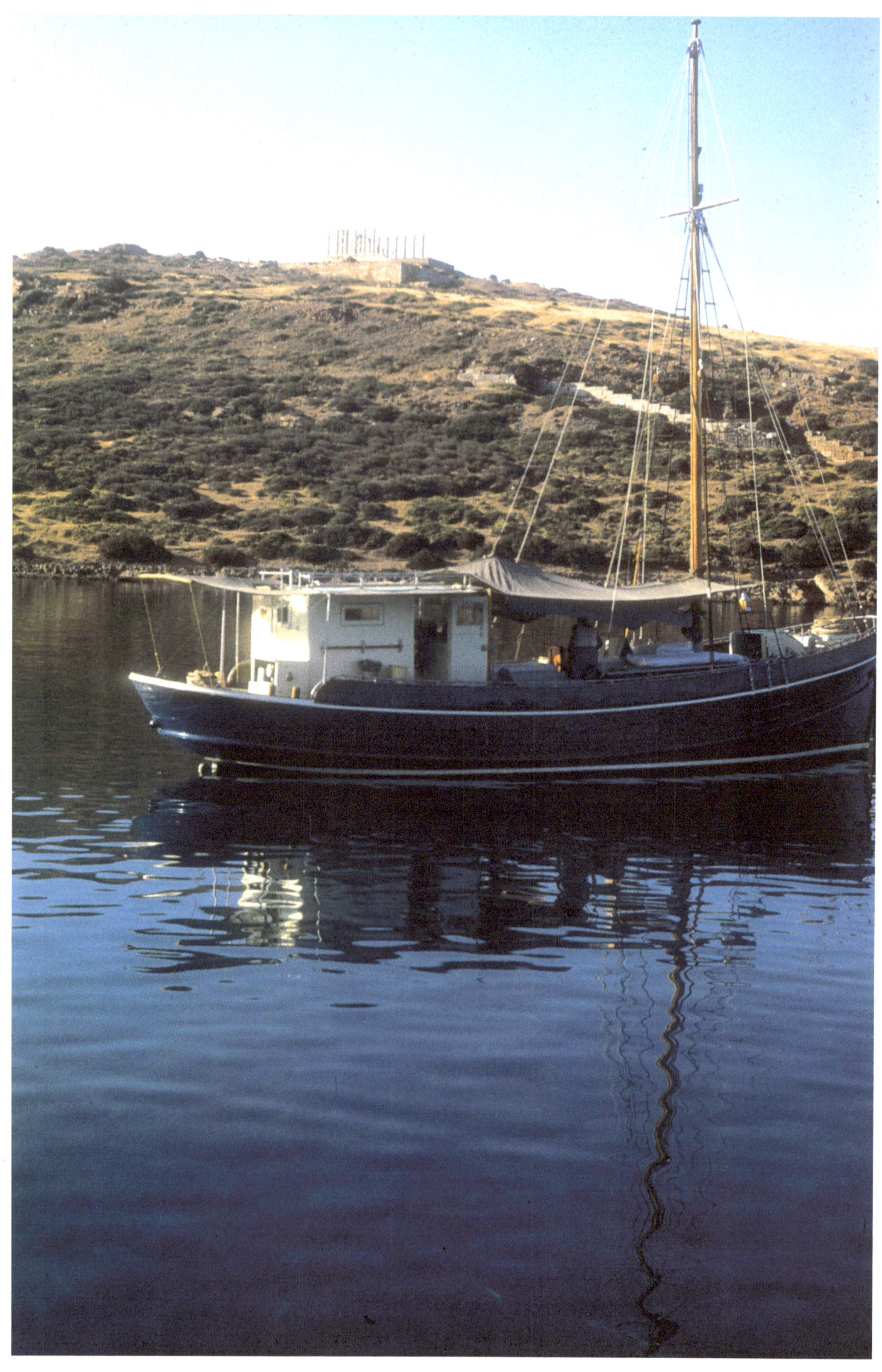

96. Sunion View on Temple

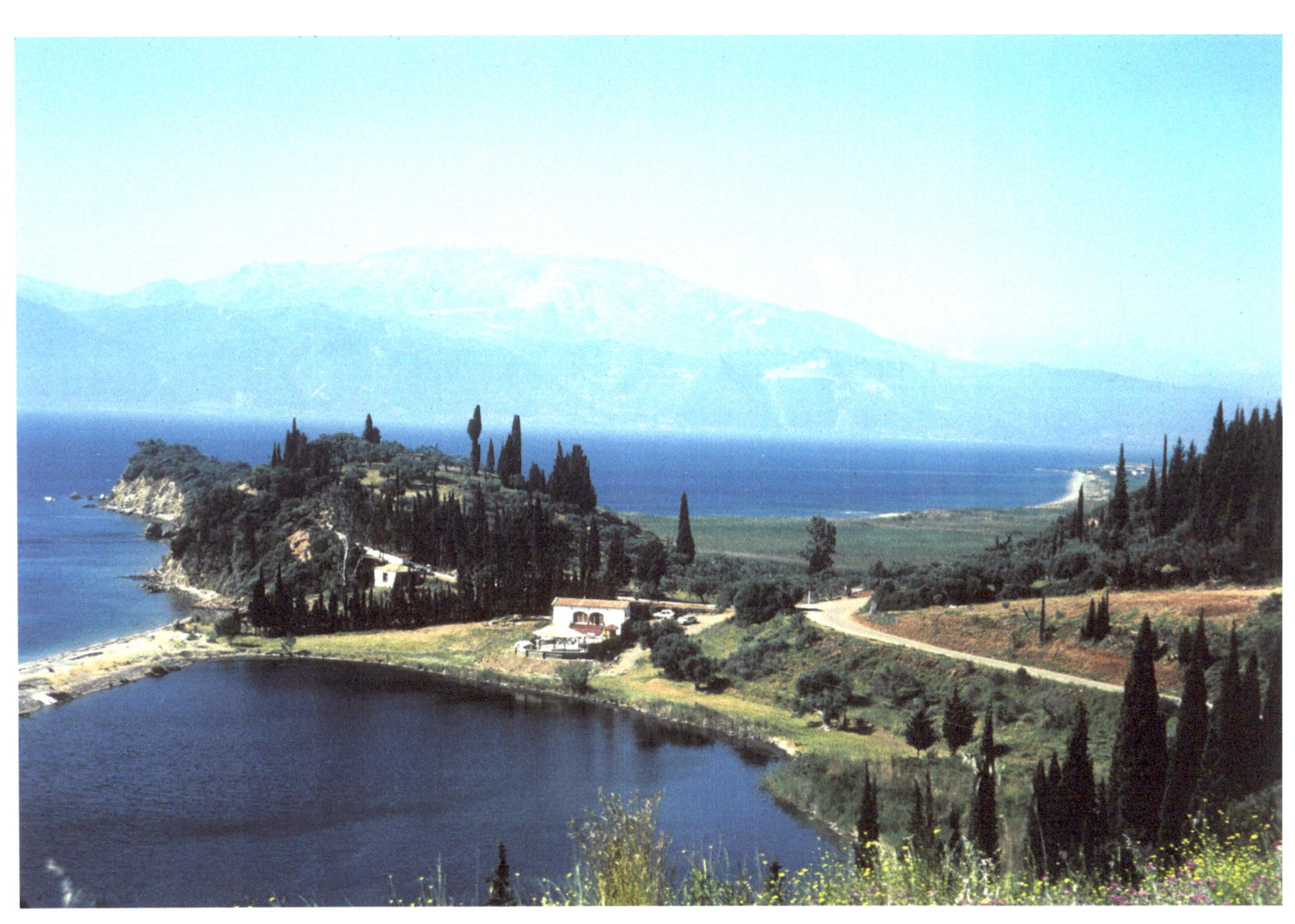

97. <u>Near Delphi</u> View on Peloponnese

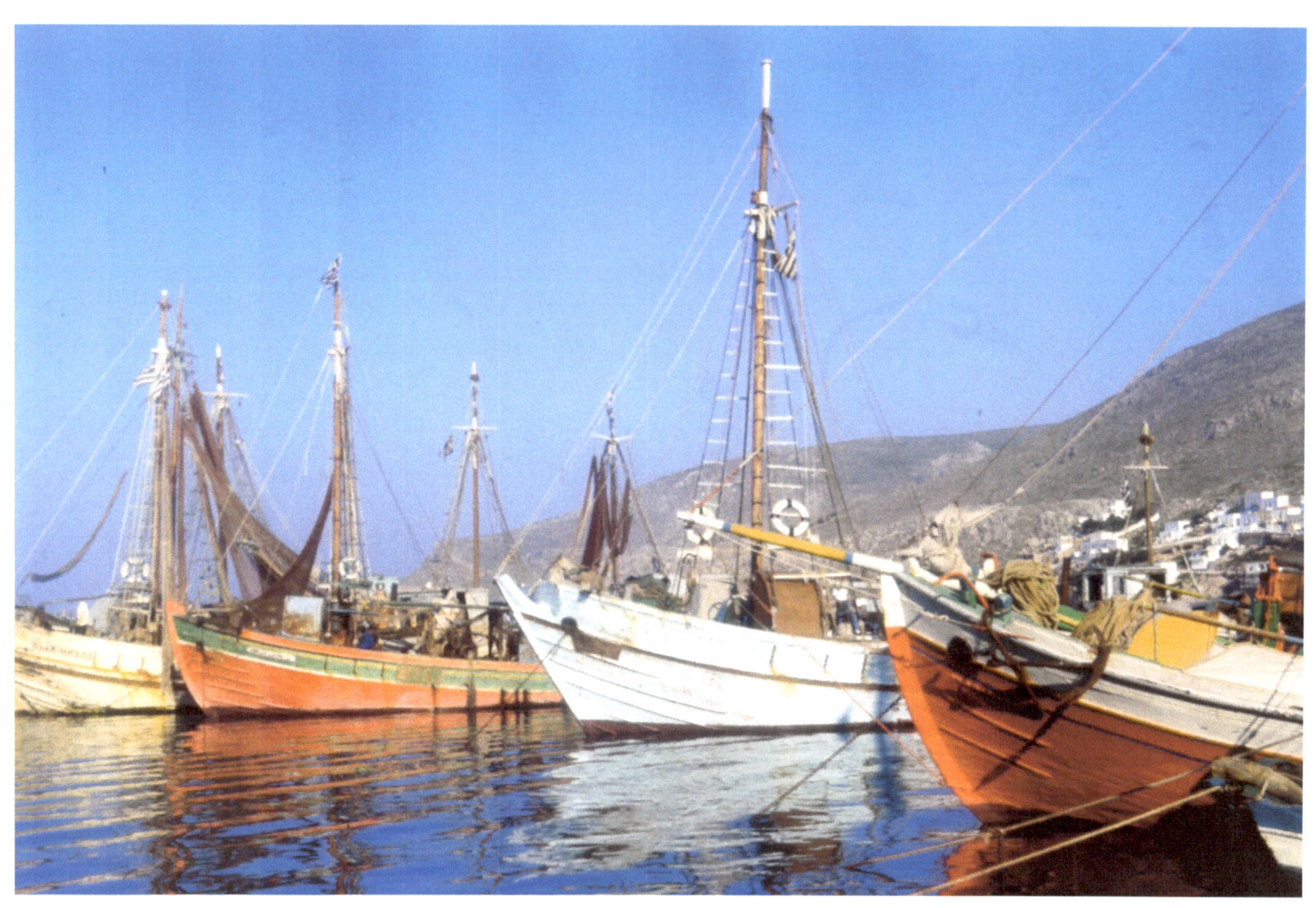

98. Kalymnos Sponge-fishing boats

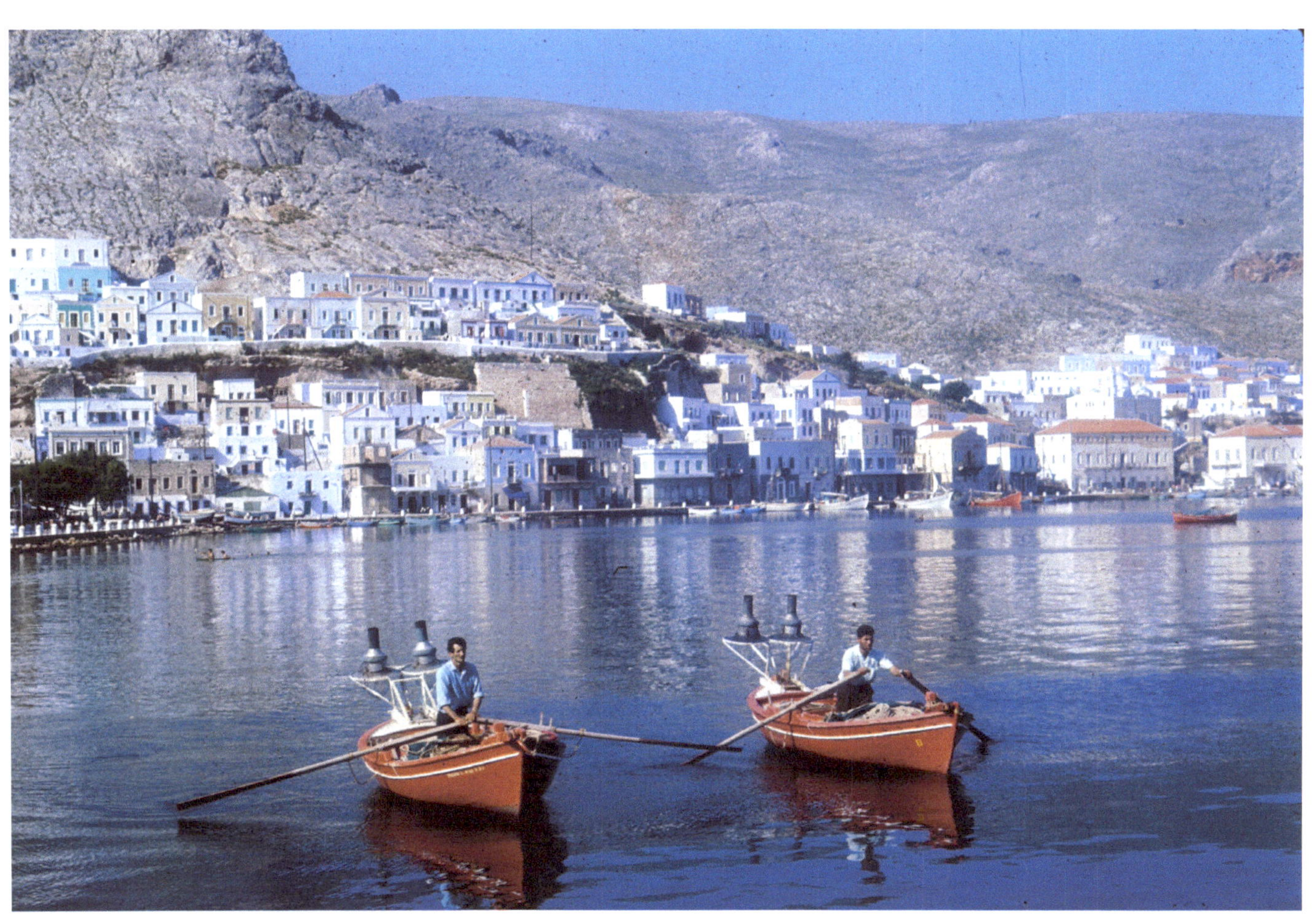

99. Kalymnos

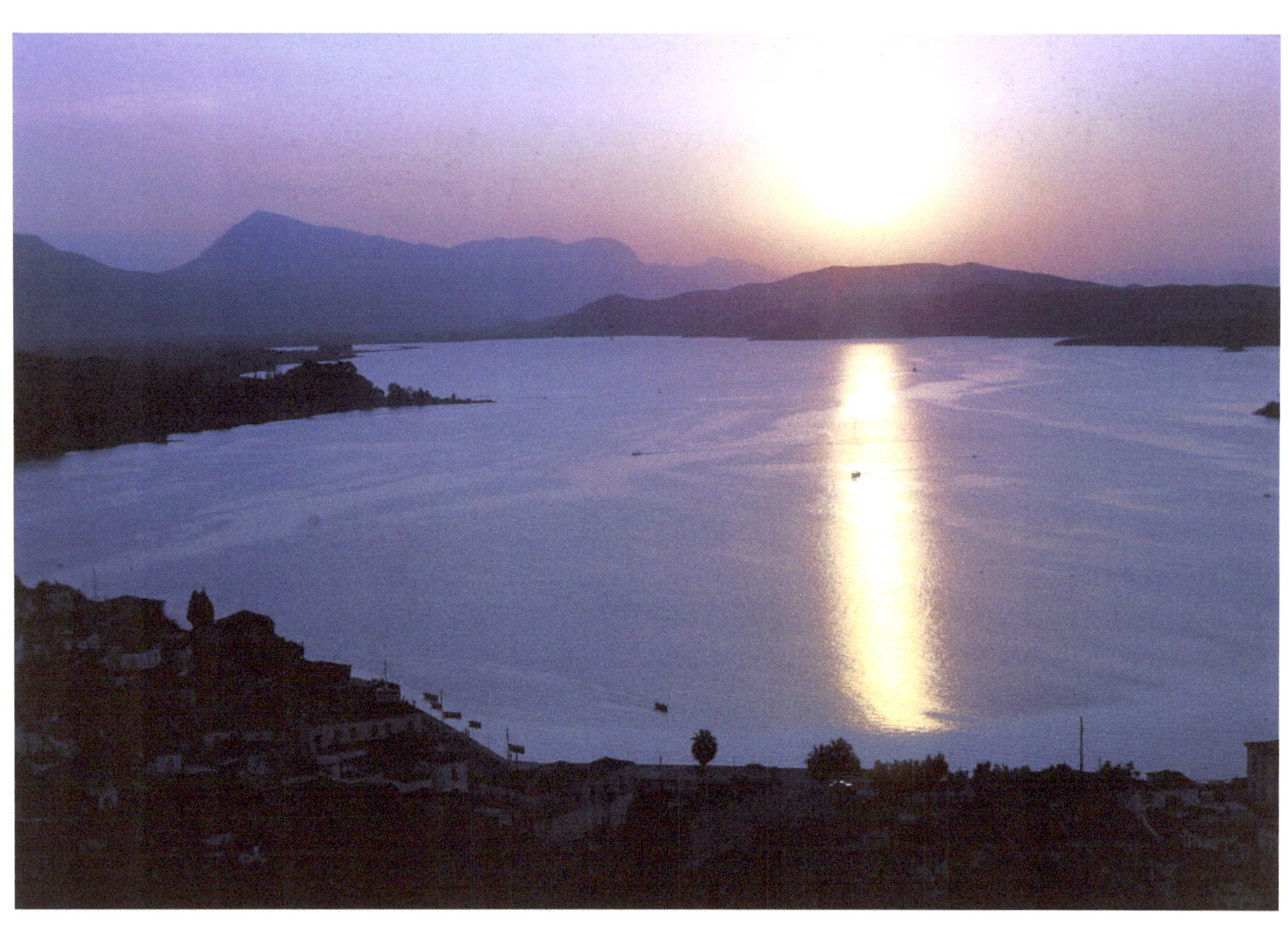

100. Poros View on Peloponnese

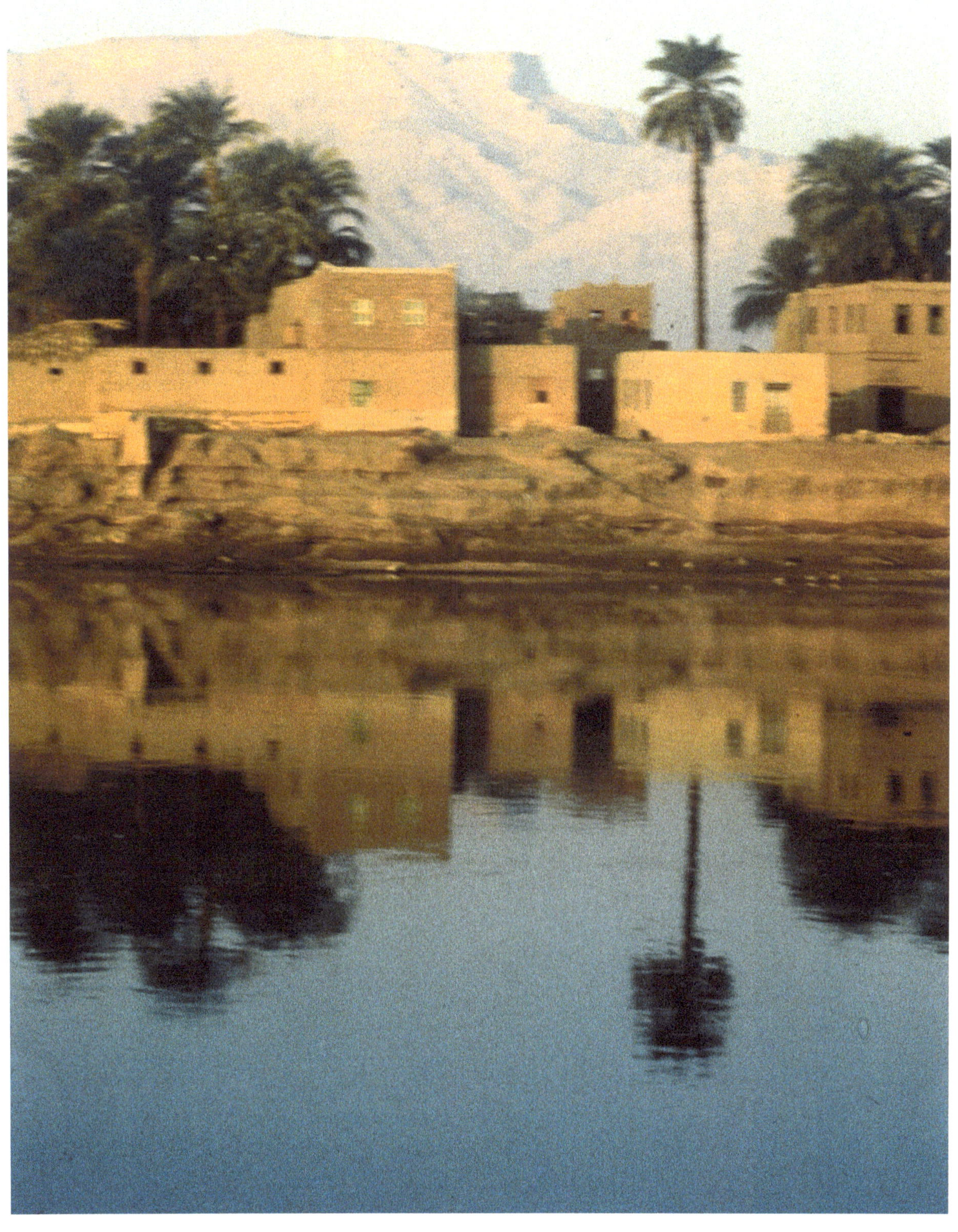

101. Dendera View from Nile

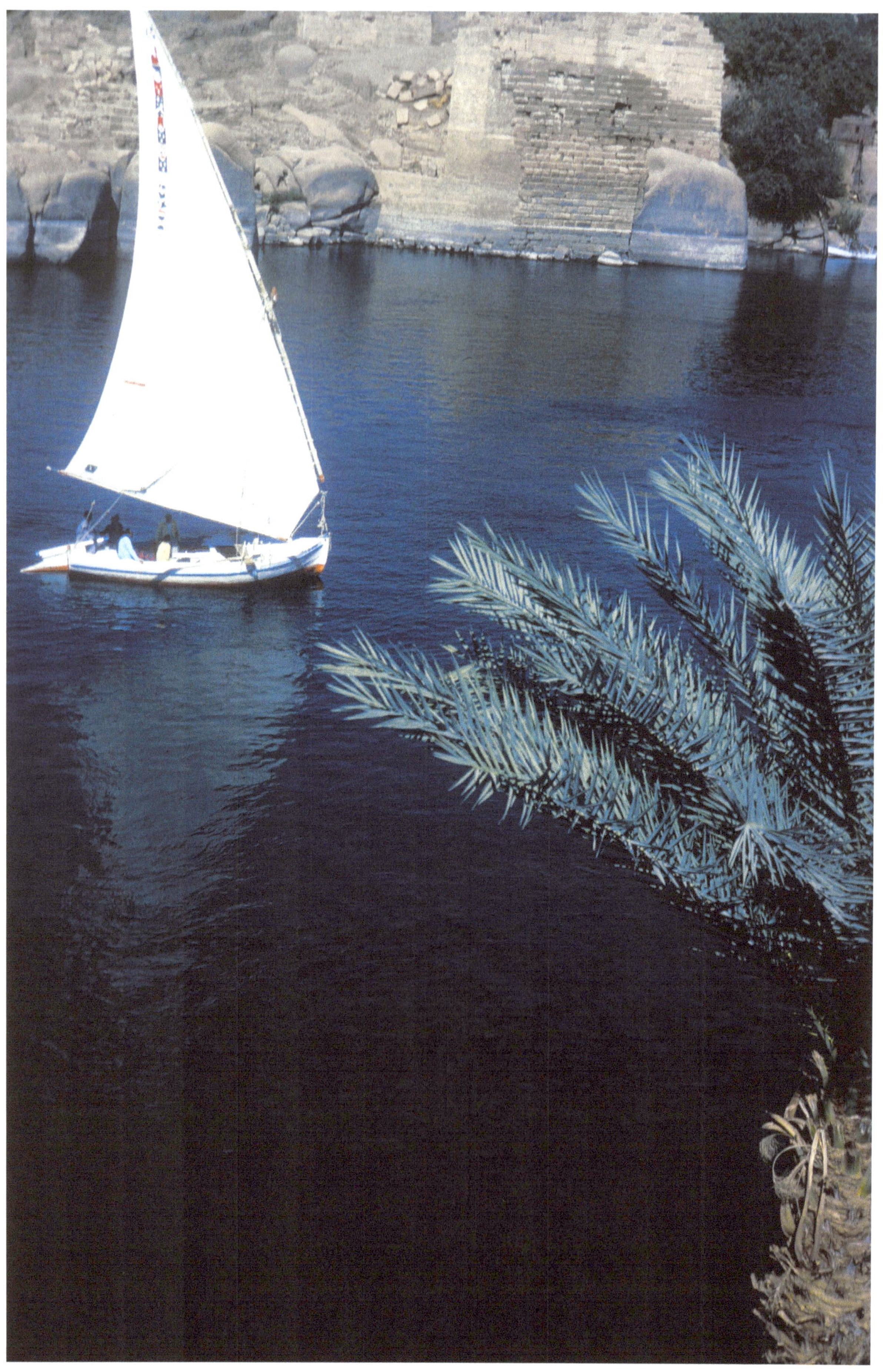

102. Assuan View on Elephantine Island

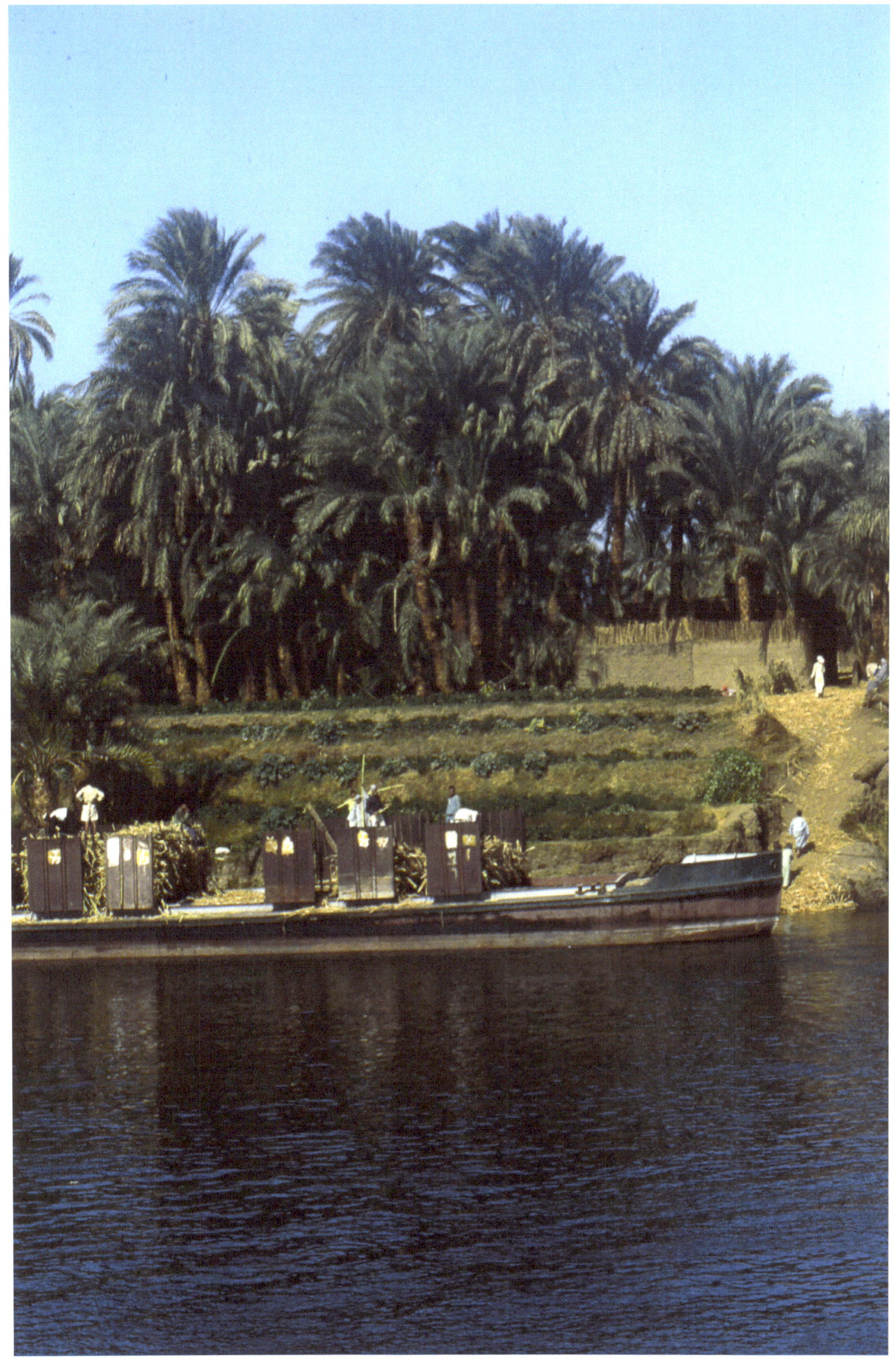

103. Near Assuan Nile

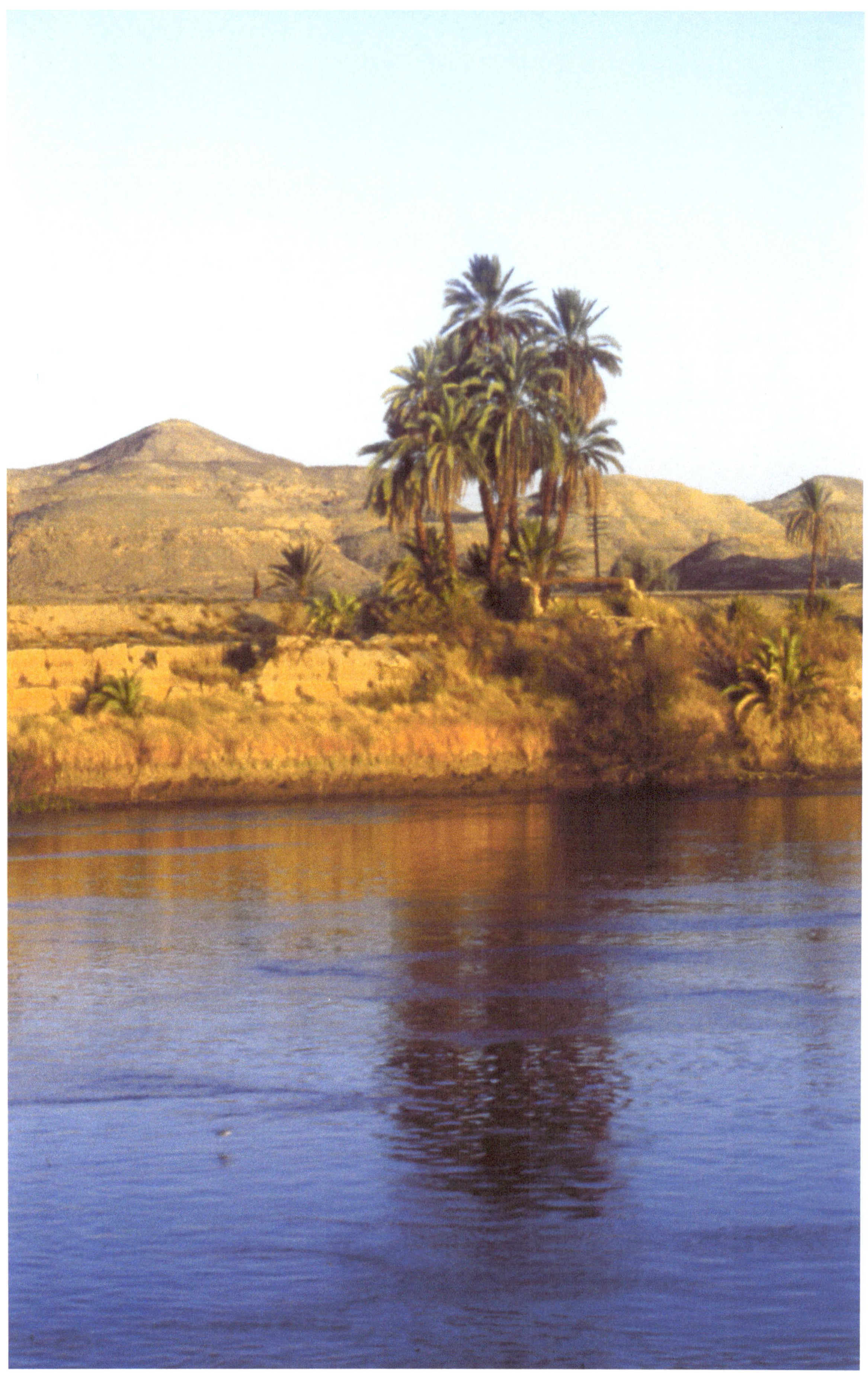

104. Nile

105. Near Assuan Nile

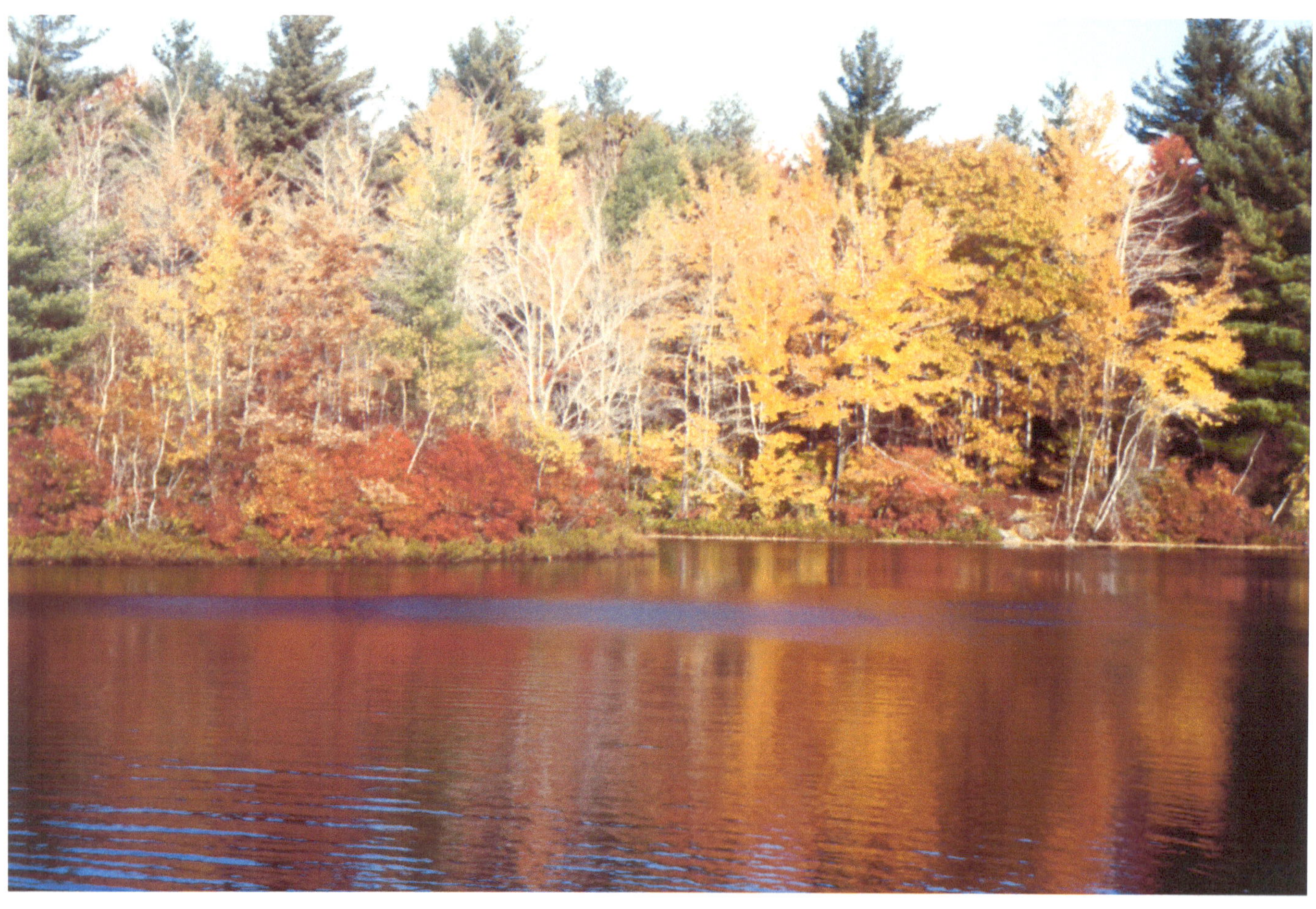

106. Pelham, MA Pond near Amherst

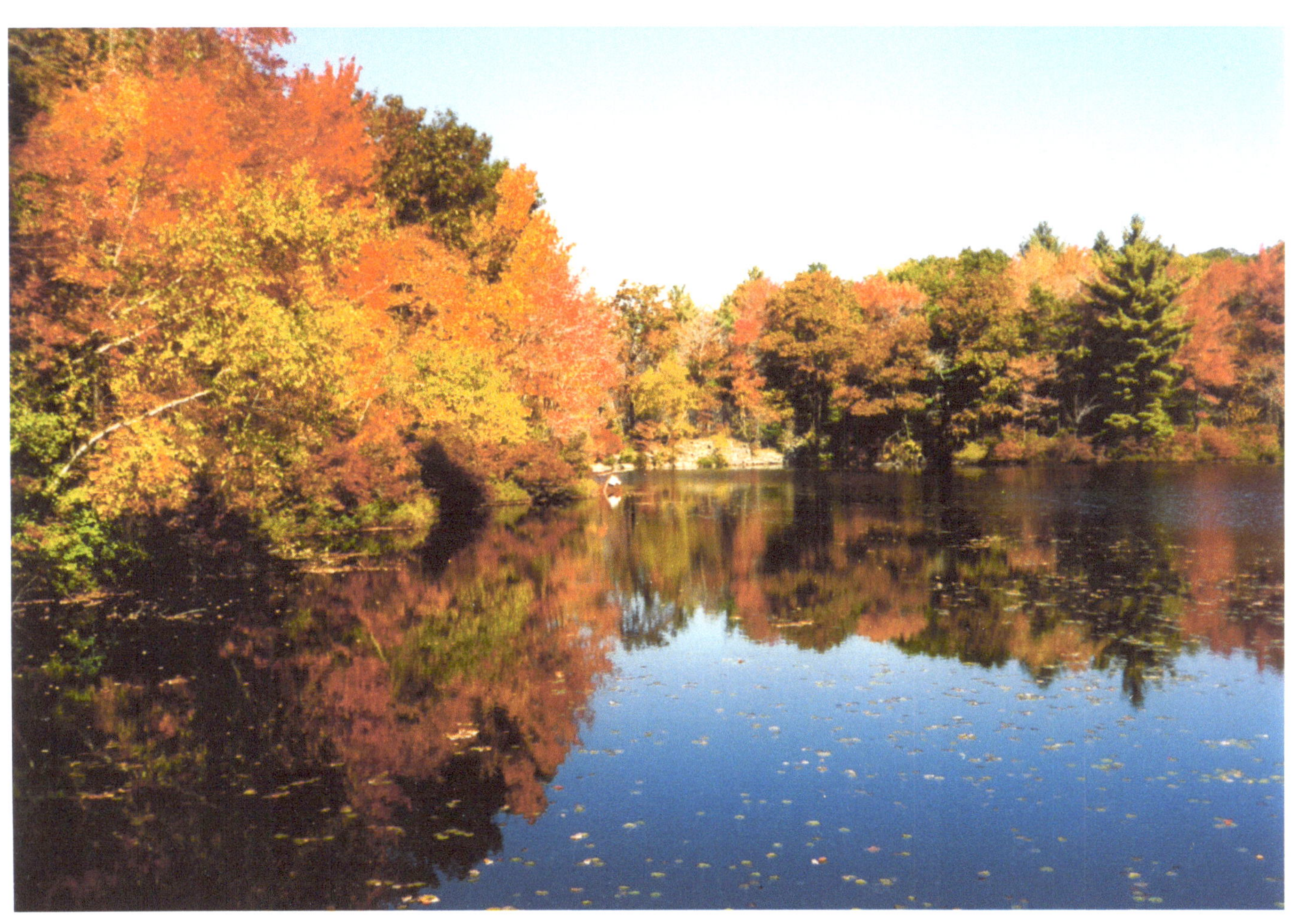

107. Pelham, MA Pond near Amherst

www.ingramcontent.com/pod-product-compliance
Lightning Source LLC
LaVergne TN
LVHW070128110826
845147LV00002B/209

* 9 7 8 0 9 7 9 2 4 5 1 6 9 *